Routledge Revivals

The Son Of A Star

Originally published in 1960, and the first of three volumes on the history of the Jews during the dispersal, this book covers briefly the period from the destruction of Jerusalem by the Romans in the year 70 down to Hadrian's suppression of Simeon's insurrection in 135. It sketches the political and religious background to the conflict between the Jewish and Graeco-Roman cultures, and the final separation of the Christian religion from its original Judaic stock; it vividly describes the general historical events involving the homeland of the Jews and portrays the principal characters in the struggle between them and the Empire, especially the insurrectionist leader Simeon Bar-Cochbar, the Son of a Star himself.

The Son Of A Star
A History of the Jews

Poul Borchsenius

First published in English in 1960 by George Allen & Unwin Ltd.

This edition first published in 2024 by Routledge
4 Park Square, Milton Park, Abingdon, Oxon, OX14 4RN

and by Routledge
605 Third Avenue, New York, NY 10158.

Routledge is an imprint of the Taylor & Francis Group, an informa business

© 1960 English Translation George Allen & Unwin Ltd.

The right of Poul Borchsenius to be identified as the author of this work has been asserted by him in accordance with sections 77 and 78 of the Copyright, Designs and Patents Act 1988.

All rights reserved. No part of this book may be reprinted or reproduced or utilised in any form or by any electronic, mechanical, or other means, now known or hereafter invented, including photocopying and recording, or in any information storage or retrieval system, without permission in writing from the publishers.

ISBN 13: 978-1-032-91012-3 (hbk)
ISBN 13: 978-1-003-56099-9 (ebk)
ISBN 13: 978-1-032-91025-3 (pbk)
Book DOI 10.4324/9781003560999

Masada

THE SON
OF A STAR

POUL BORCHSENIUS

TRANSLATED BY F. H. LYON

Ruskin House
GEORGE ALLEN & UNWIN LTD
MUSEUM STREET LONDON

FIRST PUBLISHED IN 1960

This book is copyright under the Berne Convention. Apart from any fair dealing for the purposes of private study, research, criticism or review, as permitted under the Copyright Act 1956, no portion may be reproduced by any process without written permission. Enquiry should be made to the publisher.

This translation © *George Allen & Unwin Ltd, 1960*

Translated from the Danish
STJERNESØNNEN
© H. Hirschprungs Forlag, 1957

PRINTED IN GREAT BRITAIN
IN 12 PT. CENTAUR TYPE
BY JARROLD AND SONS LTD
NORWICH

CONTENTS

I	Judaea Capta	11
II	He That Should Come	40
III	Caesarea	70
IV	A New Day Dawns	93
V	In the Dispersion	116
VI	The Horizon in Flames	133
VII	A Sceptic on the Throne	145
VIII	A Rock in Israel	160
IX	In the Balance	170
X	The Son of a Star	180
XI	In the Valley of the Shadow of Death	199
XII	As the Stars of Heaven	210
	Index	221

ILLUSTRATIONS

Masada	*frontispiece*
2. The rock of Masada as seen from the east	*facing page* 32
3. View from the top of Masada to the Dead Sea Ancient terraces in the Jordan hills	33
4. Cliff near Sodom on the Dead Sea called Lot's Wife Wilderness of Judaea	48
5. Caesarea, Herod's port	49
6. Roman statue at Caesarea Roman Emperor's statue at Caesarea	64
7. The ruins at Caesarea Excavations at Capernaum	65
8. Wilderness of Judaea and the River Jordan Near the Dead Sea	112
9. Ancient tombs of the Sanhedrin Detail of the Sanhedrin's tombs	113
10. Titus Hadrian	128
11. Vespasian Antinous	129
12. Trajan	176
13. River Jordan north of the Lake of Genesareth River Jordan south of the Lake of Genesareth	177
14. Lake of Genesareth Mountain of Beatitudes	192
15. Ancient coins	193

I

JUDAEA CAPTA

THE stars over the Dead Sea were fading slowly as the last hours of night passed. Behind the mountains of Moab, over on the eastern shore, the first glimmer of morning light appeared: the dawn was breaking. The rays of the sun glittered like lightning over the mountains: for a few minutes they caught the night mists and set them aflame. Then the ball of the sun climbed over the peaks, freed itself from the jagged silhouette of the ridge and rose high into the sky. A vast landscape lay bathed in morning light.

Eleazar's tall figure appeared on the top of the tower: he took the few steps forward to the parapet and stood motionless at that dizzy height, looking out westward, his eyes following the direction of the sun's rays. Before him lay the desert of Judaea with its miles and miles of jagged rocks broken only by deep ravines, a wild stony country stretching as far as the eye could see.

It was seven years now since he had first climbed the steep flight of steps to the top of the tower, and day after day he had been up at his post to see if the enemy was venturing out into his trackless waste. Once more he breathed a sigh of relief, for there was not a sign of life. So the Romans were far away. Could they have given up the idea of winning the last little free patch of ground Israel possessed, the mountain fortress of Masada on the western shore of the Dead Sea, where Eleazar, the son of Jair, had taken refuge with the scattered remnants of Israel's army?

Three years ago the last sparks of resistance had been quenched among the smoking ruins of Jerusalem. The noise of

THE SON OF A STAR

battle had been stilled, and the cries and groans of dying men and prisoners were no longer heard. The only sound was the clatter of iron-shod shoes on the stony road by which the victorious Roman troops were marching down from the hills, back to Lydda and Caesarea. They sang and laughed, for they had survived a terrible war, and now the triumph in Rome was due to them. After that, easy garrison duty awaited them on the distant frontiers of the empire, to stand on guard against barbaric peoples without.

But the victory was not yet complete. When Roman scouting parties entered the Judaean desert, far away to the south, they perceived on the horizon a solitary rock with high towers on its summit like a crown. This was Masada, the only place in the country still in Jewish hands. And the Emperor's son Titus, who had captured Jerusalem, had given, before he went home, strict orders for the subjugation of the whole of Judaea.

The Romans hesitated for a long time. When the war council assembled in the Governor's palace at Caesarea, the Masada problem was always on the order of the day. But the difficulties were great, and they were always put forward by senior officers of experience. Was not Masada said to be impregnable? The Judaean desert was a terrible place: its Hebrew name was Jeshimon, which meant devastation. And it was worthy of its name. Even today, two thousand years after these events, it lies desolate, without roads and—what is worse—without water; nothing but stones and stones, on which a pitiless sun beats from morning till night, so burning hot that it almost hurts to set foot on them. Acrobatic skill is needed to cross the deep ravines which cut the hill paths and make progress almost impossible. There are places where steam rises from the earth and boiling springs bubble up, but the water tastes sulphurous and bitter. 'It comes from the gates of Gehenna', say the poor nomads who make their venturesome way through the desert.

Amid this desolate country rises the solitary rock of Masada, with a steep drop on every side, overwhelmingly impressive. It is well suited to its surroundings: a Medusa's head magnified to the size of a mountain.

JUDAEA CAPTA

From time immemorial outlaws had made their way out into these regions when the weapons of those in power were directed against them. David wandered about here when Saul wished to kill him, and here John the Baptist found the solitude which brought him near God. Now Eleazar held Israel's last redoubt here at Masada.

The great King Herod had taken refuge here a hundred years earlier. The crown sat loose on his head, and he judged that it would be prudent to find a really safe place for himself. More than another hundred years before his time the Maccabaean prince Jonathan had found that at Masada he felt secure in time of danger. Like all who rule by force, Herod feared the people he ruled: he knew too that Cleopatra, the great queen of Egypt, hated him and was egging Antony on to destroy Israel's Idumaean prince.

So Herod built his fortress in one of the most inaccessible places in the world. Only two narrow paths led up to Masada. From the eastern side, from the Dead Sea, the Snake Path, as it was well called, wound its way up the almost perpendicular cliff. One would have thought that only mountain goats could follow the track as it curled about among the sharp rocks. For some stretches of the path a dizzy abyss yawned both to right and left, and any man who ventured along it must have nerves of steel.

The ascent from the west was a little easier. Here there was a kind of promontory called 'the white cliff', the light colour of which contrasted sharply with the brown and grey rock walls. It was a little lower than the fortress and was like an enormous step, but here too the path lay along the verge of the abyss.

On the top of this solitary rock, nature, by one of her queer caprices, had formed a large flat plateau, nearly 750 yards long and 200 yards wide. Herod, with his trained military eye, saw its possibilities and fortified the whole hill-top with a long, high wall, protected by thirty-seven towers. And inside the wall he gave his pleasure in architecture and his artistic talent full play. Here he erected his palace, so wonderful that only the royal palace in Jerusalem excelled it in beauty. In reading old accounts we still find the enchantment which filled all who saw Masada, its great halls, colonnades and bathrooms. The walls and floors were ornamented with richly coloured mosaics, and every column was cut in one piece. Round the palace lay men's quarters and houses. And in many places Herod had had large tanks cut in the rock: these collected the water in winter and kept it hidden till the long rainless season, so that the fortress was provided with water as if it contained secret springs.

The garrison was not to suffer hardship. On the plateau itself there was rich and fertile soil, and the King had ordered the men to grow corn on it, so that they should not need to run short of food even during a long and close siege. But over and above this he had amassed huge supplies in the cellars, quantities of corn, beans, dates, oil and wine, enough to last many years. When Jewish fighters for freedom outwitted the defenders and made themselves masters of the fortress, they found to their surprise that these provisions, which had lain there for a hundred years, were just as fresh as on the day they were brought in. The dry air had preserved them. But Herod had taken thought for other things as well. He had amassed weapons, enough to arm 10,000 men, as well as an immense treasure in silver, copper and lead.

The Romans had not kept a close enough watch on Masada. They counted absolutely on no enemy attempting to capture such an impregnable fortress. But they miscalculated. When the rising against the Romans in Jerusalem was only in embryo, and the decision between peace and war hung in the balance, the Zealot leader Menahem made himself master of the fortress by a stratagem. How he did this is unfortunately not recorded, but we know that he equipped his men from the abundant stores there and marched to Jerusalem, where his intervention proved disastrous. In the prevailing confusion and internal strife Menahem himself was murdered, but his young relative Eleazar escaped from the city and had held Masada firmly throughout the years that followed.

JUDAEA CAPTA

He had not been sitting there during the war as a passive spectator. Again and again he sent out his irregulars from Masada. Whenever they saw an opportunity they fell upon the Romans from the rear, made surprise attacks on solitary posts and cut off their supplies. The Romans never felt secure against the partisans from Masada.

Jerusalem fell, and the real war was over. A few scattered parties of the last defenders of Jerusalem escaped and with their families reached Masada, where they were absorbed into the garrison. After that things became quieter in the fortress. Eleazar limited his operations to patrolling the Judaean desert, and of course he had his spies in Hebron, keeping an eye on any military movements which might be directed against Masada. And now the only thing to do was to wait and see what would happen.

The last years had set unmistakable signs on Eleazar's face. A few sharp wrinkles between the eyes and deep furrows from the nose to the corners of the mouth showed under what a strain he had been living. His lips were thin, and his eyes had the keen, cold expression that marks a man who has made up his mind and sees his way ahead of him. Eleazar knew that the road would become narrower and ever steeper till it ended at the inevitable abyss. But he would follow that road: for him there was no other; he felt as though he had inherited it from his forebears. And while he sat alone in meditation, he saw a long series of pictures of events at which he himself had been present or of which he had heard in his boyhood, when the old members of the family told tales of long ago.

An inextinguishable love of freedom ran like a red thread through several generations of his family. He had inherited from his ancestors his defiance and his ice-cold hatred of the godless foreigners who were oppressing God's people.

The most renowned of Eleazar's forefathers was Judas the Galilean, who had kindled the flame of rebellion in Herod's time. His father, also called Judas, had rebelled before him. Herod made short work of the father, but the son's contribution was of lasting importance.

THE SON OF A STAR

The Romans soon saw that the Jewish people would not let itself be subdued without a struggle. From St Luke's Gospel we remember Quirinius, who was legate in Syria and ordered his famous census, a perfectly normal proceeding which was the foundation of the Roman administration and the levying of taxes. But the people realized that it could signify the establishment of a foreign domination, and far and wide in the country feelings began to smoulder in a manner that boded ill. At such moments there are always cautious, anxious men who advocate submission, co-operating politicians who try to keep quiet. There were people of this kind at the top in Israel. The high priest was one of them, and he actually persuaded the mass of the people to submit. But under the surface there was a ferment of bitterness, and when Judas organized the insurrectionary movement the rebellion blazed up and chaotic conditions prevailed in both Jerusalem and Galilee.

The Romans struck hard and without mercy. Judas was captured and tortured to death, and the country became quiet again. The revolt became just an episode among many others. But one thing was left which contained life and hope for the future, the party of the Zealots. They were well named. They spoke bitterly against countrymen who paid the Roman taxes and by doing so admitted that they tolerated mortal rulers, when the Lord should be their only king. These young anti-Romans—as always, the young people were the first to band themselves together in this resistance movement—could not sit passively waiting for Israel's expectations of a Messiah to be realized in God's own, perhaps remote time. They wished to bring that great day nearer, sword in hand, in battle to the death with the foreigners. It was the Zealots who under the ashes kept the spark alive which sixty years later, with elemental violence, set the country ablaze.

The family of Judas of Galilee gave the Zealots a succession of leaders—and martyrs. Two of his sons were crucified by the Romans, and others had to live as outlaws in caves and among the mountains. One of his grandsons was that Menahem who captured Masada. He was the leader of the notorious *sicarii*, a

JUDAEA CAPTA

short time before the great rebellion broke out. The name comes from the Latin word for a knife or dagger, *sica*, this being their favourite weapon. It was very handy in the underground war they were forced to carry on, and could easily be concealed under the outer clothes.

The Roman procurators used the severest measures to quench the unrest, and even at this date we find Gestapo methods among them in full flower. And, as always, violence bred violence. The 'dagger-men' became the Jewish reaction: they were a kind of Zealots, an antique form of liquidation groups. They fought bitterly not only against the Romans but also against their countrymen who favoured a policy of co-operation. They liked to operate where people collected in numbers at the great festivals, especially in the Temple square. Here they mingled with the crowds with their daggers hidden and ready. Unseen themselves, they inflicted a fatal stab and stole swiftly away through the crowd. They were accused of camouflaging themselves by loud expressions of anger when their bleeding victims were carried away. No one could feel that his life was safe: even the high priest Jonathan was murdered by them, and a general feeling of panic spread among the population.

Of course, religious fanaticism went hand in hand with terrorism. Wild visionaries, seeing their chance of fishing in troubled waters, appeared in the streets and squares with fantastic prophecies and promises. In the Acts of the Apostles, xxi. 38, we read that when Paul was arrested in Jerusalem he was suspected of being the Egyptian who a little while before had started an uproar and led 4,000 'dagger-men' out into the desert. But this was only one of many incidents.

The Roman yoke lay heavy on the oppressed peoples of the East. But in no other country did the people dare to murmur against the foreigners as they did in Judaea. The first manifestation of the revolutionary spirit was, as always, whispering campaigns in which mysterious predictions and phrases went from mouth to mouth. All through the eastern countries men were told: a man will come from Judaea and conquer the world! It sounded quite improbable, but it gained credence just for that reason: the miraculous element in the prophecy excited the fanaticism of the masses all the more. The belief that the Jews would head the struggle for supremacy was in the air everywhere.

In this atmosphere of excitement and anticipation the *sicarii* raised their banner with the kindling watchwords: 'God alone is lord, death does not matter, freedom is all!' The leaders of the nation, the collaborators and quislings of all kinds hated and feared them, and many of the best people in the country saw with mingled admiration and fear how the propaganda of the 'dagger-men' gained ground when, time after time, the news of some sensational exploit threw light on their activities.

It was of bad omen for the national future that it proved impossible to combine the *sicarii* with the more steady-going resistance movement. Thus many incidents ended in unbridled savagery which was bound to lead to disaster. Menahem's last experiences were a terrible warning of all that was to come.

As stated above, Menahem took possession of Masada and marched to Jerusalem with his men. The insurrection there was on the point of breaking out, and a detachment of Roman soldiers was surrounded. They opened negotiations and offered to surrender: they were willing to hand over their arms and equipment on condition that they were allowed to withdraw. A formal agreement was entered into and sworn to. At first all went well. The Romans marched along the street while the people watched quietly. But they had hardly surrendered their arms and begun to march out of the city when Menahem ordered his 'dagger-men' to attack them. They flung themselves upon the defenceless soldiers and began to cut them down. There followed a scene of savagery which was never forgotten. The soldiers died like true Romans. They offered no resistance and did not beg for mercy. They just stood still, shouting in chorus: 'Oath! covenant!' The chorus grew weaker and weaker as the voices became fewer. At last one single man was left crying 'Oath! covenant!' Then he too fell silent.

This event made the breach final. Now neither mercy nor negotiations could be expected from Rome. New internal quarrels broke out in Jerusalem, and in these Menahem met his

JUDAEA CAPTA

death, but Eleazar and his men succeeded in getting away to Masada. But of course the outbreak of war was the result of long-term developments and deeper causes than agitation and fanaticism.

Palestine has always been one of the sensitive nerve centres of world politics: it is today, and it was the same two thousand years ago. Great roads met there and it was the scene of crucial contacts: Judaea was an important line of communication in the empire between east, west, south and north. In those first two centuries of our era Eastern politics were always on the order of the day in Rome. The Parthian kingdom (the present Persia and the country round the Euphrates and Tigris) was the only competitor for world supremacy equal to Rome: it was always a potential and often a real enemy. And the way to it ran through Palestine. Moreover, millions of Jews scattered about in the great cities of the empire looked to Jerusalem as their spiritual capital. Therefore Judaea obtained an influence in the Roman empire quite disproportionate to the smallness of the country. So there were important considerations in favour of a cautious policy in Judaea.

But Rome could never see this. The Romans did not grasp that the very existence of Roman sovereignty was a standing mockery of the Jewish idea of Israel as a theocracy with the Lord alone as king. Time after time Rome contemptuously trod these feelings under foot. A single example is enough.

The Emperor Caligula had the insane notion of having his statue erected in the Temple of Jerusalem. It happened that at that time Syria had a reasonable and moderate governor, Petronius. He realized what frightful consequences the imperial order could have, and tried to delay the matter. And the Jews by their behaviour showed clearly that he was right.

Petronius came to Ptolemais, the present Accho, whence the statue was to be sent to Jerusalem. Tens of thousands of Jews made their way quietly to the town and assembled there, 'covering all Phoenicia like a cloud'. They stood drawn up in good order, in six detachments—old men, young men, boys, old women, younger women and girls—crying and lamenting without cessation. They carried no weapons and would make no resistance. But if the Emperor's statue was to be carried up to the holy city, it would be over their bodies. Petronius would have received orders to cut them down if his dispatch on the crisis had come into Caligula's hands. Before it arrived the mad Emperor had been murdered by his bodyguard.

But the Jews were not only in constant fear of religious encroachments: they were misgoverned in every other walk of life. An agricultural country like theirs needed peace, order and stability. It was just these things that Roman rule failed to give them: it levied unreasonably high taxes, sent out brutal, unjust officials, and afforded but little public security. The continually changing Roman governors were a set of exploiters who thought only of filling their own pockets. When we follow the developments in the first sixty years of our era, one has the impression of a tragedy moving forward inexorably to its climax. The fuel was collected: only a spark was needed to set it alight. And it came.

Gessius Florus was the last Roman procurator of Judaea, and he was the worst. Compared with him even the worst of his predecessors seemed models of rectitude. He behaved as if he was 'an executioner who was there to punish criminals'. In his time plundering was a daily occurrence, and thieves went unpunished so long as they shared their booty with Florus and his minions. When the citizens saw their lives and property unprotected, a general exodus from Judaea started and gathered speed. Florus' proceedings in Caesarea will be described later. But when he had the audacity to levy a tax of seventeen talents —an enormous sum—on the Temple treasure, patience was exhausted. There were demonstrations in the streets of Jerusalem, and some wags hit on the idea of going round with baskets collecting for 'the wretched pauper Florus'.

He took a bloody revenge. He entered Jerusalem with a detachment of troops, set aside a part of the city for looting, seized a large number of well-known citizens at random and had them crucified. When two more cohorts were about to arrive

JUDAEA CAPTA

from Caesarea, he demanded that the citizens should go to meet them and receive them with ceremony to show their penitence. The town council of Jerusalem indeed consented to this monstrous demand, but when the citizens went to meet the troops as they were compelled to do, the soldiers, acting upon orders, did not return their greetings. This fresh insult was too much. Abuse of Florus filled the air. He sent his soldiers out looting again, but now the people rose. The Romans could not deploy their full strength in the narrow streets. Stones and arrows rained from the roofs on the crowded mass of soldiers, and Florus found himself compelled to withdraw from the capital.

At this time Menahem captured Masada and came to Jerusalem. And two events of decisive importance occurred. The Roman soldiers were cut down, and the city council took the vital decision to stop the daily offerings for the Emperor in the Temple. The die was cast: this was a theocratic form of declaring war.

Of course, the Jewish leaders knew that the fight was hopeless. Sooner or later Rome would mobilize her overwhelming strength and crush all resistance. When Judaea nevertheless took up arms, it was not because the Jews were so naïve as to think themselves stronger than Rome. No, their reason was quite otherwise: they were sure that the God of Israel would intervene! In old times there had been such wonderful happenings in the people's history, whenever its need had been greatest. Had the people not been freed from Egypt and taken to the Promised Land? How had Sennacherib fared when he lay before Jerusalem, and had not the Maccabaeans waged war victoriously against Antiochus Epiphanes? God would do the same now. And the great decision was taken in full confidence that God would intervene.

And their faith was rewarded. The legate of Syria, Cestius Gallus, moved into the rebel country with the Twelfth Legion and numerous auxiliary troops. To his great surprise these Roman crack troops were violently attacked on the march towards Jerusalem. The enemy seemed to have both beak and

THE SON OF A STAR

claws. But he reached Jerusalem without great difficulty and attacked at once. Everything went according to plan. He captured one of the suburbs despite furious resistance and was ready to deliver the decisive assault on the great walls of the temple square.

And then it happened. The defenders of Jerusalem thought at first that it was an optical illusion—but it was real. The Romans struck camp and marched away, down the old military road through the hills of Judaea. The Jews followed them hesitatingly: there might be an ambush. But the retreat was real enough, and the pursuit was pressed with all possible vigour.

What lay behind Gallus' decision is not known today. It was late in the year and the rainy season was about to set in, so that supplies would be difficult. Perhaps, too, he realized that he had not troops enough to deal with so desperate an enemy, and thought it would be better to wait till the spring.

But there was no next time for him. When the army entered the narrow ravines at Beth Horon—near Gibeon, where the sun stood still during the battle in Joshua's time—the Jews were in readiness on the steep slopes of the pass. The heavily armed and not very mobile Roman soldiers were deluged with arrows, while great boulders were rolled down on to them and created havoc in their ranks. Gallus himself was killed, and the whole army narrowly escaped destruction. Only by abandoning all its heavy equipment, and thanks to the self-sacrifice of the rearguard, was the main force able to withdraw with severe losses.

This was the greatest military reverse Rome had suffered since Varrus' legions were destroyed in the trackless forests of Germany. A Roman army defeated by unorganized insurgents of a small nation! Roman prestige sank to a low ebb in the eastern provinces of the Empire.

But to the Jews, returning to Jerusalem in triumph, the victory was a clear revelation of the Lord's might. As soon as the heathen laid hand on his holy temple they were flung into

JUDAEA CAPTA

confusion and lost over 6,000 of their best troops. Before such a manifestation of divine help the Jews' last hesitations disappeared. All rifts in the nation were closed, a provisional government assumed the direction of affairs and took measures to defend the people's newly won freedom.

The news of the disaster reached the Emperor Nero in Greece in the middle of his great artistic tour, on which he was hailed as a singer at the Olympic games. Once again he displayed some of the energy and statesmanship which he undoubtedly possessed, but which were wellnigh submerged under all kinds of vice and incipient madness. Can he have known that he was both saving the Empire and indicating his successor when he appointed the ageing, long retired general Flavius Vespasianus commander-in-chief of the army of the East? A better choice could hardly have been made. Vespasian was full of energy, a shrewd man, and the result showed him to be one of the great generals of the Empire. He hastened to Alexandria with his son Titus and began to assemble the necessary troops for the Jewish campaign.

There are not many events in ancient history of which we know so much as the Roman-Jewish war in the years 66–70. One of the finest of writers took part in this unhappy war, on both sides in fact—first one, then the other—and his book teems with intimate experiences and is as full of tingling life as a work can only be when written by a man who has himself taken part in the events described. I mean, of course, Flavius Josephus and his *History of the Jewish War*. His intervention in the course of the war was of a decisive nature, so we are bound to listen to his story. Moreover, his mentality was so baffling that historians and psychologists throughout the ages have sought with keen interest to plumb its depths.

The name by which he is usually known is a Latinization of a Hebrew original. His real name was Joseph, son of Matthew, but the Latin version is in itself an indication of the split in his life.

He was born in Jerusalem about A.D. 38 of an old and

distinguished family which traced its ancestry back to the Maccabaean princes. He was intended to be a priest, and received a careful education: as a boy of only fourteen he attracted attention by his knowledge and intelligence. But not content to go through both Sadducean and Pharisean educational courses, at the age of sixteen he went out into the desert to live with a hermit called Banus and by mystical practices to attain complete enlightenment on the secret of life. When he returned to the capital three years later he publicly attached himself to the Pharisees. In the year 64 he was sent to Rome as a kind of envoy to obtain the release of three eminent priests whom the Romans were keeping closely imprisoned for a trifling reason. And there he met his fate. The young Pharisee lived in the great world centre for two years, and to carry out his mission he sought contacts in the highest circles. The 'star' actor Alityrus, by birth a Jew, introduced him to the Empress Poppaea, Nero's beautiful and refined consort, and he obtained a first-hand knowledge of Graeco-Roman culture.

Of course the whole of this unknown milieu was bound to make a deep impression on a receptive young man who hitherto had lived in pious Pharisaic circles in distant Jerusalem. When he went home he carried with him a deep conviction of the invincible strength of the world empire and the political genius of Rome. He felt that heaven itself had decided to let Rome rule the world—'God lives in Italy', as he expressed it. Judaea could live only by linking her destiny with that of Rome. What she lost thereby in political freedom she would gain in culture.

He came home in the year 66. The revolution was imminent: the clock showed five minutes to twelve. What happened in his mind in those decisive days we do not know. He himself declares that he advised against war to the last, and it may be supposed that the Jewish aristocracy joined the rebellion only under compulsion. Perhaps the storm of enthusiasm after the miraculous victory over Cestius carried him away. But it is a fact that the provisional government entrusted to him, the pro-Roman, the most responsible post in the impending conflict.

JUDAEA CAPTA

He was appointed Governor of Galilee, which would take the first blow when once the legions were on the move.

He set about his task in two minds. And as weak men often do, he displayed a busy, restless activity, fortified the towns and called up men, till he had in all 100,000 at his disposal. But the local conditions were difficult, with Gentiles and Jews living all intermingled. Zealot extremists were agitating, and large towns were ready to surrender to the first Roman soldier who showed himself.

Josephus was a moderate and tried to do what was impossible —to sit on the fence. He was surrounded by continual intrigues and met with concealed or open opposition. So when at last Vespasian ordered an advance, he met a commander who believed in Roman invincibility more than in his own cause.

The mere rumour of the Romans' arrival was enough to scatter the bulk of the loosely organized troops of the Galilee army. But when all seemed lost, Josephus summoned up courage to undertake the desperate and famous defence of the mountain fortress of Jotapata, in the Galilean highlands. It stood on a steep cliff surrounded by deep ravines and there he displayed both skill and bravery.

He himself gives a vivid account of the defence of Jotapata and does not conceal his own high qualities as a commander. The prolongation of the siege for months was no doubt due largely to the inaccessibility of the place and the bravery of the Jewish soldiers. But Josephus' keen intelligence hit upon thousands of ingenious devices which irritated and delayed the enemy. He hung sodden animals' skins over the walls, which caught the Romans' blazing arrows and gave the impression that the defenders of Jotapata did not lack water—of which in fact they were very short. When the enemy began to run their battering rams against the wall of the town, the Jews let down sacks of hay and straw in front of the wall to intercept the blows. Vigorous sorties and furious shooting alternated: once Vespasian himself was wounded by an arrow from the wall.

But it was all in vain: the fortress' fate was sealed. A

deserter told the Romans how exhausted the defenders were, especially in the morning after a sleepless night. Vespasian made use of this information and delivered his main attack early one morning. The sleepy sentries were cut down, and the fortress fell.

Josephus, with forty soldiers, took refuge in a tank. They resolved to die together, but in the drawing of lots, by what he called 'a lucky chance', he was to be the last to die. Then he surrendered to Vespasian. At the meeting between the defeated and victorious generals Josephus assumed a prophetic mien and foretold that Vespasian would become Emperor. It may have been these flattering words that made Vespasian spare his enemy's life. But it is just as likely that he saw how useful Josephus could be in the further course of the war. It would be wise to keep this man, with his knowledge of the Jews, as an adviser. So Josephus became a turncoat and went through the last phase of the war on the side of the Romans.

When Vespasian set him free he gave Josephus permission to bear his own family name, which is why we know him as Flavius Josephus. After the fall of Jerusalem, Titus allowed him to take what he liked from the conquered city. He chose only a few sacred books, but asked that the lives of a large number of friends and relations might be spared. His request was granted: in fact three men who had already been crucified were taken down again.

After the war he was a man of high standing at court. He wrote his books there and lived till about A.D. 100. But a wall of contempt separated him from his countrymen: in their eyes he had betrayed his country. Was he a deliberate traitor? That is the riddle of his life. There can be no doubt that he was vain and self-centred to an exceptional degree; his books reveal it again and again. But he sturdily defends himself against the charge of treachery. The most that we shall ever be able to do is to convict him of a conspicuous want of character, which can explain his unhappy oscillation between the two fronts.

On the other hand, we have to thank him for our knowledge

JUDAEA CAPTA

of the war and for a great deal of information about the Jewish people. Certainly his books have many defects and must be read with a critical eye. But he was a brilliant, vivid writer, and his writings have survived nineteen centuries. It is a pity that the later rebellions had no Josephus of their own.

Revolutions, like everything else in the universe, follow certain laws. One of them lays down that forces once unleashed sooner or later seize power from those who unleashed them, and get out of control. In almost all revolutions, therefore, there is a period of terror: the Jewish revolution is no exception to the rule. The catastrophe in Galilee and Josephus' betrayal shook Jerusalem and flung the unhappy city into a fearful turmoil. The extremists seized power, and the old aristocracy were ruthlessly murdered. The civil war gathered impetus and blood flowed in the streets of the holy city.

When the Roman intelligence service reported this news to the supreme command, Vespasian's generals urged him to take advantage of the chaos in Jerusalem and deliver a swift attack which could put an end to the troublesome war. But this did not appeal to Vespasian. He was one of these men who can wait and let the fruit ripen: who would, indeed, rather let it fall to the ground of itself. He contented himself with securing all the surrounding areas and was soon in control of all Judaea except the capital.

This silent, slow man had higher aims. It was not only in Judaea that the barometer indicated storm: in Rome political events were moving swiftly towards chaos. Nero committed suicide, and three emperors in quick succession ascended the throne: the different armies proclaimed their favourite generals Emperor, and civil wars were bringing the Empire to the verge of the abyss.

At last the army of the East took the initiative and proclaimed Vespasian Emperor. He accepted the dignity with reluctance: the soldiers had to threaten to kill him if he did not accede to their wishes. A short, fierce war with his rivals for the throne was decisive, and the man of simple origin had reached the goal it had seemed so improbable that he could attain: the world empire bowed before him and acknowledged him as its ruler. Vespasian hastened to Rome, handing over the command in Judaea to Titus.

The pause in the war and the long drawn out crises had lasted for several years, and Vespasian's hesitating, uncertain strategy had strengthened the Jews' hope that the Lord was fighting on their side. But Jerusalem had not made use of the time of grace: on the contrary, internal anarchy had reached heights unseen before. Different leaders fought for power: this went so far that they burnt one another's food supplies, which would have helped the city through the coming siege.

And now came the Roman advance, swift and vigorous. The newly chosen Flavian dynasty needed a brilliant victory for the sake of prestige. At Easter of the year 70, when Jerusalem was crowded with hundreds of thousands of pilgrims, Titus established his headquarters on Mount Scopus, north of the city, and the fifth act of the great tragedy began. In their extreme peril the hostile factions in Jerusalem at last united. Old enemies joined hands and stood side by side on the walls in the most heroic defence in the world's history.

The desperation with which the Jews fought their hopeless fight exceeded the Romans' worst anticipations. Again and again the balance swung to and fro. Once Titus narrowly escaped being taken prisoner: another time, on the Mount of Olives, the Tenth Legion wavered before an unexpected assault: only Titus' arrival at the last moment averted disaster. The siege engines were suddenly attacked and set on fire or undermined so that they collapsed.

Jerusalem was not a single fortress, but was divided by walls and separate, very strong forts, the Antonia, the Temple and Herod's palace with massive towers. The city could not be captured simply by breaking through the outer wall, but had to be overcome section by section. This was just the kind of war to which the Jews were best suited. The legionaries advanced only step by step, with enormous losses.

The Jews could have held out for years if one of the most

JUDAEA CAPTA

elemental forces—hunger—had not been working against them. The overcrowded city was cut off from the rest of the country—the Romans had built a wall all round it—and its food stocks had unfortunately been burnt, so that famine became acute. The pale spectre of starvation penetrated into every house, even those of the richest, who for a long time had been able to buy in the black market at fantastic prices. Grey-faced people, their bodies swollen with hunger, fell down dying in the open street. Whole families died silently and slowly, one by one, and there was not strength enough in them to weep over the dead. Jerusalem was like a cemetery: a deathly silence hung over it. But the starving warriors still stood on the walls, ready to die but not to surrender. Outside were triumphant Roman soldiers holding up delicious, tempting food for them to see.

Then the Romans launched the decisive attack. The Antonia fell, but not till the capture of the Temple was the Jewish resistance broken. Titus' staff had decided to spare this unique monument, but in the heat of the battle it was set on fire. Josephus tries to convey the atmosphere of this scene, the frightful culminating point of the war:

'The Temple Hill seemed one glowing mass right from the ground, enveloped in fire as it was from all sides. But the stream of blood seemed to flow even more strongly than the stream of fire. The earth could not be seen for bodies, and Roman soldiers were still pursuing fugitives over regular mountains of corpses.' The words convey to us vividly the shiver of horror which ran through every Jew who saw it all.

What had the Temple in Jerusalem not meant to the Jews! Shining in white and gold it lay there, like a snow mountain. It contained immense treasures, the talk of the whole world. There was the seven-branched golden candelabra, whose lights signified the sun and moon and the planets Mercury, Venus, Mars, Jupiter and Saturn. There was the table with the twelve shewbreads symbolizing the zodiac and at the same time the course of the year, and there stood the carriage with the thirteen kinds of incense from the sea, the uninhabited deserts and the cultivated land, which proclaimed that all came from

THE SON OF A STAR

God and was for God. From all over the world the warmest thoughts of the Jews flew to the Temple where the invisible God had his holy habitation. And now flames and smoke were sweeping over the white roof. Now the great event must take place.

But the miracle did not happen. The revolt had been started to protect the Temple in particular and the war raged in confident hope that it would prove inviolable. And now the heathen were defiling its most sacred buildings with Israelite blood and setting fire to the house of the Lord. But the Lord was silent; he answered not, nor did the Messiah come down from heaven and destroy the ungodly with the breath of his mouth. Instead were heard the victorious Roman soldiers, shouting in chorus as they hailed Titus with a thundering 'Imperator!' the title belonging by right to a victorious general.

With the fall of the Temple the Jewish resistance collapsed. The last phase of the struggle—for the upper city and Herod's palace—was short. After this was stormed the rest of Jerusalem was in flames. The fire raged for a day and a night, and 'next morning the sun rose over the smoking ruins of Jerusalem'. The city was in the hands of the Romans after a five months' siege, devastated, burned down and streaming with blood.

Josephus says that 97,000 prisoners were taken and that there were over a million dead. Of course these figures cannot be checked, but it was a tremendous battle. It has been said that 'it was not so much a heroic victory as a victory over heroes'. It cannot be put better.

The prisoners were sold as slaves—there was a slump in the price of slaves in the following years—or used for popular amusement in the arena, where they were flung to wild beasts or made to cut each other down as gladiators. This tradition throws just a scrap of light on the human tragedies which followed in the wake of defeat. A brother and sister belonging to a good family in Jerusalem came separately into the possession of two neighbours. Their owners, not knowing of the relationship, decided to marry the proud, well-built slave to the pretty slave girl. When they were brought together at night they recognized each other and were so horrified that they killed themselves.

But there were darker passages still, and no picture would be accurate which did not include them.

The last members of the Maccabaean royal family, King Agrippa and his sister Berenice, looked down on their people's death struggle from the headquarters on Mount Scopus. These are the couple we read of in the Acts of the Apostles. They visited the procurator Festus at Caesarea, and he brought before them his interesting prisoner, the apostle Paul. It was then that Paul described his life to them and showed them the way to Christ, to which Agrippa replied with the famous words: 'Almost thou persuadest me to be a Christian!'

This was presumably meant sarcastically. At any rate, this would be most in keeping with the King's character—or lack of character. He was openly indifferent to religious matters, and his inherited Jewishness was as superficial as could be. He had been brought up in Rome, and throughout his life truckled to the Roman emperors. When the insurrection broke out in Jerusalem, he made a still-born attempt to stifle it, and afterwards stood firmly on the Romans' side with his auxiliary troops. He maintained an unconcealed liaison with his sister Berenice, but such things were not uncommon in the East.

Titus was immediately fascinated by the strange Eastern princess and without doubt was genuinely in love with her. She gave herself willingly, and had she not been a Jewess she would certainly have become Empress. Titus, however, was obliged to consider anti-Semitic feelings in Rome, and dismissed her. She was probably not very faithful to her imperial lover. At any rate the consul Caecina was put to death because he was suspected of having enjoyed her favours.

This was the end of the last scions of the royal house of Israel. They were descended from the old Hasmonaean princes through the marriage of Herod the Great with Mariamme. But they themselves were in the enemy's camp. A river which springs fresh and strong from its source in the mountains often

THE SON OF A STAR

spreads out into turbid stagnant swamps before it glides slowly into the sea and into oblivion.

For almost nineteen centuries the destruction of the Temple was the greatest and most decisive event in Jewish history. It was not overshadowed till the setting up of the State of Israel in 1948. And to this very day we are confronted with memorials of it, both dead and living. When we see them, against the background of eternity, we feel the passage of two thousand years as a faint ripple on the ocean of time.

Titus' triumphal arch in Rome was not completed till after the Emperor's early death, and it has survived all the violent happenings that have shaken the Eternal City. We see the Goddess of Victory crowning Titus, and captured Jews being driven past with the shewbread table and the seven-branched candelabra. We know from this sculpture what these precious objects looked like, but they themselves have disappeared. Vespasian had them preserved in the temple of the Goddess of Victory which he built after the fall of the city. Probably the Vandals carried them off to Africa when they sacked Rome in 455. A few hundred years later the might of the Vandals was broken and the booty was transferred to Constantinople. An ancient historian narrates that a Jew saw them there when visiting the Emperor Justinian and pointed out to the Emperor that so far they had brought misfortune to those who possessed them wrongfully: both Rome and Carthage had been captured. Thereupon the Emperor hastened to send them to Jerusalem. Who knows that they may not one day reappear?

In Jerusalem the three towers of Herod's palace, Phasael, Hippicus and Mariamme, remained standing. Tradition says that they were spared to show the generations to come what a mighty city Titus had been able to conquer. One of these towers stands to this day by the Jaffa gate: it is now called David's Tower, Migdal David. And the western part of the wall of the fortress, with its huge ancient stones, where the Tenth Legion was encamped as army of occupation, is still standing. This is the present-day praying wall in Jerusalem, the

2. The rock of Masada as seen from the east

Ancient terraces in the Jordan hills

3. View from the top of Masada to the Dead Sea

JUDAEA CAPTA

centre of Jewish life for uncounted generations after Jews were again allowed to visit Jerusalem.

But living memorials are more than stone ones, and in peoples wedded to tradition they are preserved and handed down from father to son. By a curious coincidence Jerusalem fell twice on the same date, the 9th of the month Ab (*Tisha be'ab* in Hebrew), first to King Nebuchadnezzar in 586 B.C. and to Titus in A.D. 70. and both times the temple was devastated. And what is still more curious, it was also on the 9th of Ab that the revolt of the Son of a Star in the year 135 came to its bloody conclusion. Three times the Jewish people lost its political independence on the same date.

This day, therefore, is still alive in Jewish memories: it still bleeds like an open wound after nearly two thousand years. Since the devastation of the Temple it has been forbidden to build any house without a corner being left unfinished, and no festival may be celebrated without remembering the loss of Zion. As a matter of course the 9th Ab is a day of mourning and a fast day. Three weeks earlier, on the 17th Tammus, the Romans penetrated into Jerusalem, and both days are fast days. On the 9th Ab the synagogue is kept in semi-darkness, and Jeremiah's Lamentations are read to the accompaniment of melancholy old tunes. As during the seven days of mourning after the death of a near relation, people sit on stools near the ground as a sign of grief. In these three weeks everything which can give enjoyment and pleasure is avoided. A person may not eat fruit he has not tasted already that year, he may not put on new clothes or move into a new house. Hair is not cut and no festival may be celebrated. On the following Sabbath the words of Isaiah are read: 'Comfort ye, comfort ye my people!' There is universal grief at the nation's deep fall, a longing to atone for the fault and win back what was lost.

Coins from those old times are still found in the soil of Palestine. Vespasian, Titus and Domitian all struck coins to commemorate the capture of Jerusalem. They show a woman wearing mourning and are inscribed *Judaea capta* (Judaea conquered) or *Judaea devicta* (Judaea overcome).

THE SON OF A STAR

Jerusalem fell. But far from the smoking ruins, down south in the Judaean desert by the Dead Sea, Masada stood proudly on its inaccessible rock, the only place where Jewish will to live still breathed.

When Eleazar stood on the top of the tower he felt like a bird flying high in the sky, with a vast panorama spread below. Far down, almost beneath his feet, the Dead Sea lay in its gorge, a brilliant deep blue like no other water on earth. He had a view of the whole length of the Sea, from the Jordan valley by Jericho far off on the misty horizon, and if he turned his eyes the other way they did not stop till the blue surface of the Sea was broken by the mountains to southward. Here and there flat spits of land and sandbanks lay along the shore, covered with a white salty deposit. And on all sides the mountains rose steeply as though cut with a knife: reddish, rose-coloured limestone, tinged lilac by the setting sun.

But Eleazar was not now absorbed in the contemplation of all this beauty: he had far more important matters on hand. The incredible had happened: the Romans lay before the fortress. Scouts had reported troop movements southward, and later one evening Eleazar had seen the Roman camp-fires far away to the west. First a little light appeared, just one. But a moment later there were more, and it was not long before the dark shadows of the mountains were dotted with hundreds of lights. So they were coming. What no one had thought feasible was now to be done. Inaccessible Masada was to be stormed and the last fragment of free Israel crushed. It was Rome Eleazar had against him—and the time had not yet come when Rome would know the word impossible.

Two thousand years later, every patch of the Jews' ancient land carries the marks of Roman power. Wherever one digs in the soil, water-pipes, sites of houses, stumps of columns are found, dating from Roman times. But no place tells of the might of the conquering nation so eloquently as Masada, where Roman will and Roman steel shattered Israel's last defences. Military historians have pronounced the battle for Masada,

JUDAEA CAPTA

both in attack and defence, to have been one of the most, if not the most remarkable and impressive the world has ever seen.

The Roman general Flavius Silva was marching with strong forces drawn from the army of occupation to carry out the Emperor's orders at all costs.

In places which only solitary shepherds had dared to traverse, he made roads right through the desert and over mountains. Most important of all, he organized a water supply. Every drop of water the army would use in those burning mountains had to be carried for many miles. The heavy siege equipment was dragged forward: it was let down into steep ravines and drawn up again on the other side.

The Roman legionaries were accustomed to do their own work, but they were not equal to this. Hordes of slave labourers were driven forward, tens of thousands of them. Roman soldiers compelled them by use of the whip to exert the last scrap of will-power they possessed and any strength that the heat and flies and fever left in their muscles. Scores of them collapsed daily and were flung off the road half dead and gasping for air. Some were not quite dead when the jackals came at night and tore the flesh from their bones. Every night the jackals howled round the camps, and by day the vultures hovered in flocks over the places where work was being done: it was just the time for them.

The Romans arrived at last, but only to see that the hardest task of all awaited them. The fortress still rose unconquered on its rock. It could not be starved out, it must be stormed and conquered sword in hand. And there was no time to be lost: Rome could not keep her soldiers out there in the desert.

The Romans built their camps, eight in all. The foundations and remains of the walls can be studied to this day as examples of Roman military organization. They had ramparts, gates, towers, main roads and by-roads, and in the commander-in-chief's tent Flavius Silva performed the daily sacrifice for the Emperor's welfare.

When the camps were ready, Silva had a wall built all round the plateau, so that the defenders were prevented from making

THE SON OF A STAR

sorties and hindering the continuation of the siege works. And at the only point where it was possible to approach the fortress, the white promontory, the legionaries heaped up a regular mountain of earth. On it they laid a foundation of great stones: the catapults were placed on this and they slung stones against the walls. Right at the top the soldiers operated with a powerful battering-ram, so high up that it could be run direct against the stout wall of Masada.

From dawn to sunset, with long intervals, were heard the dull thuds which shook the whole fortress. The battering-ram rushed forward at the wall, then drew back, was put into position again and sprang forward to deliver a fresh blow. Even the thickest walls must give way in time before such a monstrous engine. The century-old defences of Masada began to crumble: large parts of the wall crashed down into the abyss, and a breach was opened which grew wider every day.

But Eleazar was energetic and untiring: he and his people would not be passive victims of the enemy's superior strength. Behind the threatened section of the wall he built a new rampart, so constructed that the enemy's machines were powerless against it. Huge beams were laid on top of and in continuation of one another, and fastened together to make a new wall. There were two rows of these, parallel to each other and connected by cross-pieces. The space between was filled with earth. When the battering-ram ran against this elastic wall all that happened was that the earth collapsed with the shook and made the rampart still stronger than before.

Masada's last day came. Silva ordered that blazing arrows should be fired at the new wooden rampart. The Romans succeeded in setting it alight. But the wind was blowing the wrong way, and flames and smoke rushed towards the Romans and their machines. It looked as if they had dug their own graves. Eleazar stood on the tower eagerly watching the course of events. For the very last time, was the miracle about to happen?

No! The wind changed suddenly, the flames took hold of the rampart; smoke and fire now swept into the fortress and drove the defenders back. The buildings too began to catch

JUDAEA CAPTA

fire. A cheer from the Romans greeted this decisive turn of events. It was growing dark, so the final assault would have to wait till next day. Strong posts were stationed at the vital points, so that no sally or attempt to escape was possible. Then the Romans withdrew to their camps to recover strength for the morrow's fighting.

Inside the fortress Eleazar mustered his men for the last time. He surveyed their ranks. He knew every man and had proved his worth. From a military standpoint they were only loosely organized and amateurishly trained partisans. But they had dared to stand up to the world's strongest military power and had defied it till now. The legionaries outside the walls were professional soldiers who had won the last battle in all their wars till now. The traditions of centuries had created a war machine which worked with the precision of clockwork. What had the Jews to oppose to it? Courage, defiance and fanaticism— and faith in the God of Israel. And now there was nothing more.

Eleazar began to speak. With despair in his voice he reminded them of their oath: freedom or death. Now only the last choice remained. The men looked at him uncertainly. Were they to kill their women and children and themselves? Then Eleazar pointed out over the burning defence works in the direction of Jerusalem. He asked them to remember what happened when the capital fell and what would happen there next day: slaughter, captivity, slavery, rape of women and murder of children. But that night they were still free men, who could die, but could keep their oath and despite everything believe in the God who had left them alone.

So the last soldiers of Israel went to their death. Each man embraced his dear ones: tears ran down the cheeks of these men of iron and they did their wives and children the last service by killing them. Then every man lay down beside his dead family, and ten men who had been chosen by lot ran their swords through the breasts of their comrades. Of these ten, one had been chosen to kill the other nine: when this had been done he threw himself upon his own sword. Nearly a thousand bodies covered the ground.

THE SON OF A STAR

It began to grow light. The trumpets sounded in the Roman camp, and the assaulting columns moved forward. When they approached the ramparts they were surprised at the silence which met them. They feared a ruse, and picked their way forward through the burned down wall. Then two women and some children appeared. They had hidden in a vault the night before and saved themselves. Now they told the Romans what had happened. It was not the day of triumph on which the victors had counted. They gazed in silence at the heaps of corpses. Those tough soldiers had seen a good deal, but never a sight like that.

The day passed and evening came on. Silva stood on the tower which had been Eleazar's post for so many years. In the faint light of the new moon he surveyed the vast landscape. The Dead Sea lay silent under his feet: it was like the darkness of death and gave him a queer uncanny feeling. From the courtyard below came the shouting of busy men. The legionaries, working by torchlight, had formed a chain from the tanks to the burning fortress and were passing along skin buckets of water to quench the last flames. They shouted and swore as they dried the mingled sweat and soot from their dirty faces. When Silva saw that the fire was out he descended from the tower.

By the light of a single torch he dictated a dispatch to the Emperor announcing his victory. The report ended with the words *Judaea capta est*, Judaea is conquered. At last the objective was attained. The dispatch rider mounted his horse and sped off through the burned gate on his way to Caesarea.

The legionaries had had enough to do all day. The dead had to be thrown over the walls to be food for the jackals, the place cleaned up and the fire put out. At last their task was over. Food and great leather jars of wine were brought from the cellars, and the victors made merry.

Silva sat deep in thought, gazing at the blackened walls. He was meditating on the long, bloody campaign. Then he gave a kick at a sooty lump of wood, muttered: 'Well, now we've stamped out the last spark in this accursed people', and went

JUDAEA CAPTA

off to join the festive board, whence shouting and singing were beginning to be audible.

The light of the torches rose high into the night sky. The Dead Sea and the Judaean desert lay in the darkness beyond. Possibly some of the Romans noticed the stars over the fortress —large bright stars, moving on their unchanging courses.

II

HE THAT SHOULD COME

FLAVIUS SILVA was richly rewarded for his achievement. In the year 81 he rose to the highest rank after that of Emperor and was elected Consul. But he was wrong in his belief that the last spark of Jewish longing for freedom had been crushed out under the heaps of corpses in the blackened ruins of Masada. He himself left conquered Judaea to follow his political career. And while he was living the brilliant life of an upper class Roman, the troops who had remained behind to guard the outposts of the Empire felt often enough that the fire was always smouldering under the ashes, and at times it burst into flames again.

LEG X FRET. These initials are found in many places in Palestine, carved in stone or simply on rocks. It is the mark of the Tenth Legion. LEG is an abbreviation of Legion, X is the Roman ten, and the last syllable FRET means Fretensis and signifies the Straits of Messina, the narrow strip of water between Sicily and the toe of Italy. The legions as a rule took their names from the places where they were permanently garrisoned, and the Tenth Legion had been at Messina for a long time. It ought almost to have changed its name, for after taking part in the Jewish war it was employed for more than a hundred years as the garrison of Judaea: traces of it are found there dating from as late as the third century of our era.

The inscriptions give us an idea of where its various detachments were stationed: in Jerusalem, at places of strategic importance from Jerusalem through the Judaean mountains, to Joppa, Lydda and Caesarea, at Tiberias on the Sea of Galilee

HE THAT SHOULD COME

and along the Galilean road system. On the Mount of Olives a large burial place, like a catacomb, has been found with numerous stones stamped LXF—the Legion's initials again—which were used to cover graves. Many of the fallen soldiers of the Legion were buried here. The legions often had a special sign, a kind of mascot: that of the Tenth Legion was a wild pig, which constantly appears in its inscriptions.

Officers and soldiers lived in the conquered country only because they had to. They never ceased to feel themselves foreigners in the land of the Jews. There was an invisible but sharply defined barrier between the Roman army of occupation and the people of the country: even in those days the policy of the cold shoulder was known. The Romans were allowed to see only the quite external sides of Jewish life, but they found enough to surprise them even in that: it was a queer alien world which filled them with mingled disgust and curiosity.

Every seventh day life came to a complete standstill. And this people did not worship gods in temples, but believed in an invisible God and observed an endless series of special customs and commands. The Roman soldiers shook their heads.

And from the Jewish side the barrier became sharper and more pronounced as the years passed, even in thousands of small things. Jewish men would not follow the barbaric custom of shaving the beard. They wore it as nature let it grow, and took the greatest care of both beard and hair. A bald man could not become a priest, and the hair of ladies of fashion was treated with ointment, scented and powdered with gold dust. Gymnastics could lead to intercourse with Gentiles, so they were avoided. For the same reason there was opposition to theatres and all kinds of public entertainment.

The rabbis were always on their guard against infection from the heathen. It was forbidden to throw a stone in honour of Mercury, to do any business with Gentiles three days before or after the festival of a false god, or to buy in shops which were decorated in honour of a false god. It was indeed forbidden to celebrate the first of January and the Emperor's birthday. A

THE SON OF A STAR

Jewish doctor might not assist at the birth of a Gentile child nor a Jewish wet-nurse give it her milk.

The line was clearly drawn. For the Tenth Legion, which sent its soldiers marching about the country, came from Rome, and Rome was Israel's enemy.

The country recovered remarkably quickly. The catastrophic events of the years from 66 to 70—the insurrection, the civil wars and the campaigns of Vespasian and Titus—left Palestine in a state of chaos. Jerusalem lay in ashes and was not rebuilt during the next sixty or seventy years; many other towns had been under martial law—more than a million people had lost their lives, and the best patriots among the survivors had fled to their countrymen in dispersion. But despite all this the year 70 was not the landmark it is commonly reputed to be. The defeat was symbolized in a humiliating manner in the imperial order to the whole of the Jewish people, both in Judaea and elsewhere, that the former voluntary contribution of half a shekel to the Temple at Jerusalem should in future be made to the temple of Jupiter on the Capitol in Rome, and Judaea was placed under the Roman governor of Syria and so lost the last glimmer of independence. But generally speaking the people lived for another sixty-five years in the old country, and even if the shadow of defeat brooded over them, life was lived with the old manners and customs. Pulses began to beat again and the blood to circulate.

In old times the country had been divided according to the settlements of the twelve tribes, and to this very day the districts are named after them. The political changes of different epochs have affected the frontiers of the provinces: one delimitation after another has been made and altered again, but generally speaking the country has been divided into four large provinces—Galilee, Samaria, Judaea and Peraea.

The northern part of Galilee consisted of high mountains, where for the most part Gentiles lived. Generally speaking, in Galilee the people of Israel were ringed round by Gentile immigrants: the very name shows it, for *galil* means a ring or circle, 'the heathen's ring'. The southern part of Galilee lay lower and was more level and fertile. Many of the Galilean Jews were made alert, self-confident and brave by the close proximity of the foreigners. And the country was rich. It was said that there were no fewer than 240 towns in Galilee. By the Sea of Galilee the soil was particularly fertile: the Sea lies more than 600 feet below the level of the Mediterranean, so that subtropical warmth prevails. Here a hard-working and efficient population had a good chance of obtaining an ample return from agriculture.

Samaria was the smallest of the provinces, but the richest. The soil was fertile and the climate good, with plenty of rain, and the water of the springs was particularly sweet. Abundant water and aromatic plants made the Samaritans' milk famous for its excellent flavour. Relations between the inhabitants and the Jews were strained. Mutual distrust and bitterness were deep-rooted, going right back to the building of the Second Temple. The Jews regarded the Samaritans as the descendants of a mongrel heathen people and accused them of worshipping false gods. The Samaritans replied with hostile acts and lost no opportunity of revenging themselves. What the two peoples preferred was to avoid one another. As is known, pilgrims from Galilee, when going to Jerusalem, liked to make the long detour east of the Jordan, so as to avoid any communication with the despised Samaritans. The rabbis forbade the Jews to buy uncooked food from Samaritans or to spend a night under the same roof with them.

Judaea was the most populous and important of the provinces: it gave its name to the country. 'Judaea the seed, Galilee the straw, east of Jordan only chaff' was a common saying. Judaea proper consisted of gloomy barren mountains, but the coastal plain was rich and fertile. Peraea was the country east of the Jordan and was not of much importance to Jewish life. It was a mountainous and in many parts a desert region, but it had important towns: the majority of the ten towns we are accustomed to call Decapolis were in Peraea.

The most important industry was agriculture, but there

were a striking number of towns. The reason for this was that a great many of the farmers collected in towns for reasons of security. A distinction was made between fortified places and towns: the latter were called large if they contained ten men so rich that they did not need to live by the work of their own hands. In the towns people lived in safety, protected by a wall or rampart with a moat in front and towers at the gates. The gate was a place of assembly in the busy life of the town. From it people had a view out into the world down the long grey road: there was shade there, and they collected and discussed public affairs or listened to words of wisdom from a rabbi.

The streets were narrow and lined with small shops: pavement was unnecessary on the stony ground. Cemeteries and tanneries, which smelt unpleasant, had to be not less than thirty-five yards outside the town.

The houses were built of sun-dried brick, rich people's of cut stone. The wood was that of the mulberry, the commonest tree in the country, but superior kinds of wood were also used, almond or cedar, often finely carved and painted. The centre of the house was the inner court, with open galleries and sometimes a fountain. The roofs were almost flat, with only slope enough for the rain-water to run off, and were edged with balustrades: on them people could seek solitude or sit in the evening when it was cool. The windows were either wide in the Phoenician or narrow in the Egyptian style and covered with lattice-work.

Outside the walls the roads ran from town to town. Country roads were only some ten feet wide, but the main roads were broad, up to forty feet, often paved and with milestones. One important road ran from the coast at Ptolemais through Galilee to Tiberias: there it swung away northwards through Capernaum, where once Matthew had sat 'at the receipt of custom', and over the Jordan to Damascus. From Jerusalem one of the oldest roads in the world ran southwards into Egypt, and the ancient coast road from Phoenicia to Egypt also passed through Palestine.

People travelled a great deal in those days, on foot, on

HE THAT SHOULD COME

mule-back or in carts, but such a journey was difficult and dangerous, so they usually preferred to join a convoy. Anyone setting out on a journey made great preparations: he provided himself with a tent and a supply of corn, dried fruit and clothes. He sent word in advance, and his host came to meet him and accompanied him along the road. People stayed with fellow-countrymen if they could: the inns were bad and often managed by Gentiles, so Jews did their best to avoid them.

Merchants travelled far, and there was an active sea trade, both export and import; ships sailed as far as India. Palestine was a rich country and sold goods of many kinds overseas; the ships came home with full cargoes, with fish from Spain, apples from Crete, beans and onions from Egypt and Cyprus, and wines from Italy. Palestine herself exported oil, honey, figs, balsam, linen and wool. We get from the Talmud an impression of trade on a large scale: it mentions 90 different kinds of export and 120 of import goods.

Palestine was first and foremost an agricultural country. Curiously enough the rabbis looked down on the simple farmer: he had no time to study and therefore did not know all the complicated ritual obligations. It was another matter with the rich landowners, who could afford to have bailiffs and men to do the field work. Many centuries of careful tending had made the country immensely fertile: it was indeed 'a land flowing with milk and honey'. Special importance was attached to irrigation, which was absolutely necessary in the long dry season from April to November.

Jewish law demanded careful work: for example, great care had to be taken to see that different kinds of corn were not mixed. It also required generosity: a seventh part of the harvest must be handed over to the poor, also whatever was spilt on the way home or fell beside the sickle when the corn was being cut. The corn was thrashed with the flail or trodden by cattle.

But it was especially fruit in which the country was rich. There were ripe figs in ten months of the year, and vines grew readily in many places. Special care was given to them: they were grafted or often renewed. The wine was drunk both before

THE SON OF A STAR

and after fermentation, either strained or diluted with water and prepared with spices. But as today, moderation was observed: drunkenness has never been one of the Jews' national failings. Wine was made also from honey and dates. The sap was drawn from the balsam tree by making a little cut in the bark, and myrrh was won from the myrrh plant in the same way.

An abundance of fruit trees—pomegranates, mulberries and almonds—grew in the gardens and along the roads. In the mountains the fruit grew on terraces, surrounded by walls. The peasants kept watchmen to guard the fruit, but passers by had the right to pick what they could eat on the spot. The olive harvest was of great importance. There were three kinds of olives—those which were picked first, those from the middle of the tree and those which fell down of their own accord: these were left lying till they were almost dissolved, and then the oil was pressed out between two stones.

Cattle formed a great part of the wealth of the country, but only clean animals: those that were unclean, such as pigs, were absolutely forbidden. Sheep were kept mainly near desolate stretches of land which could be used for grazing. They were watched over from towers and folded at night. The animals were watered from tanks and driven home in winter. Oxen were reared for beef, but could also be used for ploughing and thrashing: they were driven not with a whip but with a pointed stick, and it was of no use for an ox to 'kick against the pricks'. Milk, both fresh and sour milk, which was turned into cheese, came from cows, goats and sheep. The camel was used for the hardest work, and its manure was valued as fuel.

The townspeople who were not rich enough to be independent earned a living by trade or by crafts. It was the duty of parents to train their children for some work, not too hard but healthy. But some crafts were despised, either because they were too hard or because they catered for luxury—such as barbers, weavers and perfumiers. Moreover, work might only be a means of earning one's daily bread, so that the real object of life, the study of the law, could be pursued.

So the land lay from the blue Mediterranean to the deep

HE THAT SHOULD COME

Jordan valley, spreading itself in wide plains and climbing over dark mountains. Men had set their traces everywhere, and diligent hands had made the country so fertile and rich that the smell of growing things filled the air. It is estimated that there were five million people in Palestine in those days, and the land provided for them amply. There was swarming life in the narrow streets of the towns, where busy craftsmen sat in workshops open to the crowds, and the merchants cried their wares aloud in their booths. People sang at their work all over the fields and orchards and plantations, and merchants and travellers with heavily laden carts and animals drove along the roads.

Then the step of men marching in time was heard, and a sharp voice ordered people to make way: a detachment of the Tenth Legion was marching by. Men turned their eyes away or exchanged swift angry looks. For the masses never forgot that this was their country, the promised land which the Lord had given them. One day he would bare his arm and drive the foreigners out and make his chosen people masters of the world, with Jerusalem as the earth's centre. And this firm belief in the one God and his intentions with the Jewish people had its centre in the learned academies at Jabneh. There Judaism was preserved despite defeat and foreign domination.

This had begun when the Romans lay before Jerusalem, besieging the city. All who had watched the development of events with a sober eye saw clearly the coming disaster. But the Zealots had established a pitiless dictatorship and were determined to wage war to the bitter end. They had forbidden people to leave the town: the penalty was death.

At this time the old rabbi Johanan Ben Zakkai was the finest teacher in Israel. He had belonged to the peace party and had always done his uttermost to avoid war. He now saw that Judaea was lost. But for him the choice did not lie between victory and defeat. A still greater disaster than the defeat of Judaea would be if the Jewish nation was crushed under the ruins of the State. The task, therefore, was to save the essence of Jewish spirit and give it the possibility of future growth. So he decided to live for the people and lay the foundations of spiritual rebirth in the midst of political catastrophe. First of all he must plan how to get out of the doomed city. How he accomplished this we know from legends to which the mists of antiquity cling.

Johanan had a nephew, Abba Sikra, who was one of the Zealot leaders. The old man met him in secret and their conversation began as follows:

'How much longer are you going to resist the Romans and let the people die of starvation?'

'You know that I cannot do anything. I have committed myself too far. If I try to draw back now, I am lost.'

'But at any rate you can help me. I have found a way of getting out of the town, so that I can negotiate with the enemy and possibly make them better disposed towards us.'

They agreed upon the plan. Johanan spread a report that he was dangerously ill, and later that he was dead. He was laid on a bier in grave-clothes and had a piece of meat hidden beneath them to spread an odour like that of a corpse. His disciples carried the bier to the gate of the city, where the sentries stopped the cortège to make sure that the man was really dead. One of them raised his spear and was going to run him through. But Sikra was standing by and checked the blow, saying:

'What will the Romans think of us, if we do not leave a teacher of Israel in peace when he is dead?'

So Johanan reached Vespasian and said to him:

'Peace be with you, O King! Peace be with you, O King!'

According to Jewish custom a crowned head had to be addressed twice. Vespasian replied:

'You have made yourself liable to the death penalty by calling me King, for I am not a king.'

'You will become King, for otherwise Jerusalem would not fall into your hands. Isaiah says that Lebanon—that means Jerusalem—shall fall by a mighty one.'

At that moment an officer entered and announced that the Senate in Rome had elected Vespasian Emperor. He was just

4. Cliff near Sodom on the Dead Sea called Lot's Wife

Wilderness of Judaea

5. Caesarea, Herod's port

sitting down and putting on his shoes, but he had only put on one. When he tried to put on the other, it had become too small. He tried to take the first shoe off, but could not. He looked up in surprise, but Johanan said:

'Be of good heart. It is because of the good news, for the saying goes: good tidings put marrow into the legs. Let one pass whom you dislike, for another saying is: an anxious spirit dries the bones.'

Vespasian told Johanan that now he must go to Rome and let another take his place before Jerusalem.

'Now what can I do for you?'

And Johanan replied:

'Give me the town of Jabneh, that I may set up my chair of learning there.'

The story is full of absurdities and errors. At the time of Johanan's escape Vespasian had been Emperor for a long time and Titus was in command of the Roman armies in the East. Another suspicious feature is that it reminds us of Josephus' meeting with Vespasian after the fall of Jotapata. None the less it is worth listening to, for its picturesque form is peculiar to Jewish narrative of that period. And at any rate it contains one historical fact. In the little town of Jabneh, on the coast near Jaffa, Johanan really opened a school during the Roman occupation, and a circle of prominent teachers and disciples found shelter there. It became a spiritual centre and the seed of the coming revival.

Historical development seldom proceeds by leaps and bounds: as a rule it advances step by step and in such a way that each new step contains the seed of the next. And so things took their course even amid the catastrophic events of this period in the life of Jewry. When Jerusalem fell Israel lost only its State, not its country. The people did not become homeless till much later, after the Son of a Star's rebellion. Of course the destruction of the Temple was a terrible loss: the whole people had attended and loved the colourful temple services. But for several centuries there had been a gradual movement away from the Temple and priests towards the law and its teachers. The

THE SON OF A STAR

charm the Temple exercised acquired by degrees a national emphasis, and the forms came to mean more than the spirit behind them. From Ezra's time there was a steady development towards what we call a nomocracy, rule of the law. There was a conspicuous new interest in the words of the law and all the traditions which had grown up round it. The written law stood fast, but the oral law took shape. This development gave Jewish life a spiritual content which could be preserved and could give strength to an existence without land and without national independence. It was firmly founded in the school at Jabneh, and Johanan Ben Zakkai is its first great name.

He was called the youngest of the great Hillel's disciples. Hillel was the famous teacher at the beginning of our era: we remember him for the many gentle and good sayings which are attributed to him. Once a stranger asked him to summarize the whole law so briefly that he could read it while standing on one leg. Hillel replied with the familiar words, 'Do not to your neighbour what you would not that he should do unto you', which Jesus later took up and formulated in a positive form. Johanan continued Hillel's work in many ways and became the next link in the unbroken chain of teachers who carried the tradition on from generation to generation. Curiously enough the Jews always find parallels between Moses and great teachers of a later date. Moses lived to be 120 years old, so Hillel, Johanan and after them the rabbi Akiba must also have reached the same venerable age. And Moses' life fell into three stages of equal length: he lived at Pharaoh's court for forty years and in the desert of Midian for forty years, and for forty years he served the people of Israel. And the same was true of the other teachers! For example, Johanan was a merchant for the first forty years of his life, then he studied for another forty years, and for his last forty years he was a teacher.

More interesting than these trivialities is what tradition can tell us about Johanan's personality. It shows us to what the school at Jabneh attached importance. Johanan never started a conversation about everyday subjects; he was the first in the lecture room and never let himself be overcome by sleep; he

HE THAT SHOULD COME

never went fifty yards without taking the law and phylacteries with him; and finally—and this is the vital point—no one ever heard him teach anything which he had not himself learnt from his teachers. When he was congratulated on reaching so great an age, he always replied that he owed it to an exact observance of tradition and diligent study of the law.

His behaviour to the Romans shows that he was a man of peace, but the most marked feature of his character was his dependence on his predecessors and his fidelity to what they had taught him. This, of course, is a polite way of saying that he lacked originality and independence. It is significant that he speaks of one of his disciples as being 'like a well-caulked tank which does not let a drop of water ooze out'. That time of acute crises, when the most urgent task was to preserve what the Jews had inherited from their forefathers, demanded just a man of this type.

When the news of the fall of Jerusalem reached Jabneh, the teachers tore their clothes and mourned as for the death of a near relation. But Johanan consoled them, saying that good deeds would now take the place of sacrifices, according to the teaching of Hosea: 'I desired mercy and not sacrifice'.

Then he took the decisive step. When Jerusalem was stormed, the Sanhedrin, the supreme authority of Israel, was destroyed in the general massacre. But Johanan chose a new one and summoned it to meet at Jabneh to replace that of Jerusalem. It was an assembly of seventy prominent and learned men, which ruled the people in both spiritual and juridical affairs. Probably it was not formally recognized by the Romans, but for the Jews it was the highest authority. Johanan was elected its president with the title of Nasi (prince).

The great change was effected very quietly. The Temple had gone, the Talmud[1] grew up in its place. Without brilliant talents, but with an immense accumulation of learning in his mind and a firm will to serve God, Johanan created the channel

---

[1] The Talmud is a collection of old Jewish traditions, discussions on the understanding of the law and decisions concerning it—the oral tradition in written form.

THE SON OF A STAR

through which the tradition of antiquity could be passed on to the teachers of the future. And it was just his lack of independence and his peacefulness that made him a natural middleman.

We find in Jabneh all the shoots which later grew and gave the Jewish people its special stamp. No lectures, properly speaking, were held in the school (*Beth hamidrash*), but conversations between teachers and pupils and among the pupils. Still, despite this informal method, exact repetition was the principle of the instruction. The word 'repeat' came simply to mean 'teach'. And the result of these discussions, and the discussions themselves, were gradually written down in the Mishna. (The word means repetition.)

The teaching fell into two branches, the Halacha and Haggada. Halacha meant current affairs and was a form of instruction in the law. The law of Moses, although so detailed, did not contain ordinances touching every side of life. So the learned men discussed the problems which cropped up and reached decisions which were collected in the Halacha. Thus the aim of the Halacha was a better understanding. But in the Haggada the imagination had free rein. It contains interpretations of the Scriptures and often arrives at curious results. We shall hear more about it later.

When Johanan was dying he became profoundly melancholy. His disciples looked at him in grave concern and asked him:

'O light of Israel, why do you weep?'

Johanan replied that he was afraid to appear before the Judge, who was no earthly king who could be satisfied, but the only righteous one, the King of Kings, who punished with eternal destruction.

'Two roads lie before me: one leads to the Garden of Eden, the other to Gehenna, and I do not know which I shall have to take. So have I not cause for weeping?'

He begged that his friends might be guided by fear of God rather than of men, and his last words were:

'Make the throne ready for Hezekiah, the king of Judah, who will soon come!'

No one had felt the fall of Israel as Johanan did, and no one had prepared the way into the future as he had. He had seen with bitter grief the hope of Messiah's coming wither like flowers in drought. But he kept the living germ hidden in his heart, and before the mists of death wrapped themselves about him he described him who was to come and deliver his people—would it be soon?

Johanan's successor was Gamaliel, usually called 'the Second' to distinguish him from his grandfather whose name also was Gamaliel. This first Gamaliel was the wise councillor who, in the discussion in the Sanhedrin on the attitude to be taken up towards the Christians, spoke for moderation. 'If this is the work of men,' he said, 'nothing will come of it, but if it is the work of God, you cannot destroy it.'

He was grandson of Hillel, so that the second Gamaliel was directly descended from the great teacher, being in fact his great-great-grandson. Thus his family was distinguished and had great prestige. Johanan pleaded with the Romans for Gamaliel and saved him from their vengeance, but the catastrophe of Jerusalem shook him so profoundly that 'he wept till the lashes fell from his eyelids'.

Gamaliel was a highly cultivated man with not only Jewish but wide general learning: he spoke both Latin and Greek and had mastered astronomy. For a Jew, and a Pharisee at that, he had unusually liberal views of foreign culture. He was able to dispute with Gentile philosophers on an equal footing, and had a human figure on his signet, a thing quite incomprehensible to the Jewish people, for ordinarily they dared not depict man, who is made in God's image. He once went into a bath-house where a statue of Venus stood. When reproached with this, he simply replied that Venus had trespassed on his ground, not he on hers. The whole of this unusual philosophy made it easier for him to talk with the Roman authorities, who recognized him as the leader of the Jewish people.

Gamaliel was the born leader: full of energy and brilliant qualities, he was made to head the new Sanhedrin at Jabneh. He was indeed the exact opposite of old Johanan. He came at the

THE SON OF A STAR

right time and carried the work farther. And there were urgent tasks enough to be tackled, great and small.

First and foremost he endeavoured to bring about cohesion and unity. As always, there were deep cleavages in the Jewish people, and many were bitterly opposed to each other. The teachers were often at variance over ridiculous trifles. Erudite men discussed with unnecessary heat such questions as whether it was permissible to offer as a sacrifice an animal which happened to have been wounded in the mouth. Note that the case was purely theoretical, since the Temple no longer existed! But such things aroused the strongest emotions. Other questions were of far-reaching practical importance—for example, the fixing of the exact time of the new moon, for on that all the festivals depended.

His work on spiritual problems had a lasting effect. Gamaliel completed the Eighteen Prayers, *Shmone essre* (the name means eighteen), consisting of eighteen praisings and prayers. Together with the ancient prayer *Shma Israel* ('Hear, Israel, the Lord our God, the Lord is one'), the password of monotheism, it is the highest point not only of the synagogue service, but also of the three daily prayers of the common man. It is the spiritual backbone of Judaism to this very day.

Gamaliel was authoritative and imperious and had the reputation of being despotic. As happens with all strong men who follow their convictions without turning aside, he was the object of tavern gossip and intrigues. He asked for it, for he was always brutal in silencing opposition, and did not shrink from harsh methods. If argument was not effective, he had recourse to disciplinary measures, sometimes humiliating to the other party and at times absolutely devastating, as when he simply expelled and outlawed his opponents.

But this was certainly not his real nature. Once an old accumulated feeling of injury carried the day, and in a violent scene of unrestrained passion he was voted down and deposed from his position as Nasi. The learned men howled and screamed at him, and furious cries of protest flew through the hall—a real Eastern scene, in which the door-keeper was thrown head over heels when people from outside came pushing in to have their say. And now that Gamaliel was overthrown a new Nasi was elected.

If he had been the dictator he was accused of being, he would surely have drawn back in dudgeon. But he quietly took his place as an ordinary member of the council and attended its meetings under the presidency of the new Nasi. It was seen before long not only that he had been unjustly treated, but that he was indispensable, so the council restored him to his old dignity.

He lived into the second century, but was spared from seeing the catastrophe which awaited his people. When he was dying he ordered his friends not to bury him in the usual expensive grave-clothes, a custom which had laid intolerable burdens on those who were left behind, but just wrapped in linen and without a sarcophagus. In memory of which, in some countries, Gamaliel is toasted to this day at a Jewish funeral.

A man of quite another type was Joshua Ben Hananiah,[1] at once Gamaliel's best colleague and most severe critic. He was of quite humble origin and had only been a Levite in the Temple services, one of the choristers. His pious mother took the cradle with the baby boy in it into the synagogue, so that he might from his earliest years be accustomed to the words of the law. After the destruction of the Temple he lived in extreme poverty and earned his living as a nail-maker. But his modest way of life did not diminish the prestige which this learned, gentle man enjoyed in the Council at Jabneh.

He was extraordinarily ugly, a fact which has given rise to many stories. When travelling he met in Rome an aristocratic

[1] The old Hebrew names seem curiously strange to us. In reality many of them can be elucidated and explained, so that we recognize in them old acquaintances. Proper names are the field in which perhaps we see most clearly how old Biblical culture is interwoven with ours. One can pick up a handful of the commonest names and see that they are Hebrew. For example Elizabeth, Jacob, Esther and Ruth. It is the same with the old teacher with the peculiar name Joshua Ben Hananiah. Joshua (which when written at full length is Jehoshua) is the same as Josva, but in Greek it is pronounced Jesus. Ben means son, and Hananiah is another form of Johannes.

lady who felt as much attracted by his intellectual conversation as she was repelled by his ugliness. Ladies could be tactless in those days as well as now, and involuntarily she burst out:

'How can so much wisdom live in so ugly a body?'

Joshua, with a cunning smile, proposed that in future the lady should keep her best wine not, as hitherto, in a clay jug, but in one of gold. She was naïve enough to follow his advice. Later she reproached him with having thus spoilt her wine, to which he replied that one was sometimes obliged to keep the most precious things in cheap, ugly vessels!

He was in sharp conflict with Gamaliel on several occasions: he was the cause of the violent scene in which the Nasi was deposed. His opposition to Gamaliel was not dictated by personal motives, but only by firm conviction, and there are pretty stories of the way in which the two great men could humble themselves before one another and shake hands as friends in spite of their differences of opinion.

Moderation and love of one's neighbours was Joshua's motto, and it was so that he found the road to happiness. Envy, unclean passions and ill-will towards one's neighbour always brought misfortune: a man should avoid bad company and find good friends. Moderation, in the sense that religious ordinances should not be exaggerated to the point of morbidity (as also in lay matters), was the first commandment in his philosophy of life, and he supported it by telling comparisons. Of certain persons who sought to improve on God's word with exaggerated inventions of their own, he said: 'They poured water into a vessel that was full of oil: so the oil ran out and was lost.'

Many years later, when political events were violently agitating men's minds, he firmly adhered to these principles. It was, therefore, his doing that the Son of a Star's rebellion was delayed. Not till Joshua, the man of peace, was dead did passions rage unchecked.

There were great men in those days whose deeds and thoughts rose above the normal level like the tallest trees in a wood. We have heard of a few, but many more could have been described. It was an epoch in the history of the Jewish people in which were

HE THAT SHOULD COME

laid the foundations of a future which was to defy many storms. It is an old experience that in such times the leaders who are needed come to maturity. But the soil from which they grew, and the low scrub at their feet, the mass of the people and its customs, its daily life and ordinary way of thinking—all that on which in the long run everything depends—is for the most part forgotten, wrapped in the mists of oblivion. And yet, when we study with care the traditions of later times, we can to some extent form an idea of popular life in the land of the Jews, before homelessness became their hard lot.

The central point and the basis of everything was God's Word. The law was studied and ransacked, for every line, indeed every stroke and stop in the Bible was of importance. But not only the law, but oral tradition too was of significance: indeed, for the mass of the people the unwritten law became by degrees more important than the written: 'Halacha is bread, Haggada water'. The oral law was received from God's hand by Moses, who gave it to Aaron. He passed it on to his sons, and they bequeathed it to the teachers of Israel. But both the written and the oral law were the source of happiness and well-being.

The Tora[1] existed before the creation of the world and was the model on which God created the world. Seven things existed before the creation of the world: the Tora, God's throne, repentance, Paradise, hell, the Temple and the name of Messiah. The most important duty in life is therefore the study of the Tora, especially in the last watch of the night, when the dawn is approaching. David had the harp hanging on the northern end of his bed. At midnight the night wind ran over the strings and drew music from them. Then David awoke and began to read the sacred scrolls. The Tora is everlasting as the tree of life: therefore Israel, which owns the Tora, can never be destroyed. When David was dying, he read the Tora without ceasing, so that the angel of death, who had been sent to fetch him, could not touch him. The angel had to

---

[1] Tora is the Hebrew word for the law and is ordinarily used in speaking of the five Mosaic books.

have recourse to a trick: he made the trees outside the window rustle, and this diverted the king's attention for a moment. The angel of death seized the opportunity and took possession of his soul.

It was believed that God judged mankind every day and at every hour. At the Passover, the 15th Nisan, God determined the size of the corn harvest; at Pentecost, that of the fruit harvest; on New Year's Day, the 1st Tishri, the fate of mankind; and at the Feast of Tabernacles, how much rain would fall in the course of the year. The great judgement on New Year's Day was given at the moment at which the Sanhedrin had fixed the new moon: the fate of Israel was decided first, then that of the other peoples.

The law stood on one side of man with its call from God. Lust and ambition, which were the source of all evil, pulled at him from the other. And the punishment was in proportion to the crime. Samson became blind because he had let his eyes wander where they should not. Absalom was vain, and therefore he was hanged by the hair. Unchastity caused dropsy, hate jaundice, covetousness brought locusts. But most of all, men should be on their guard against denial of God or the Scriptures, for that brought not temporary, but everlasting punishment.

True riches did not consist in money, but in satisfaction with what one had. Discontent led to thieving, and this was a greater sin than robbery with violence, for it showed more fear of men than of God. For this same reason the use of false measures and weights deserved heavier punishment than simple thieving. Gluttony and drunkenness, which 'made a man first red and then pale', were a cause of sorrow. But chastity was one of the finest virtues. To preserve one's chastity was just as brave as for a poor man to restore something he had found, or for a rich man to pay tithe secretly. It was therefore unseemly to hold unnecessary conversation with women, or to take notice of their clothes and hair. But the most dangerous organ was the tongue, and that was why it was hidden behind a double wall, first the cheeks and then the teeth.

In the popular conception mankind was split between good

and evil: every person had a good and an evil tendency. The latter was at first as thin as a thread, but gradually became as strong as a rope: it came as a pilgrim, took up its habitation as a guest and ended as master. But God had given his law to help mankind. He gave Israel 613 Precepts, of which 365, the number of days in the year—were positive, 'thou shalt', and 248, the number of bones in the body, 'thou shalt not'.

The people of Israel traced their descent back to the same ancestor: everyone was descended from Abraham, they were one great clan. This gave them a unique feeling of cohesion: they all shared the same historical development through 1,000 years, and all were the products of a common national character. Jews were not isolated individuals, but small parts of one mighty unit. Modern individualism would have been quite alien to the old-time Jews. To us modern Western Europeans every single person, at any rate every generation, is a unit. But in Israel the people were a unit from Abraham downwards through all the changing generations, and all shared in common both God's blessing and his punishment.

And the connecting link in this chain was marriage and the family, the most central institution of life. Marriage was arranged in heaven; God decided whom a child was to marry forty days before its birth. An unmarried man was looked down on: he had no blessing, peace or happiness; indeed, he could scarcely be called a man. Jewish conceptions often have a gleam of humour in them, and satire and irony have always been to them a natural form of expression. Thus woman had a certain amount to put up with. God created woman, not from Adam's head, lest she should become haughty; not from his eye, lest she should be covetous; nor from his ear, lest she should be inquisitive; nor from his mouth, lest she should be loquacious; nor from his hand, lest she should be greedy; nor, finally, from his foot, lest she should gad about. But he created her from the rib, which is always hidden! Yes, from the rib of all things, while man was created from the dust of the earth. That is why it is always the man who seeks the woman, and not the reverse; he seeks for what he has lost. This explains, too, why

THE SON OF A STAR

man is more companionable than woman: he is made of soft stuff, she of hard bone!

Comparing the Jewish view of woman with that of the other peoples of antiquity, one comes to the conclusion that the Hebrew woman's standing was high, though the picture had its dark corners: polygamy existed, and the practice of divorce was loose.

Girls were minors till twelve, boys till they were thirteen years and a day old. Marriage was preceded by betrothal, at which the conditions of marriage, for example the size of the dowry, were arranged in detail. The period of betrothal was twelve months and was spent in preparations for the marriage. And the wedding day itself was the greatest day of rejoicing in life. The bridegroom with his friends fetched the bride and took her to his house, where feasting went on for several days. The wedding as a rule took place on a Wednesday, so that there were three days after the Sabbath to complete the arrangements, and on Thursday the magistrates of the town ordinarily met; if the bridegroom had found his bride unchaste, he had the chance of lodging a complaint at once. The bride wore a wreath of myrtle and had a veil over her eyes, and her hair loose. Seed was dealt out to the guests, and two birds were carried before the young couple, all this expressing good wishes for the fertility of the marriage.

The rabbis were in dispute as to what grounds could justify divorce. The school which took the matter most lightly was satisfied with such reasons as that the wife burnt the food, or talked so loud that the neighbours could hear—or simply that the husband had found another woman who attracted him more! But the woman also had the right to ask for a divorce—if, for example, her husband became a leper or took up particularly dirty work, such as tanning.

A mother suckled her child until it was two. She was entirely responsible for the bringing up of girls. They had to learn only the written law, not the oral, which would bring them too much into contact with the other sex. A boy was circumcised on the eighth day, even if it was the Sabbath, and

HE THAT SHOULD COME

was then given his name. He was taught at home until he was six, and then went to school.

There were plenty of schools: one tradition says that before its destruction Jerusalem had 480 schools, each with three classes. School occupied a central position in the life of this bookish people, and teachers were highly respected. It was a teacher's duty to win the confidence, affection and respect of his pupils: he might not beat them with a stick, but he might with a strap. The alphabet was taught by writing the letters on a board: later there was instruction in both the Tora and the Talmud. Everything was learnt by heart, with the help of numerous aids to memory. Kindness and chastity were specially insisted upon, and a pupil owed his teacher greater reverence than his father.

There was slavery in Israel, as in all ancient communities. This was no kind of problem, but a matter of course and a necessity in order to get work done. But the Jews treated their slaves well, almost as members of the family, and any act of cruelty to a slave automatically gave him his freedom.

It was said that there were seventy languages in the whole world, but of course Hebrew was the only one the study of which was of any real interest to a Jew. Hebrew had disappeared as a spoken language of daily intercourse several centuries before. That part of the people which returned from the captivity in Babylon spoke a West Aramaic dialect. The purest speech was in Judaea: in Galilee the language approximated to Syrian, in which the gutturals were more indistinct. It will be remembered from the New Testament account of Simon Peter in the court of the high priest that his dialect showed him to come from Galilee. But Hebrew was always the sacred language and remained so until modern Israel revived it as the tongue of daily use.

Despite all efforts to maintain the belief in the one true God, relics of old superstition were of course deeply rooted in the popular mind, and infection from heathendom trickled in unnoticed. There were things which had to be guarded against. The number two was dangerous, as being subject to Ashmedai,

THE SON OF A STAR

the prince of the spirits; it was unlucky to eat two eggs or drink two or four cups. It was advisable not to pass between two dogs, pigs, snakes or women, but to go outside them. Specially malignant spirits lived in caper bushes, but luckily they were blind, so that it was not difficult to slip by. Other evil spirits lived in uncanny places, in deserts or among ruins. To hold the feet crossed while they were being washed was to risk becoming forgetful. On the other hand, a person who dipped his finger first in salt and then in water would have a good memory. Generally speaking, people had to be on their guard against evil spirits, but fortunately there were ways of dealing with them: many protected themselves with amulets and wore small scraps of parchment on which specially efficacious passages from the Scriptures were written.

In old times Hebrew culture never produced any painter or sculptor. This was the result of the Old Testament fear of pictorial representation of the human body, as something approaching idolatry. But poetry and music were favourite arts in Israel, and in these fields, in the course of time, a special Jewish art of great value was created. This applied also to the popular method of expression. Proverbs were freely used, and many of these, typical of the Hebrew mentality with its dry humour and its disposition to look events soberly in the face, have survived the passage of 3,000 years and are as fresh today as in ancient times. Here are a few samples.

A small coin in an empty bottle makes a lot of noise.
With the measure you measure with it shall be measured into you.
You can get to know a man in three ways: over a drink, when you are doing business with him, and when he is angry.
Every kind of wood gives its special sound when it catches fire. The briar says: I too am a tree.

The following is an old Hebrew fable:

When Noah was going to plant his vineyard, Satan came to him and asked: 'What are you planting here?'

HE THAT SHOULD COME

Noah answered that it was to be a vineyard.

'What will you grow in it?' Satan asked.

'Grapes,' Noah replied, 'for they are sweet, both when fresh and when dried, and wine, which gladdens the heart, can be made from them.'

Then Satan made his proposal: 'So we will work together.'

Noah agreed, and the devil brought four animals, a lamb, a lion, a pig and a monkey, killed them, and poured out their blood in the vineyard. The result is well known. When a man begins to drink, he is at first as mild as a lamb, then as brave as a lion—'is there my equal in the whole world?'—then he is like the pig, rolling in dirt, and at last he becomes like the monkey, jumping about and not knowing what he is doing.

The Tenth Legion felt ill at ease in Judaea: there was no security. Granted that this queer crazy people was different from all other peoples the Legion had known. Granted that the legionaries never ceased to feel themselves foreigners, that people looked through them as if they did not exist, and everything was strange and incomprehensible. But down the spine of even the bravest there crept a chill uncanny feeling, as if something unknown was impending, and anything whatever might be expected.

In the headquarters at Caesarea old reports were taken out of the files and studied afresh. They told of strange, fantastic reactions among the Jews. What was it that had happened that August day when Titus' victorious legions—the Tenth among them—stormed the white Temple in Jerusalem, which had defied them for so long? Why, the Romans had positively had to set it on fire before they could overcome the resistance. And in it, under one of the arcades, they found the carbonized remains of a multitude of people. Inquiries after the storming revealed that 6,000 persons, including many women and children, had perished miserably in the flames. It had been impossible to make them leave the arcade even when the fire had eaten its way right into their midst. All because a 'prophet' had declared that at just this place, when their need was

THE SON OF A STAR

greatest, they would receive a sign from heaven that the liberator was coming.

The files also contained the story of Theudas, fanatic and prophet, who had begun to enrol people to follow him to the Jordan. There the miracle would happen: the old marvel from the Red Sea, which parted itself in two before Moses' staff, would be repeated. The water of the Jordan would cease to flow, and when they had crossed its bed dry-shod, the Roman soldiers, who by that time were sure to be following them, would drown miserably like Pharaoh's army. But how had this adventure ended? When the Roman procurator heard the story, he at once dispatched a party of cavalry. They took the crazy fanatics by surprise and hewed them down. Theudas himself was killed and his head cut off and sent to Caesarea.

And there was the mad Egyptian who enticed people up on to the Mount of Olives, promising them that the walls of Jerusalem would fall down before him and that the Romans would be cut to pieces. He paid dearly for his prank along with hundreds of his credulous followers.

There were many other incidents. And it was always the same—crazy expectation of a sign from heaven. The Romans felt as if they were in a madhouse, or rather as if they were walking on a volcano, whose crater might open its fiery jaws under their feet at any moment. There was always unrest somewhere. People swarmed together in the towns and villages, and from the centre of the crowd a hoarse, shrill voice was heard uttering fervid promises and prophecies of fearful events about to happen and a glorious future for the chosen people.

All reasonable people, the Romans said to themselves, had believed that this mischief was stamped out for good and all. But no, the nation was still in a feverish mood of exaltation, a chronic state of excitement in which anything might happen.

The Tenth Legion was compelled to be on the alert and keep a sharp look-out. It had to do garrison duty in a country in which expectations of a Messiah were always alive. And if we wish to understand this strange time and the tragic events which continued to afflict Israel, we must first grasp this idea,

Roman Emperor's statue at Caesarea

6. Roman statue at Caesarea

7. The ruins at Caesarea

Excavations at Capernaum

which so permeated the people's lives that, even in the most common everyday affairs, they lived in an atmosphere of crisis.

In times of antiquity disasters had happened and ended. Nebuchadnezzar stormed Jerusalem and carried the people away to captivity in Babylon. But it was only seventy years before the hour of liberation came. Then God intervened and turned the great king Cyrus' heart, so that he allowed Israel to return to its old country.

But the years of happiness were short, and the time of Ezra and Nehemiah, when the Temple was set up again and the walls of Jerusalem built, was like scattered sunshine on a winter day. Then the sky began to darken again, and clouds as black as night drove up from every quarter.

When everything seemed hopeless once more, the Maccabees' rising broke out—a spontaneous outburst of combined faith in God and patriotism. Heathendom had to give way before this shock, and everything seemed to indicate that the great promises of an idyllic future made by the prophets were about to be fulfilled.

But in the course of a hundred years the tide had ebbed, and the naked reality was the harsh domination of Rome. And it seemed that this would never end. Why? What could the intention be? Men cudgelled their brains and searched their hearts, but all cogitation ended in the same painful question: Lord, how long?

In this endless period of tension—it lasted fully three centuries, from the Maccabees to the Son of a Star—the so-called Apocryphal literature sprang up. It is a long series of curious books, filled with a mixture of highly-strung political and religious excitement and dreamlike visions of the future that awaits Israel. They are inspired by the books of the old prophets and seek to identify themselves with them. The book of Daniel, dating from the Maccabaean era, resembles them, and like it they choose old personages of high repute from times long past as a kind of speaking-tube: Enoch, Baruch, Solomon, Ezra, even the heathen Sibyl, are pressed into service. They are the literary

THE SON OF A STAR

sediment of the Messianic idea, and it is through them that we know it as well as we do.

The kernel of the idea is the conflict, the eternal conflict between dream and reality. In this tragic collision steel struck against flint, and the sparks drifted far. The great promises of the prophets set men dreaming: imagination took wings and feasted on visions of the great time, the golden age, that would come when the kingdom of God was established with Israel as its centre and the mistress of the other races. In the popular mind these prophecies were projected down to earth: the promises became material and extremely worldly, so that everything became comprehensible and close at hand.

Messiah is a Hebrew word, meaning the anointed one. The reference is to the kings of Israel, who were anointed before they took over the government. And it was this future king who was to bring in the great time. He was to be of the Jewish race, of David's line, and was to come from David's town, Bethlehem. This Messiah was to take up arms against the world power and crush its King Armilius, certainly a perversion of Romulus. His time had been foretold by Elijah. After the great victory Jerusalem would become the queen of the world, and there the other races would bow down before Israel.

But these dreams were elaborated in detail. God created not one, but two eras. The first was the present one, and that could be viewed only with the most profound pessimism. The prince of this world was the devil, and apostate, inimical powers ruled the peoples. But the second era was approaching, in which the power of God would gain the mastery. And when our era was ebbing out, its close would be marked by terrible struggles and anguish. The new world would be born in pain.

This is a field in which fantasy has always had free play. And the dreams of a Messiah are no different from so many others which have revelled in the terrors of the last days. People would see a sword in heaven, the sun would be extinguished in the midst of its course, wood would drip blood, stones would begin to speak. But among men too there would be signs that the end of the world was near. Truth and loyalty would fail; human bodies would wither and the great would become small; children under a year old would speak plainly; women would give birth to monsters; fresh springs would give salt water; sown ground would suddenly become as if left fallow, and full store-rooms would be found empty.

But in the day when their need was sorest Messiah would come. He would take his stand in the middle of Israel, and when the enemy attacked he would destroy them with the breath of his mouth. The wicked would be condemned, and Israel would govern the world with justice. Her rule would endure for a thousand years of happiness and would replenish the earth.

The Messianic visions have no kind of unity. The most heterogeneous elements are woven together, from crassly material expectations to deep presentiments with a real gleam of spirituality. There were not only inflamed, enthusiastic patriots, looking for him who should free the nation from the Roman yoke. The old prophecies of Isaiah about the Suffering Servant of the Lord, bruised and wounded for our transgressions, he who took our chastisement upon himself that we might have peace, played their part. And there were those who dreamed of a mystic, half divine Messiah, who would redeem men from their sins.

In so fertile a soil trees of very different kinds could take root. And among them was Christianity. Its original connection with late Jewish Messianic ideas is obvious. When the word Messiah is translated into Greek, the language in which the New Testament is written, it is Christos. So we understand the triumph that rang out in the confession 'We have found Messiah!' But Jesus of Nazareth, of whom these words were spoken, was quite different from the popular idea of the Messiah. And so we can feel the nervous anxiety of the uncertain, doubting John the Baptist, who asked Jesus from his prison: 'Art thou he that should come, or do we look for another?'

Deep down in this half-light of spiritual wrestling, fervent expectation and desperate conflict the tragedy took place: the two great religions, the Jewish and the Christian, came to the fatal parting of the ways. They were branches of the same tree, but moved farther and farther apart. It began one night in Jerusalem, when Jesus said these words: 'My kingdom is not of this world.'

Christianity has found the Messiah: he once lived on this earth, and the Christian faith looks back to the historic revelation of God in him. But the Jews look forward to him who has not yet come, but will come some day. In the minds of Jewry, despite all its catastrophes, there dwells the unconquerable conviction that the divine impact upon the world's history lies not in the past, but in the future. Some day the Lord's chosen people will experience its great future. Therefore its thinkers, poets and prophets are always on the look-out: their eyes shielded by their hands, ever peering ahead for a sight of what will happen in God's own time.

But the night was long and dark, and they would have to wait and wait, till the late morning grew grey at last. Wait and hope, as in the famous passage from 2 Esdras iv, in which the author cannot conceal his impatient longing for the Messianic time, of which there is nowhere a sign, and God's answer comes: 'Do not thou hasten above the most Highest.'

But times of longing can be so long that people can wait no longer. They take a hand themselves, and things begin to move. So it happened in Israel. The popular impatience burst its bonds with elemental violence, and in the ferment of longing revolution germinated.

To an outside observer it was madness to suppose that a little people like the Jews could have a brilliant future in store for it. But deep in every Jewish soul lay the assurance that the Lord had promised his people a special place above all others. They did not doubt, therefore, but just went forward. It was as if a line had to run right out, whatever the cost might be.

In the years after the fall of Jerusalem people in Israel counted on their fingers. After the first fall of Jerusalem, had not seventy years passed before the people were liberated? Had not the liberation, indeed, begun before the seventy years had run their course?

HE THAT SHOULD COME

As the years passed, and the new century entered its first and second decades, expectation grew. Now liberation was approaching. The fire broke out among the Jews of the dispersion, but was ruthlessly trampled to ashes. When the fourth decade arrived, there was the great explosion in Palestine. The days of the Son of a Star had come.

The Tenth Legion had the best of reasons to be on its guard.

III

CAESAREA

ON a quiet sunny spring morning a couple of years ago my car was running over the northern part of the plain of Sharon, towards the sea. Newly built colonies, consisting of scores of pretty little uniform toy houses, and swarming with busy people, slid past us, then came cultivated fields and green orchards. Far to the north rose Mount Carmel's broad heavy silhouette: on the top I could see the white houses in the new quarters of Haifa. Gradually, as we approached the sea, the character of the landscape changed: fertility disappeared, there were longer intervals between the fields; rocks and sandy soil, with withered thistles from last year and gaily coloured fresh weeds, met the eye as we looked ahead. We drove over a low ridge, and there lay the sea in full view from north to south.

By the roadside lay the stump of a column, and then another. Then I discovered that the irregularities in the surface were old cut stones and remains of walls: they lay scattered everywhere, half covered by sand and earth on which red poppies swayed in the wind. A large board stood by the road marked 'Caesarea' in both Hebrew and Latin characters. So we had arrived: here once lay Caesarea apud marem, the imperial town on the sea. Once, long ago—and now, of the splendour which two thousand years ago had excited the admiration of the world and caused the place to be called 'the second Rome', faint traces of ruins remained.

Ruins are always desolate, but never have I felt such loneliness as among the mouldering stones of Caesarea. Where once the great city spread its streets far and wide and raised towers

CAESAREA

and palaces high into the sky, with its 200,000 swarming inhabitants, not a soul was to be seen. The only sounds heard were the cries of the sea-birds over the rocks on the edge of the shore and the dry rustling of dead stalks among the stones.

I found my way about with the aid of a map. These stones must be the remains of the theatre in which King Agrippa I performed and died on the stage: here the great temple had been, there the racecourse, and, far beyond, the city walls with towers and gates. A few rocks ran out into the water, forming a kind of peninsula, with the waves washing lazily against them, a new sound in my ears. Then I found more columns and stones which had been piled up on the rocks on the shore to make them higher and turn them into a kind of mole under which small fishing craft could find shelter. These, then, were the relics of the world-renowned harbour and Strato's tower.

Far away, up in the mountains, lay Jerusalem, today a large and growing city, full of life. Nineteen hundred years ago the legions had marched out through the gates of Caesarea and on to Jerusalem to crush the holy city. They came from the centre of the Graeco-Roman heathen power in Palestine, and the goddesses of victory smiled on them. Cold strength and violence triumphed over spirit and faith. But today Caesarea lies more dead than any cemetery. No one misses it, no one mourns for it. When it is remembered, it is because the apostle Paul was kept there for a couple of years as a prisoner before he was taken to Rome.

Jerusalem survived, Caesarea faded out.

Where Strato's tower had raised its head defiantly on the shore from time immemorial, King Herod the Great built the city which he named after his imperial protector and friend. As a rule towns grow up organically, little by little. But Caesarea was built in one burst: the work was done during the years 24 to 12 before our era. Herod erected the seat of Roman power in Palestine on a grandiose plan, with the harbour as centre. The place was of strategic importance: for the imperial sea power the harbour was the connecting link between the naval bases in Phoenicia and those in Egypt, and it was the starting-point of the trade routes to the distant kingdom beyond the deserts east of the Jordan.

This great work was a severe strain on the King's finances, for no expense was to be spared. The result was indeed splendid: the city became one of the most populous in the East, with a prosperous trade, and the seat of the Roman procurator in Judaea. From it a strong garrison dominated the country. The king took great pains to make the harbour the best possible. A large mole always sheltered it from the waves: its position in the city was so central that all the streets led towards it: great arcades afforded lodging to sailors. Not even Piraeus, the port of Athens, was larger. Herod also adorned the city with all the finest products of Graeco-Roman culture—temples, a theatre, a racecourse, a governor's palace, and huge aqueducts which brought it fresh water. It even had drainage, a most uncommon thing in those times. To this day beautiful statues are being dug up out of the soil in which they have lain hidden for nearly two thousand years, and a great deal more research work will have to be undertaken before it can be said that the secrets of Caesarea have been disclosed.

It was there that the war between Judaea and Rome broke out in the year 66. The Jewish population was only 40 per cent of the whole, against 60 per cent of Romans and Greeks. But the Jews had long been in power in the city council. The electoral system gave votes according to economic circumstances, and many Jews were rich. This caused continuous friction and complaints to the Imperial Court. The heathen accused the Jews of governing arbitrarily and of sending disproportionately large contributions from the city funds to the Temple in Jerusalem. At last Rome came to a decision and supported the heathen. The Jews lost their majority.

Their success made the Greeks aggressive: they scoffed at the Jews and, as always, found their most sensitive point, their religion. The chief Jewish synagogue was situated on land belonging to a Greek. Of course, the Jews tried to buy the land, but the owner would not sell it at any price. Instead he got the

CAESAREA

better of the Jews by putting up some workshops so close to the synagogue that when they wanted to attend service only a quite narrow entrance would be left to them. A band of young Jewish hotheads took the law into their own hands, drove the workmen home and stopped the building. Disturbances took place, and Florus, the anti-Jewish governor, of whose exploits we have already heard, intervened sharply.

When the people assembled for prayer next Sabbath, a Greek was sacrificing a bird just outside the door of the synagogue. The Jews could not have been more grossly insulted. Such a sacrifice was offered only for a leper, when he had been cured. It was, therefore, an allusion to the malicious reports that Israel had its origin in an Egyptian leper.

The infuriated Jews attacked the man, and a violent affray was the result. Roman cavalry tried vainly to intervene. The end of the business was that the Jews hastily collected their sacred books and carried them off to a neighbouring town. Fearful pogroms began: it is reckoned that in those few days 20,000 Jews were killed in Caesarea. And Florus let things take their course. He remained a long way off at Sebaste, watching developments with malicious pleasure. He had a Jewish deputation, which waited on him to beg for help, thrown into prison. But these events were the spark which started the blaze. The war began.

From Caesarea a bitter wind blew over the Jews' land. Heathen Rome triumphed over a defeated, divided people. Jupiter had been victorious over Jehovah. Greek and Roman culture followed in the footsteps of the legionaries. And it found itself at home in Palestine. It has been said that Palestine was made of 'such stuff as dreams are made of'. And it was not only the dreams and ideas of a revealed religion that impregnated the land which not without reason is called Holy. Heathendom too, ancient and quite modern, let fall its coloured veil of dreams and legends so beautiful and bewitching that to this very day they fascinate the traveller through the regions where once they were born.

Pan first played on his flute in the cave where the springs of

THE SON OF A STAR

the Jordan rise. At Jaffa anyone could see the rock on which Andromeda lay bound till Perseus came to free her on his winged Pegasus, and Minerva gave her a place among the stars. In Ascalon, in ancient times, Semiramis, half queen half goddess, was born. Up in the north, on the Phoenician border, springs of a curious reddish colour rise in the spring-time and flow into the Adonis river. This is the blood shed in the encounter in which Adonis, Aphrodite's lover, received his mortal wound. The deep-red anemones which grow in profusion, in huge clumps, in this region are the heart's blood of the same passionate youth.

And Tyre, the frontier city, which sent its seamen and colonizers all the way to Carthage and Cadiz, came into existence in this fantastic manner: two rocks came floating along carrying between them a large olive tree, and in its branches sat an eagle. Melcarth (so the local divinity was called) taught his worshippers to bind the floating rocks together, and on them he built the city which later took the sea in its embrace.

Stories like these the mothers of Caesarea told to their children. And ships came into the harbour from far-off lands, and in the unloading and loading of their cargoes the scents of rare foreign goods were spread abroad. Soldiers of the Tenth Legion wandered about the streets, looking at the shops and the girls and dropping into the taverns. Messengers with news from the Court or the frontiers of the Empire hurried into the old Governor's Palace, now the residence of the commander of the Legion. And the years passed, one thing was added to another—while yet again the clouds began to darken the sky of Palestine.

Vespasian saved the Roman Empire from chaos. But no one would have dreamed that Vespasian of all people would end his days as Emperor. His origin was humble: he came of a Sabine peasant family. None the less he managed to work his way up to the command of a legion in Germany: he was Consul in Rome for a time and for a short period a governor in Africa. But all the same fortune never really smiled on him: he was always so poor that he was driven to horse-dealing. Popular humour nicknamed him 'the mule-driver'. There was a fiasco when he

CAESAREA

accompanied Nero on the imperial artistic tour to Greece. It was necessary to keep close to the Emperor in order to acquire his good will. Unhappily, the elderly general had no feeling for Nero's art. At a concert, in which the Emperor himself was taking part, Vespasian fell asleep and snored so loud that a painful sensation was created.

Yet, when the insurrection in Judaea broke out and a capable general had to be found to suppress it, the Emperor's choice fell upon Vespasian. It sometimes happens that blind chance chooses right.

When Vespasian became Emperor, there were matters enough to be put in order, But he set to work and tackled them with all his robust energy. On the throne he remained its man of the people. His speech retained its common accent, and his coarseness and unpolished manners offended the Roman aristocracy—and his refined son Titus. And yet he was not devoid of all feeling for higher culture. He was a soldier, but not a mere swashbuckler, straightforward and with no diplomatic finesse. He demanded absolutely the fulfilment of duty, first of himself and then of others. In war he was up and about both day and night: he lived with the soldiers, ate their rations and shared their dangers. His rule was marked by strict economy. Nor was he fastidious. When he put a tax on the public lavatories in Rome, Titus criticized him: he said it was too dirty a way for an Emperor to raise money. 'Money doesn't smell,' Vespasian replied.

He died in true Roman style. When he felt that the end was approaching, he said, with a shadow of the stern smile his entourage knew so well:

'I suppose I'll become a god now!'

Then he ordered his servants to lift him out of bed and hold him up: a Roman Emperor should die standing.

Titus was thirty-nine when he succeeded his father on the throne. In his earliest boyhood he had known only the rather shabby poverty of the parental home. This was suddenly exchanged for splendour when the Emperor Claudius took the seven-year-old boy to be a member of his court and had him

THE SON OF A STAR

educated with the Prince Imperial, Britannicus. This nearly cost him his life. Titus was sixteen when Nero had Britannicus poisoned. Britannicus died half-way through a meal; Titus had drunk from the same cup and was dangerously ill for a long time.

Nature and art both seemed to have made Titus their favourite to an extraordinary degree. His face was handsome, and even if not tall, he had a commanding character: he was immensely strong, unexcelled in the use of weapons and horses, brave, and had a charming demeanour. He spoke both Latin and Greek well and was a brilliant improviser. It is known that he had a curious gift for imitating other people's handwriting: he once said, with a smile, that a great forger had been lost to the world in him.

The traditional Roman view is that he was a mild and good-natured ruler. He might have been suspected of becoming another Nero, for ominous rumours of his licentiousness and cruelty had been in circulation. But he died two years after he ascended the throne, so his reign never got beyond the honeymoon stage. It was said that he regarded as wasted a day on which he had done nothing good. The Empire suffered grievous blows in his days. The famous eruption of the hitherto slumbering Vesuvius took place in the year 79 and buried three flourishing towns, one of them Pompeii. Rome too was devastated by fire and plague. Of course, the Jews saw in these visitations a divine punishment of the ruler who had defiled Jerusalem.

For Jewish tradition draws quite another picture from that current in Rome. In Judaea he was remembered as the hard man who dared to enter the Lord's temple, and he cut the curtain of the Sanctuary with his sword so that it began to bleed. The Jews nicknamed him Rasha, the godless one, the evil one. Israel has had many oppressors in its three thousand years' history, but none but Titus was given this most terrible of all names.

The Jews pursued him in their legends with an undying hate: they never forgot the misery and shame he had brought upon

CAESAREA

them. I choose this tradition from among many horrible stories. The Jews declared that Titus' body was burnt and his ashes strewn over seven seas so that he might escape the last judgement. But he did not. A necromancer once summoned up his soul and asked him how things were on the other side of the grave.

'Who is honoured in the next world?' Titus was asked.

'The Israelites!' he replied.

'How are you judged over there?' the necromancer continued.

'The way I chose myself. Every day I am burned and the ashes spread over the seas. Then my ashes are collected and I am judged again. And I am burned and the ashes scattered. And so it will go on to all eternity.'

The Flavian imperial house began very promisingly, but its sun had a bloody setting. When Vespasian's youngest son, Domitian, succeeded his brother, much was expected of him, but the dream of a new golden age was miserably unfulfilled. Those who came to know him well began to suspect—and certainly not altogether unjustly—that he had poisoned Titus. He had been overshadowed by his brother all his life, but burned to possess power and taste its sweets.

The Empire did not prosper in his time. He fought an unsuccessful war against the Dacians on the lower Danube, in what is now Rumania. Then he did the one thing a Roman Emperor could not do: he made peace and bound Rome to pay the Dacians a sum of money yearly. Thus Rome came to pay tribute to barbarians, and Domitian had let his most important weapon, prestige, slip from his hands.

He replied to criticism with unparalleled cruelty. Mass arrests, interrogation with torture, and executions rained down upon the Roman aristocracy: they followed one another so closely that at last people ceased to take count of them. A poet said caustically that 'nothing is so rare as an old nobleman'. Spies and hired assassins were at work everywhere, and no man who was in a public position or possessed wealth could be sure that he was safe. Jews and Christians also were sought out and fell beneath the executioner's sword. The Emperor was so

THE SON OF A STAR

suspicious that he had mirrors set up in the audience chamber so that he could see what was happening behind his back. Even near relations of the imperial house lost their lives in those terrible years.

It ended as it was bound to end. The Empress Domitia had been unfaithful to Domitian: she had fallen madly in love with an actor. When the Emperor learned of the affair, he put her away, but discovered later that he loved her too much to do without her. Tragically enough she, the only person in whom the suspicious man showed confidence, became the cause of his death. She saw by accident a list of proscribed persons with her own name on it. She must strike first. She allied herself with some courtiers whose fall also was impending, and a plan was laid.

One of the conspirators sought an audience of the Emperor, saying that he wished to hand over a document to him in person. To avert suspicion he had his arm bound up, and his dagger was hidden under the bandage. While Domitian was reading the document the courtier drew out his dagger by stealth and wounded the Emperor in the abdomen, but not mortally. Domitian was a man of tremendous strength: he flung himself on his assailant and threw him head over heels on the floor. He shouted to a child who was always near him to pass him the sword which hung over his bed. But this had been foreseen: the blade had been taken away, only the hilt was there. The child ran out to call the guard, but all the doors were locked.

All this time a life and death struggle was taking place between the two men. Domitian pressed his blood-stained fingers into the other man's eyes and tried to wrench the dagger out of his hands. But now the other conspirators arrived and killed the Emperor. This horrible scene is typical of the manner in which several Emperors ended their lives, and an early sign of the degeneration of the mighty Empire.

The senators breathed a sigh of relief at the tyrant's fall: they had all felt themselves to be in the danger zone, and willingly elected the conspirators' candidate for the throne, the

CAESAREA

old senator Nerva. He was a jurist, a wise and cautious man, who had learnt the difficult art of steering between the rocks in Domitian's time, a dangerous one for all those in high places. He tried to remedy the worst injustices, but his rule was not securely founded. The legions were not disposed to obey an old senator, a pronounced civilian. He was shrewd enough to see his weakness and played his cards accordingly. He took up the most popular general, the Spaniard Marcus Ulpius Trajanus, and nominated him as his successor. This pacified the army.

Nerva's reign was quite short, only a year and a half, but he was long remembered for his mildness and justice. The Jews obtained a better lot as well as others: the payment of tax to the image of Jupiter on the Capitol had naturally been most deeply wounding to them. Nerva did not release them from the tax, but allowed them not to pay it to the heathen temple. We still have coins struck in memory of this: they bear the figure of a palm tree with hanging fruit and the inscription *Fisci Judaici calumnia sublata*, 'the shame of the Jewish tax is removed'.

And when the old Emperor died in 98, Trajan took the reins in a firm hand.

Never before or since has the world seen such a power as the Roman Empire. It stretched from the fells and mist-clad mountains of Scotland to the sun-baked Sahara desert, from the storm-beaten Atlantic coasts to the distant borders of the Parthian kingdom. Outside its frontiers only wild, unknown barbarians lived. Within the Empire the *Pax Romana*, the Roman peace, prevailed. Earlier land frontiers were rubbed out, and old enemies lived at peace with one another under the mighty wings of the Roman eagle. Strong ties bound the remotest provinces of the Empire together—roads, trade and shipping, the common languages Greek and Latin—and the vigorous, purposeful administration gave security, order and regularity. Pliny said that the whole earth was one with the majesty of Roman rule, and he was certainly right. In those happy times no one gave a thought to the possibility that this peace would not last for ever, but would in the course of a few centuries be dissolved from within and broken from without.

All roads lead to Rome, it was said. They spread out from Rome too and ran to the remotest frontiers: they were the veins that kept the blood in circulation. They ran through deserts and over mountains: they crossed the passes of the Alps and the snow-clad mountains of Asia Minor. Strategic considerations and care for trade communications determined their direction. Impressive engineering skill was employed in making them. They lay so deeply and solidly fixed in the earth that they resembled more than anything a wall with a road on the top. They can still be found in all the countries over which Rome ruled: they seem to have been built for all eternity. They were long and even, with gently rounded curves. Where modern roads in England have been made over them motorists enjoy driving: their straightness allows cars to run at their top speed. When, in 1850, a French general climbed with his troops over a pass in the Atlas mountains, he held it for a tremendous achievement and thought he was the first who had dared to cross those impassable heights. But then he found an inscription on a rock showing that the Third Legion had made a road there!

Augustus always maintained fleets ready for action and built naval bases to keep the shipping routes clear of pirates. But the ships were small and seafaring dangerous. In winter they lay in their home ports: it was thought rash to defy the winter storms. No voyages were made between November 11th and March 10th. On March 5th Isis' ship was initiated on all the coasts of the Mediterranean: Isis was the guardian goddess of sailors. Processions went to the harbour, where they decorated and loaded a ship in Isis' honour and sent the vessel out to sea. After that the other ships were put into the water.

It was unpleasant to be shipwrecked. The inhabitants of a country as a rule exercised strict shore rights: they stole cargoes and sold shipwrecked people as slaves. St Paul's account in the Acts of the Apostles of the journey from Caesarea to Rome gives a vivid impression of the dangers and hardships of a sailor's life. It was no exception to the general rule.

CAESAREA

Modern seamen make for the open sea: they feel safest there. But the sailors of antiquity preferred not to get out of sight of land, so that they could put into harbour quickly in case of necessity. They had neither compasses nor chronometers to guide them, and when clouds hid the stars they sailed blind.

When Virgil was going to sail from Italy to Greece, a day's voyage over the sea which carried more traffic than any other, Horace wrote a farewell poem as if his friend was going into the utmost danger. And Juvenal tells of a Roman senator's wife who ran away with a gladiator. What most astonished him was that she could bear sea-sickness and the smell of water in the ship's hold. But what would a woman in love not endure?

Life was impregnated with religion: it followed mankind from the cradle to the grave. There were gods who watched over every step in life. One god took a boy to school, another brought him home; there was one god to teach him to count, another to teach him to sing; one looked after his physical development and one his understanding. Every person had his guardian deity, and an evil and good genius stood at his side and contended for his life.

To the Romans religion was primarily a question of right. Men had to fulfil their obligations to the gods, and it was the duty of the gods to make a return. As time passed more warmth came into religious practice: the Greek mythology gave colour and life to the abstract Roman divinities, and the Greeks taught the Romans to take art into the service of religion. And even if it is only a faint echo of the past we hear when looking at the ancient temples in Rome, Athens and Ephesus, we are unwittingly fascinated by the beauty and splendour the men of old lavished on their divine worship.

Religious tolerance prevailed everywhere. So long as the Empire and the State obtained their due, people could worship what gods they liked. In the Forum Romanum there stands to this day a rough black stone. It was the symbol of the savage and senseless worship of the Phrygian goddess Cybele: she paid her tribute to Rome with this stone.

THE SON OF A STAR

But doubt was creeping into men's minds. Philosophers fed it when imparting their profound or—often—cheaply acquired wisdom. Philosophical street preachers wandered about the squares and streets and disputed with anyone who was willing to listen to them. They wore rough cloaks, with knapsacks and cudgels, and called themselves God's emissaries or spies. Not infrequently there were among them highly gifted, independent men, whose philosophy has held its ground for centuries. There were the Epicureans, who made enjoyment the object of life, and the Stoics, who taught that wisdom was the highest good. The Cynics had great influence. They were the begging monks of antiquity. They went from town to town in threadbare cloaks, with wallet and staff, and scoffed at the divine mythology. They taught the masses to despise the old gods.

Officially the old Roman religion was maintained. And nothing more was demanded. If only due worship was performed at the right time, all was well. Everyone knew quite well that this form of religion was worn out, but the unity of the Empire demanded religious expressions; even the sceptics admitted that. It gradually took the form of emperor-worship.

And here was something tangible, something that could be felt. As an Athenian put it when the Emperor entered his city: 'The other gods are far away. Either they cannot hear, or they do not exist, or they do not trouble about us. But you we see with our eyes, not made of wood or stone, but living. Therefore we worship you.' Augustus had freed the Empire from civil war, chaos and ruin. He was the saviour and lord who had shown himself more powerful than anyone who had ever lived. From this time onwards emperor-worship swept forward with irresistible strength. When the Emperor's corpse was burned, an eagle was released from the pyre. It flew skywards, symbolizing the freed spirit of the Emperor ascending to heaven.

But the chief cause of the religious unrest was the mystical eastern religions which in these years were making a triumphal progress through the Empire. The Roman priests were only masters of the ceremonies, while those from the east were spiritual guides. There was something misty and veiled about these eastern religions that made it easier for clear, cold brains to make submission to them, and the insistence on ruin and death which lay at the heart of them appealed to a generation which, hopeless and despairing, had been trying to feel its way forward to find a way to the light.

The worship of Isis came from Egypt and was the most popular religion under the Empire. It told in mystical pictures of the sufferings, death and resurrection of the deity and the life of the initiated after death under the care of a maternal, all-powerful goddess. Isis was going about seeking for the dismembered body of her husband Osiris. She put the pieces together and fanned them with her wings. And Osiris rose up again to a new life as ruler of the kingdom of the dead. Everyone through death became as Osiris and entered his holy realm.

This was a drama everyone could understand, and it stirred human feelings most profoundly. Isis sought for the mutilated body amid the lamentations of the faithful, and the crowd cheered when she woke the god to new life. Their grief and jubilation had a deeper meaning: it was not only the god who suffered but the human race with him: snatched from the jaws of destruction, it became one with the god.

The priests of Isis knew their people and went to work quietly, making good use of their religious experience, so that the cult gained greater and greater power over men's minds. With its daily services, and its precepts of abstinence and asceticism, it controlled the whole of human life, and educated its devotees by systematic exercises.

The priests assembled the people every day. While they were singing hymns, the temple was opened, the holy fire was kindled, the holy water poured out and the images of the gods displayed. And when the temple was to be closed of an evening, there was another service. The gods were not far off, so that they were only sought for when there was real use for them: on the contrary, they were near, and accompanied mankind in all its daily activities.

The new religions, therefore, also began to employ technical resources to grip people's feelings and appeal to their imagination. The deep notes of water organs accompanied the holy scenes of the mysteries. Lighting effects were used, and the lamp obtained a regular place in divine worship: its light represented the deity itself, it lit up the darkness and cast over existence a glamour from the eternity whence the light itself came: life was raised into a higher sphere.

A contemporary writer who had tasted the mystery of initiation thus described his experience:

'I approached the frontier of death and stood on Proserpine's threshold, I turned back after I had travelled through all the elements. I saw the sun's rays in the middle of the night like a shining light. I went in before the gods both of the lower world and of heaven and worshipped them.'

No religion obtains power over men's minds and hearts if it does not lay restrictions and burdens upon them. The new religions demanded long and thorough cleansings and complicated ceremonies amounting even to wild asceticism and self-flagellation. Juvenal describes how in winter the worshippers of Isis had to plunge three times into the cold waters of the Tiber and drag themselves round the divinity on their bleeding knees.

But this repulsive element was far more pronounced in others of the eastern religions—in the first place, in the worship of Magna Mater, the great mother, and her son and lover Attis. The great mother lived in the mountains of Asia Minor. Her power revealed itself in nature: she cared for the wild animals. In the many pictures of her which are known to us a lion is always in attendance. Magna Mater and Attis were the protectors of nature's breeding power: savage ceremonies were performed in their honour which bore the stamp of the eastern peoples' inclination to wild and orgiastic worship.

The legends about them are manifold, and often contradict one another. But in the main they amount to this. Cybele—another name for the great mother—had a lover, but the gods made him impotent. They flung his testicles down on the ground, where they fertilized the soil so that an almond tree grew up. Nana, the river-god's daughter, plucked the almonds from the tree and so mysteriously conceived a son. She gave birth to Attis and exposed him in the mountains. He received his first care from a he-goat and grew up to be a handsome youth. Cybele caught sight of him, and all her wild passion was aroused. But Attis knew her and fled up into the mountains, mad with terror. Here he castrated himself in a fit of delirium and bled to death under a pine tree. Violets sprang from his blood. Cybele sought for him with despair in her heart. At last she stood by her dead lover under the tree which had heard him draw his last breath.

The worship of Attis was on the border-line between religion and sexuality. Primitive instincts, which most in ordinary circumstances veil and hide, were suddenly realized and exercised a dangerous fascination. These were religious instincts of great antiquity, all the feelings which the mutations of nature have awakened in men from time immemorial. The changes of the seasons, the awakening and death of leaves and flowers, had the same rhythm as the god's death and resurrection: they were parallel to sorrow and joy, death and life, and caught the innermost chords of the human heart in a grip as firm as it was mysterious. It will be seen how, when the ecstasy of the participants rose to its dizziest heights, streams from quite different sources flowed to join one another in the rite of worship.

One day at the end of March, at the spring equinox, a pine was felled in the sacred grove. It was decorated with coloured ribbons and the first spring flowers, Attis' violets, thus symbolizing the dead Attis, and was carried in procession to the temple. The faithful had fasted the day before: now they walked as mourners behind the dead god, with tambourines in their hands and singing. The song swelled and became shrill and wild. The priests began to scream, and young men swung whips over their naked bodies and beat them till the blood flowed. Naked girls and men performed a dance full of sexual incitement. Then a young man appeared, driven by ritual ecstasy to the zenith of delirium. Madly gnashing his teeth, he suddenly cut off his genital organs and flung them at the feet of the god. He had made the supreme sacrifice, and collapsed with blood streaming from his body. Now he was one of the priests of the god.

A nocturnal festival followed, in which the initiated were united with the great mother. When day dawned at last, new feasts began, now of rejoicing, at which the reawakening of Attis was celebrated with tumultuous joy and copious banqueting. Last of all the image of the great mother was carried down to the river, where it was given a cleansing bath. The multitude, thrilled to the core, followed the brilliant spectacle as the goddess's car glided past, music rang out, and long lines of priests advanced in splendid robes, with amulets hung round their necks. Last came the white-clad believers bearing the insignia of the goddess.

Here there was something to see, and shattering experiences to be followed at close quarters. Everyone could understand what was happening and let his own feelings take part in the drama. The goddess who lost her loved one, who died in the spring-time of youth, like the grass and flowers when burned by the sun—was there not food for lamentation in this? But then came the rejoicing when he returned to life. So they would die themselves, but they too would rise again. When they came into the brooding darkness of the mystical chamber, beams of light suddenly shot forth, and the priest whispered in their ears: 'Be consoled, you too shall find peace after your pain!'

The sky arched itself over the earth, the sun stretched its bow all day over the vault of the sky, and at night the moon and stars drew strange figures which the fancy could interpret as pictures. Were not, perhaps, the answers to life's deepest questions to be read in the sky? It is known that from the most ancient times some of the profoundest thinkers have sought the solution of life's riddle in the stars. The sun and moon were used to measure time, but could not their movements also give an idea of what was to happen in the future? When the sun was darkened, or a ring appeared round the moon, it must be a sign. But above all the constellations of the zodiac were full of prophecies. And even in antiquity a good deal was known about these things.

At the New Year the gods were gathered in council. Then the fate of the year was decided, and the gods revealed their decisions in the firmament to all who could interpret the courses of the stars. Mars was the war god, so his star portended strife and disaster, Saturn was the enemy of all living things, but Venus, as the goddess of love and fertility, was good and kind. The names of the stars, the shapes of the constellations and their position in the path of the sun all had significance.

The strange art of astrology grew out of all this and became more and more developed and refined. The answers to all questions could be obtained by working out the parallelogram of forces, which gave the answer to every question. The different forces could be read clearly from the positions of the planets in the constellations and their mutual relationship.

It had been established from time immemorial that the rising and setting of the stars coincided with the mutations of the climate and the seasonal changes of vegetable life. There must be a connection, and each year's experience seemed to confirm that the stars were the cause of everything that happened: currents of warmth and strength from the heavenly bodies streamed down over the earth. And gradually the astrologers put together a whole picture of the world.

The world was divided into seven spheres: each of the five planets had one, and the sun and moon had one each. But above these spheres was the highest sphere, the eternal immovable world of the fixed stars, and under the moon was the lowest, the world, in which men lived on the earth. In the seven planetary spheres regularity prevailed, but on the earth there was continual variation and mutability, which was determined by Fate, the ensemble of the heavenly powers.

Matter consisted of four elements: fire, air, water and earth. It was here that the powers exercised their influence. When all the planets were assembled in the sign of the Crab, it meant a world conflagration, and when they were in the sign of the He-goat, the world was to be flooded. And since the stars, as all knew, returned to their courses, these great events must go on repeating themselves—again and again. The course of the world was always turning back. As the preacher said: 'What was shall be, and there is nothing new under the sun.'

In old times men already had an idea that the souls of the dead lingered on in space or in the stars. The new star religions brought triumphant confirmation to this belief. After death the immortal part of men returned to its right place. In space it was cleansed by the winds: sensual desires and passions, which otherwise would have clung to it, were washed away by the rain and burned by the lightning. Thus the soul reached its eternal goal, peace in the stillness of the ether.

All this astrological picture of the world is still impressive today for its consistent and majestic clarity of thought. The world was full of gods: planets, signs of the zodiac, stars, even periods of time, were personal gods. But there were also evil forces, demons, wandering about in space: they were stronger than men, but inferior to the gods. The source of all things was Aion, eternity. The sphere of the fixed stars was the seat of divine power. Heaven itself was a god, the highest god. But he was so great that the name did not suffice, but was reinforced with additional names, superlative piled on superlative. The highest god in astrology is *summus exsuperantissimus*, the highest, the all-dominating!

The worship of the sun, which came from Syria, was related to the star religions of astrology. Everyone knew that the sun was the most important of all the heavenly bodies: the movements of the other planets depended on it, and the moon borrowed its light from the sun. The sun was the leader, about whom the other planets turned, and it determined the courses of the stars.

The sun-god was king and lord of the world. He was like fire, which gave the world warmth and light, and light was the religious expression for strength and reason. The sun too had its death and resurrection. It sank in the autumn, but in the winter solstice it was born again to new life. December 25th, therefore, was celebrated as the birthday of the unconquered sun. At midnight the call was heard: 'The virgin has given birth, the light is increasing.' In an antique calendar there stood against December 25th: 'Birth of the sun, light increases.'

It was a strictly regulated world. Everything was ruled by unchangeable laws from beginning to end. There was no room for a personal god: the substance of astrology and sun-worship was the most rigid determinism. And the inevitability of all that could be read in and calculated from the firmament was directly contrary to the innermost religious needs and keenest longings of mankind. 'Fate directs the world, fixed laws rule everything', it was said.

But things being as they were, men would do their utmost to peer into the future and interpret the signs. Interpreters of dreams and soothsayers had a golden time, and the temple priests ransacked the entrails of the sacrificed animals to read what signs were there. A soothsayer looked into the lamp-light and stared so long that at last he saw God or a holy symbol.

Others read signs in water. For this they used as medium an innocent boy who had kept himself free from all contagion. He lay down on his stomach with his face over a vessel full of water mixed with oil. His eyes must be shut or his head wrapped up. Holy pictures and screeds lay on the vessel, or it was smeared with magic ointment. Fervent prayers were offered and supernatural forces conjured up. Then, and not till then, the medium's eyes were opened and he looked down into the water. If he saw a light, the incantations were continued, and now the medium saw clearly in the water and invoked beings, dead people or gods.

In the introduction to the Epistle to the Romans Paul draws a ghastly picture of moral dissolution at the beginning of the Empire. If one compares it with other documents from that period one quickly comes to the conclusion that Paul does not exaggerate, and that all 'natural' and unnatural vices did really

THE SON OF A STAR

flourish. Whether this gloomy picture had general application is quite another matter—one that it is never easy to decide. Imagine the morals of our time under research workers' microscopes in two thousand years time—what nice results there might be! If the morals of the middle of the twentieth century were to be judged exclusively from ordinary Society gossip, or the extravagance and debauchery of a Farouk, we should appear no better than ancient Rome.

Certainly a rot had set in in Graeco-Roman culture. All our sources indicate a world which was swiftly and irresistibly going downhill to ruin. The depths of poverty on one side and mad gluttony among the few at the top, sexual laxity and unbridled brutality, created an atmosphere of scepticism and hopelessness. The suicide figures rose to undreamed of heights, always a certain sign of dissolution. Exposure of children was a natural and permitted thing. Augustus exposed his own daughter's children, and abortion was frequent.

Slavery was one of the darkest shadows in the picture. It is estimated that half the population of the Empire were slaves: the whole of antique civilization was simply based on slavery. A slave had no rights: he was not a person, but a thing. A Roman author divides the farmer's chattels into three categories: dumb, i.e. ploughs, carts, etc: those unable to speak, i.e. oxen and other animals, and those which could speak, i.e. the slaves. They were used for everything, even to satisfy the sexual requirements of both their master and their mistress. Martial tells of the matron Marulla, the features of whose seven children showed clearly which of the family slaves was the father of each: the Moorish cook, the flat-nosed athlete, the sore-eyed baker, the Cretan with a pointed head and long ears, the black flute-player, the red-haired bailiff—and the master's favourite boy.

The prevalent brutality took horrible forms. A slave tried to kill his master. He failed, and he was tortured to death as a matter of course. But the remaining eighty slaves of the household, who ought to have known of the event and prevented it, suffered the same fate.

CAESAREA

The death sentence was carried out in the most ingenious ways and was a popular amusement. Sometimes it was done in the theatre. The condemned persons learnt parts and appeared in expensive cloth of gold tunics ornamented with golden wreaths. Suddenly flames burst from their clothes and set them on fire: their faces had previously been smeared with phosphorus. 'The uncomfortable toga' appealed to popular humour.

In the arena wild animals were trained to be man-eaters. Those condemned to die were tied to posts, quite defenceless, or obtained a short respite by carrying weapons. If the wounds inflicted were so huge that the entrails hung out, doctors ran forward to study the internal functions of the body, which otherwise were unknown ground to the medicine of antiquity.

Pessimism, misery and hopelessness—these are the headlines to human destiny in the period of Graeco-Roman culture. We can still read numerous epitaphs such as these:

'I was not, and came into existence. I was and am no longer. That is all.'

'I was nothing and am nothing. And you who read this: eat, drink and be merry!'

'What I have eaten and drunk I have taken with me. What I left behind I have lost.'

A world and a state of imposing strength and glittering beauty: but with a snake-bite in the marrow and on the way to disappear in rottenness and decay.

On the coast of Palestine, in the everlasting ferment of the East, Caesarea lay as a solid bastion of Roman might and the old heathen culture. From Caesarea the Romans delivered one crushing blow after another at Jewish rebellion and Hebrew culture and belief. The Jewish state collapsed, but the eternal substance of Judaism went purified through the fire and became from one generation to another a peculiar and indispensable leaven in the lives of the nations.

And even before the fall of Jerusalem there was appearing, both in Caesarea and all over the far-flung Roman dominions, a new-born spiritual force, which would prove vigorous enough both to survive the Empire, and to advance swiftly as a

THE SON OF A STAR

civilizing influence. Caesarea became one of the centres of the rising Christian church.

In the year 128 Caesarea was smitten by a natural catastrophe. A violent earthquake struck the city and devastated a great part of it.

It was taken as an omen.

IV

A NEW DAY DAWNS

THE port of Caesarea was Palestine's outlet. From it shipping lanes led out into the great world, and the ships carried a steady stream of travellers on their way to or from Palestine.

The exact dates and year of this incident are not known to us, and it was an ordinary occurrence, not specially noted in the historians' annals, when one day a ship entered the harbour and a few passengers came ashore. They collected their luggage, took it on their backs and went from the harbour quarter straight up into the town: they evidently knew where they were going.

In one of the streets they found the house they were looking for. A man named Philip lived there with his four daughters. The visitors were cordially welcomed. It was not the first time the oldest of the party, Saul of Tarsus, now known as the apostle Paul, had stayed with this Philip, who had brought Christianity to Caesarea many years before: these two were old acquaintances.

But this time Paul had the doctor Luke with him. How he had met him is not known. It is known, on the other hand, that Paul had bad health; there are references in his epistles to chronic eye trouble, and he may also have suffered from a kind of epilepsy. This sickness had attacked Paul on one of his laborious journeys, no doubt in Asia Minor, and he had sent for the nearest doctor.

And it was the Greek, Luke, who had treated the apostle. His professional aid must have been effective. Paul was able to continue his journey. But this was a turning point in Luke's life: he gave up his practice and accompanied Paul. The patient had something to give the doctor, something he had not known before. Luke was baptized and received into the Christian Church.

He was not contented with acting as a kind of physician-in-ordinary to the apostle. A highly educated man, he undertook a piece of literary work which has been absolutely invaluable to posterity: he wrote his books, one on the life of Jesus, which we call the Gospel of St Luke, and the Acts of the Apostles, the first history of the Church. He was planning to write a third book, a continuation of his history of the Church with further accounts of Paul's experiences after his imprisonment in Rome. It is not known whether the plan was carried out: if it was, the book has been lost.

In the Acts of the Apostles are the so-called 'We passages', in which the author is describing not things which had happened to others, but events in which he himself had taken part. Of course we read these passages with special attention: personal impressions, set down by an able and sensitive writer, are always of value. And the arrival at Caesarea is one of the 'We passages'. So Luke was one of the party, and he tells how they stayed with Philip before going on to Jerusalem—the stay in the capital which had such fatal consequences for the apostle.

Luke was looking for material for his books. He begins his Gospel by relating how he had sought out those who 'from the beginning' were eye-witnesses, and had not begun to write till he had 'perfect understanding of all things from the very first'. By doing so he saved a good deal of oral tradition which otherwise would have been lost. It is certainly no mere chance that he is just the one of the Evangelists who tells the beautiful stories of the Annunciation and the Christmas night at Bethlehem. He found his way to Jesus' elderly mother and listened to her experiences. And the earliest history of the Church in Caesarea we know solely from his handing down of the tradition—a fruit of his conversations with Philip.

Some of the great names of the infant Church are linked with

A NEW DAY DAWNS

the congregation in Caesarea. Philip lived there with his four unmarried daughters, who 'prophesied' and were held in esteem by the congregation. Philip himself was one of the celebrated seven relief officers in Jerusalem: he thus belonged to the circle of the first martyr, Stephen, and a certain amount is known about his activities. It was he who met the Ethiopian courtier on 'the desert road' between Jerusalem and Gaza and baptized him. After this journey he came to Caesarea and settled there: and a Christian congregation grew up round him. This was the usual way in which Christianity was spread in those earliest times. A Christian came to a new place—and the process began all of itself.

Simon Peter occupied a still more central position, and he had a decisive experience in Caesarea. 'A devout man, and one that feared God', Cornelius, was an officer in the garrison of the city, in 'the band called the Italian band', and tradition relates how he was in a miraculous manner impelled to send a message to Joppa, where Simon Peter was staying.

Here Luke works in his description of Peter, who, on the flat roof of Simon the tanner's house, had just had the vision of the clean and unclean animals and therefore felt justified in immediately giving the heathen Cornelius Christian baptism. We shall understand later why Luke, Paul's close colleague, so strongly underlines Peter's action. But it is important to establish that the Church in Caesarea could thus trace its origin directly back to the leading figure in the apostolic circle. Moreover, Paul came to the city several times: he passed through it on one of his first journeys, and he later spent two years there as a prisoner of the Procurator.

This is all that the New Testament has to tell us. But Josephus relates that at the outbreak of war in 66 all the Jews in Caesarea were massacred, and during the war, with its changes of fortune, the place remained firmly in Roman hands. The congregation must therefore have consisted mainly of Gentile Christians. And so it is that the determining lines in the young Christian Church cross just at this point.

The Church in Caesarea was so near Jerusalem that it was

within range of the source of Christianity. The development of the Mother Church was taking place near by, and there was constant opportunity for intimate companionship and personal contact. And sheltered behind Roman spears it survived the war, which everywhere else had catastrophical results for the Church in Palestine.

But Caesarea's proximity to Jerusalem was only geographical: in reality it belonged to quite another world. For the Church this meant that the narrow Jewish-Christian views which were dominant in Jerusalem never really obtained a foothold in Caesarea: there fresher breezes were blowing. Its Christians had formerly been heathen, so that their relationship to Judaism was mainly of theoretical interest and was not of vital importance. They lived in the city with a view over the sea, and the ships brought strangers with a smack of distant countries about them. And the personages who set the tone had the Pauline, universalist view of the determining principles of Christianity and its whole future.

It was the conflict between these opposing views that fixed the course of the Christian Church in the first stage of its development. And so they had far-reaching effects.

One of the old fathers of the Church compared it to a river whose stream ran through the changing landscapes of time and received tributaries on both sides. There were periods when it rushed impatiently through narrows, and at others it flowed slowly and spread itself at its ease, so that it came to resemble a peaceful, idyllic lake. Often it split into different streams, which ran in separate channels but in the direction of the same sea. And there came times at which it simply disappeared: it was as though it glided down into an underground stream and did not come to the surface again till after the passage of years. But it was always the same river, and it was never stopped either by narrows or stagnation: soon or later it made a way forward for itself into the ocean of eternity. Its springs were in the mountains, high and remote, so that the river ran dry.

One of these curious periods—'tunnel periods' they might

A NEW DAY DAWNS

be called—may be observed in the years which cover the great Jewish war. Here are twenty or thirty years of Church history which have simply dropped out, vanished into a covered tunnel. And the remarkable thing was that something decisive happened while the stream was out of sight. The river which came out again into the light of day was different in essentials from the one we knew before. The contradiction between Judaism and Christianity had been clarified.

In its earliest childhood the Christian Church had been strictly centralized. A number of strong personalities sat at the helm in Jerusalem and did their best to keep even the distant mission to the heathen under their control. No less a person than Jesus' brother James, nicknamed the Righteous, was the real leader. It was said that his knees were as hardened as a camel's from kneeling so often in prayer.

James the Righteous was a man of deep conviction: he knew what course to take. For him Christianity had grown out of Judaism, and it would always carry ineffaceable marks of this near relationship. The Christians would observe the Mosaic law in all its rigour, and as long as the Temple stood service in it would be dear to them. Of course conflicts arose between the old Judaism and the new Christianity. One or two of them even led to bloodshed: both Stephen and James, son of Zebedee, were martyred. But they were exceptions. Taken all round, the Church in Palestine enjoyed a steady and peaceful development and growth. There were even indications that certain elements in the Jewish Church, especially among the Pharisees, regarded the new movement with a certain sympathy.

But inside the Church tension increased. Paul was a Jew, like all the first champions of Christianity. And he was a complete Jew, by birth and education. This stamp never left him: his epistles are impregnated with Old Testament spirit, and he argues as well as any rabbi. But his religious experiences, the dramatic awakening outside the gate of Damascus, and later the sight of heathen openly receiving the gospel, broke the Jewish mould.

Paul, like all Jews, had awaited the Messiah: throughout his youth he had a fiery longing for him who should come and was ever on the watch for him. And the Messiah came to him from heaven and revealed his will. Jesus of Nazareth was the Messiah, i.e. Christ. Paul had never expected him in the form in which he appeared, and for a long time he kicked against the pricks. But at last he was convinced, first crushed, then raised up and sent out with the Gospel, And he remained true to that heavenly vision for the rest of his life. He travelled far and wide with the message of Jesus Christ, first to the Jews, then to the Gentiles. But the road was the same for both: it went straight to God, without any halting-place in Judaism. Therefore heathen should not be circumcised before they were baptized, for circumcision was the symbol of recognition of the Tora. Christendom must not be isolated in Judaism: it was universal in its belief and its aim.

So sharp had the controversy become. It is not surprising that the first crisis of Christendom, the dispute between James and Paul, made a deep and painful cut. There were fierce collisions. Paul says openly in the Epistle to the Galatians how he had been in conflict with the eminent leaders from Jerusalem. And Luke also, though in a more cautious form and often indirectly, makes reference to the dispute in the Acts of the Apostles: his narratives from Caesarea are examples of this.

On the whole the dispute was moving towards a solution in favour of Jerusalem and James. Paul himself was brutally torn away from the scene of action by his arrest and two years' detention. It was his visions and inspirations which had created a new type of Christianity. It stepped over all national and religious barriers and proclaimed Jesus of Nazareth to be the Messiah in the sight of all men. And now it was thrust aside: it can indeed be said that it suffered a decisive defeat.

If something quite unexpected had not happened which was going to turn everything upside down, posterity would only have known a Church which was a Jewish-Messianic sect, centralized in Jerusalem and so strongly national that the road to the swarming millions of heathen would have been barred for all time.

A NEW DAY DAWNS

But just at this point the river glided down into the tunnel, the war broke out, and all outlines vanished in flames and smoke for many years. And when the Church came out into the light of day again, everything was different. The later books of the New Testament and the documents of the post-apostolic time give us the new picture. The Mother Church, with its combination of Judaism and Christianity, had been defeated, so decisively that thenceforward it simply disappeared from the scene of action of the World Church, and Paul's ideas had been victorious.

There are not many periods in the history of mankind in which the issues have been so clear cut as at this time. There had been a state of quivering tension between two diametrically opposed types of Church, that of James and that of Paul. It was relaxed by one side being reduced to insignificance. The road was now clear for a rejuvenated Christendom.

What would have happened if there had not been this turning point can be only guesswork. The Church in Jerusalem had tried to keep the new wine in old bottles. This would have led to undernourishment and lingering death. Now the bottles were smashed, and the new wine flowed out to new places where it duly matured.

But is nothing at all known of what happened to the mother congregation during the war and its later history in isolation, when it was slowly drying up and gradually disappearing?

Yet again we have to turn to Caesarea to find light on these remote, obscure times. The Bishop of Caesarea, the ecclesiastical historian Eusebius, died in the year 340. In his time Christianity had become the recognized State religion, and the Bishop administered his Palestinian diocese from the same city which had been the stronghold of heathendom. But what has made Eusebius memorable is not his work as a bishop, but the history of the Church which bears his name and is an invaluable source to every student of the free Church's history. Even if it has to be read with a critical eye, it contains so much ancient tradition and is so often our only source that the old Bishop deserves all thanks for his industry.

THE SON OF A STAR

It was he who preserved the often quoted tradition that before the war the Church in Jerusalem was ordered in a divine revelation to betake itself to the town of Pella, while 'God's judgment in the form of the Roman armies fell upon Judaea and Jerusalem and struck the unbelieving Jews'. There certainly was a town called Pella in the Decapolis, i.e. east of the Jordan. It was said that no less a person than Alexander the Great had founded it and named it so in memory of his Macedonian birthplace.

Unfortunately this story must have a note of interrogation set against it. It does not sound probable that devout Jews—and the Christians in Jerusalem were certainly that—would choose an absolutely heathen town as a place of refuge. And how could so many people get through a country swarming with military patrols, with the war either just on the point of breaking out or in full swing? How could they cross the Jordan and make their way through trackless mountains with their baggage and children and old people? For it was more than sixty miles from Jerusalem to Pella. And there are further objections. We know that at the beginning of the war the Jews captured the town and burned it to the ground in revenge for massacres at other places. But a couple of years later the Romans recaptured Pella and took a bloody vengeance on the Jewish garrison. What fate would all these terrible events have not brought upon the Christian Church?

It would seem more likely that the Church in Judaea fled to Egypt; Israel had so often turned that way in case of need. Both the Assyrians and the Babylonians had frightened many Jews into seeking refuge there. It was not surprising that a rich Jewish life had come into flower in Egypt. And there is early evidence that many Egyptian Jews were baptized. Of course this young Church had its roots in Palestine. What would have been more natural than for Christian homes to open their doors to refugee brethren?

Whether the greater part went eastward or westward, the strong general impression is that the Church in Judaea disappeared, either by splitting or scattering. But some survived, and others returned to Judaea when peace had gradually

A NEW DAY DAWNS

returned to that maltreated country. Eusebius' book gives further information.

He tells of Simeon, son of Klopas, for a long time the natural leader of the Christians. He was martyred at a very great age in the year 107, when Trajan was Emperor. Between this year and 135 Eusebius enumerated no fewer than thirteen bishops of Jerusalem. If this is to be taken literally, and these clerics followed one another in succession, the post of bishop in the Holy City must have been uncommonly unhealthy: in any case each of them ruled only for a very short time. But the solution is probably that the bearers of these names figured in the college of presbyters, a kind of Christian Sanhedrin, and that now one was prominent, now another: perhaps the senior member was elected president.

And within its narrow limits the Jewish-Christian Church in Jerusalem was both live and active. We know that these Nazarites—so the Christians were called in Judaea—took up the theological debate with the Jews most vigorously. And now they were well armed. They pointed to the ruins of the temple and reminded their opponents of Jesus' prophecy which had been so terribly fulfilled, for literally not a stone had been left standing on another. And the whole priesthood had disappeared. Was that not evidence that Jesus the Messiah was about to initiate a new era? They quoted industriously old passages in the prophets, which both sides recognized as the highest authority, to support their arguments.

But the Jews did not fail to reply. The rabbis invented a special word for heretics: they called them minim, a word often found in old Jewish tradition. The Christians were certainly minim. To defend themselves against the Christians the rabbis tried with all their might to set limits to the canon of the Old Testament so that it should be determined which of its books could be recognized as biblical and which were not. And of course the Christian books, including some of the Gospels, which had begun to circulate among the Jews, were banned. The bitter violence with which the rabbis carried on the dispute shows that the Christian propaganda was not ineffective. We know too that even prominent teachers were suspected of secretly sympathizing with the minim.

After the war the provincial stamp became more conspicuous in Judaea. The conscious, deliberate isolation of the people gave life a small town atmosphere. Experience tells us that all conflicts, both personal and objective, become specially bitter in small restricted communities where the horizon is narrow. It was so in Palestine in these years, and therefore the quarrels between the Nazarites and rabbis are interesting only as a curiosity. The real events were happening elsewhere: in Judaea people busied themselves for the most part with trivialities. But it is after all worth while to study life in Judaea: one comes across quite curious things. Here are one or two examples from this debate.

One of the most famous passages in the book of the prophet Daniel describes Judgement Day: 'I beheld again, and suddenly thrones were set forward, and an Ancient of Days did sit.' The word 'throne' is in the plural, so there was more than one. For whom were they set forward? Of course one was for God, the 'Ancient of Days'. But the others? Here there was ample scope for interpretations. Certain rabbis maintained that there were only two thrones: thus the plural was defensible. The other must be for him who is described as 'a son of man'. But this was just the term the Christians used of Jesus of Nazareth! He had, indeed, often used it of himself, even in a decisive context, in the examination on the night before Good Friday: 'Hereafter shall the Son of Man sit on the right hand of the power of God': as in Daniel, on the throne beside the Almighty! Curiously enough one of the principal rabbis, Rabbi Akiba, of whom more will be heard later, took the view that the second throne was set forward for David, i.e. great David's greater son, Messiah. This interpretation too was taken up and exploited by the Christians. For this reason most of the rabbis found it unacceptable, indeed blasphemous. When Akiba offered it furious protests rang out: 'How long will you profane God's majesty?'

We have heard how the great leader of the Sanhedrin at Jabneh, Gamaliel the Second, had the famous eighteenth prayer

A NEW DAY DAWNS

composed. But he added a nineteenth prayer, aimed at the Christians: 'Let there be no hope for the apostates, and may their insolent kingdom be plucked up by the roots in our time, and may the Nazarites and heretics (minim) in a moment be destroyed and wiped out of the book of life and not entered along with the righteous. Blessed be thou, O Lord, that humblest the insolent.' The object of this temperamental prayer, which was to be used both in daily prayer and in the synagogue service, was of course to prevent the Christians from taking part in divine service, where they would have been able to use their influence.

None the less Christian teaching crept into the synagogue. There were the passages which the Nazarites quoted so often that even the reading of them evoked recollections of their Christian interpretation. Characteristically enough the prophecy in Isaiah liii about the Suffering Servant of the Lord, which was one of the Christians' main proofs that the crucifixion had been predicted by the greatest of all the prophets, was omitted in reading in the synagogue.

But the best people do not care about remaining in a backwater, thick with duckweed: they want to get out into the fresh current. And as the Palestinian Church gradually became petrified in narrowmindedness and futile discussion, some of its liveliest members disappeared. Philip and his daughters left the country: we meet them again in Asia Minor and they are constantly quoted right into the second century.

The most notable of these emigrants was the evangelist John, the very disciple whom the Master had loved, and who at the foundation of holy communion leaned his head against Jesus' breast. For many years he was head of the congregation in Ephesus, one of the most important cities of the Empire. During the persecution under Domitian he was deported to the island of Patmos, where presumably the old man worked as a slave in a quarry, until Nerva's humane regime gave him his freedom. He lived almost to the end of the century and according to tradition he was the author of some important parts of the New Testament.

THE SON OF A STAR

But the arrows which pointed in from Palestine towards the central parts of the Roman Empire were comparatively few. Many more were aimed outwards, at the countries beyond the frontier. Not much is known about this, but the glimpses that now and then are afforded give some indication of the movement. The Ethiopian courtier whom Philip baptized may well stimulate the imagination. And in the description of Pentecost in the Acts of the Apostles people from Mesopotamia and Parthians, Medes and Elamites are mentioned. Perhaps some of them carried the Gospel to their distant homes.

Curiously enough, most of the apostles vanish into the mist. We know that James, son of Zebedee, was executed, and there are traces of the further careers of Peter and John. But all the others—Andrew, Thomas, Bartholomew and the rest? Of course legend has filled the gaps. Thus Thomas and Matthew went to India, and Andrew's death gave the saint's name to a particular form of cross. But it is all pure legend.

The apocryphal correspondence between Jesus and the king of Edessa belongs to the same category. The King was suffering from an incurable disease. He wrote to Jesus asking him to come and help him. But Jesus wrote back that he was prevented at the moment, but would send one of his disciples, who would cure the King and bring salvation to him and his people. The whole of this fantastic story is doubtless a legendary elaboration of the fact that long afterwards a king of Edessa was really baptized. His name was Abgar, and he has the honour of being the first Christian prince.

The future belonged to Pauline Christianity. The apostle, burning with zeal, endeavoured to get all round the world: each time a goal was reached, the next shone out on the horizon. The aim of his strategy was to establish vigorous congregations in the great cities, from which, as centres of Christianity, they could work in the surrounding country. He covered practically the whole of the known world. Like an eagle escaping from a narrow cage, the Christian message rose skyward and flew from land to land.

A NEW DAY DAWNS

Among the Jews in the dispersion the expectations of the Messiah were just as keen as in the homeland. And Paul, who came with the message that Jesus was the Messiah, began with the Jews in each new city. He often met 'hard hearts', and some of his bitterest enemies came from the synagogues. None the less the Jewish colonies were as a rule strongholds of the Christian message. There were always some Jews who accepted the Gospel. But particularly in wide circles among the Gentiles the Jewish mission had aroused a longing for the one true God. Here was fertile soil for the seed of the Gospel, which later ripened to form a great Christian army.

But before Paul became active the report of the new faith had travelled round the Empire by a thousand secret routes, and of course it had reached Rome, the capital of the world.

Who first brought the gospel to Rome nobody knows. Neither the New Testament nor any contemporary historian has spoken of it. But the Imperial City was in active communication with the East. People of every language and every religion met there, and news came 'as if carried by the birds of the air': so Christianity had probably arrived by this, the most natural of all routes. We also know a good deal about the intimate contact between the Roman Jews and Jerusalem, so the first Christian missionaries in Rome are sure to have been Jews.

Dramatic events must have taken place in connection with the Christian mission in Rome. As early as the year 49 the authorities intervened when the preaching of Christianity led to stormy scenes in the synagogue. A Roman historian narrates that the Emperor Claudius expelled the Jews from Rome in that year because 'they caused continual disturbances, in which the ringleader was one Kristus'. This is the first time in which the name of Christ is met with outside the New Testament. Note, too, that the authorities still did not know the difference between the Jews and Christians.

The Christian congregation in Rome was fairly considerable. Paul writes in the Epistle to the Romans that 'your obedience is come abroad unto all men', so it would appear that a number of heathen joined it at an early date. And Paul himself lived

THE SON OF A STAR

as a prisoner in the city in good conditions: he 'was suffered to dwell by himself with a soldier that kept him', and 'he dwelt two whole years in his own hired house and received all that came in unto him, preaching the kingdom of God, and teaching those things which concern the Lord Jesus Christ, with all confidence, no man forbidding him'.

But in the year 64 the Roman Church emerged for the first time into the full light of day. In the middle of the summer a huge fire broke out in the city: it reduced two-thirds of the capital to ashes and rendered hundreds of thousands homeless. It was rumoured that Nero himself was the author of the catastrophe: he sought for a scapegoat and found one in the Christians. The historian Tacitus gives a vivid description of this, the first great persecution of the Christians. Certainly he was only ten years old at the time and did not even live in Rome. But the events were so sensational that he could have collected information later from numerous eye-witnesses. This part of Tacitus' history is the basis of our knowledge of the Christian Church at this epoch and is so vividly written that it deserves to be quoted in full:

'The Emperor denounced as guilty, and inflicted the most refined punishments upon those who were hated for their malpractices, and whom the people called Christians. The name Christians comes from Christ, whom the governor Pontius Pilate caused to be executed in the reign of Tiberius. This mischievous superstition had been suppressed from that moment, but now broke out again, not only in the Jews' country, the homeland of the evil, but also in Rome, where all that is evil and shameful streams together from all sides and finds supporters. First individuals were taken, who confessed, and then, on their information, a great number, who were proved to be guilty, if not of arson, at any rate of hatred of mankind. To their punishments mockery was added. The Christians were sewn up in animals' skins to be torn to pieces by savage dogs, or they were nailed to crosses, or they were smeared with pitch and lighted as torches, when darkness fell. Nero had opened his gardens for this spectacle, and at the same time he had plays performed on

A NEW DAY DAWNS

the racecourse, in which he himself, dressed as a coachman, either mingled with the people or drove his own carriage. For this reason people began to feel compassion for the victims, who indeed deserved the severest punishment, but who were being done to death not for the public good, but to satisfy the cruel instincts of one man.'

The Christians gained their first adherents among the slaves and poor people of Rome. This was natural seeing that these were by far the most numerous class. Of Rome's million and a half inhabitants at least half were slaves, and only fifty thousand belonged to the bourgeoisie. Christianity was still only a despised and persecuted religion, and later times have allowed a fertile growth of legend about these earliest days to spring up unchecked. But it is only a legend that Paul had a secret adherent in the philosopher Seneca and converted one of Nero's mistresses. Yet there are legends which stand in a class by themselves—those which contain everlasting truths. The story of Peter's attempt to flee from Rome and his meeting with Christ on the Appian Way belongs to this category. Peter asked 'Quo vadis, Domine?' (Where goest thou, Lord?) and the Saviour replied, 'To Rome, to be crucified again.' So Peter turned back and met with a martyr's death. Probably both he and Paul were killed in one of Nero's persecutions.

In Domitian's time the searchlight was again turned on both Jews and Christians. The morbidly suspicious Emperor was expecting a new Jewish insurrection and kept the Jews down with an iron hand. The Christians suffered along with them. When Domitian heard that descendants of David and blood relations of Jesus were still living in Palestine, he had them summoned to Rome. But their behaviour was so simple and unpretentious, their character so modest, and their hands so rough and marked by hard toil that even Domitian was persuaded that he had nothing to fear from them, and he let them go home again.

But there were Christians in high positions as well. Flavius Clemens, who had been Consul in the year 95, and his wife, Flavia Domitilla, probably Vespasian's granddaughter, were charged with 'godlessness, like many others who have been led into Jewish ways'. Clemens lost his life and Domitilla was banished. Their two young sons had been designated as the Emperor's successors. What became of these boys is only guesswork: most likely they shared their parents' fate. There are several indications that this family was not Jewish, but Christian: the name of Domitilla is found in one of the oldest Christian cemeteries in Rome.

This is also true of another eminent man, Acilius Glabrio, who was accused of 'Judaism and godlessness'. At any rate his family owned a burial-place in another Christian catacomb, Priscilla's churchyard. He was flung to the lions, but killed the lion that attacked him, and did it so skilfully that the Emperor, who was looking on, envied him. But this did not help him: he had to die.

But Christianity, as is seen, was no longer confined to the lowest stratum of the people. It had got through the hard early stages and had begun to gain admission to the aristocracy, even to the imperial family. Only half a century after the faith arrived in Rome, and thirty years after Nero's persecutions, the chosen heirs to the throne were Christians. One cannot help wondering how history would have shaped itself if these boys had lived and in time ascended the throne. Now it was more than two centuries before a Christian Emperor came to the throne, and for this long period Christianity had almost continually to struggle against imperial opposition, which often took the form of persecution.

Why did the State nourish this eternal ill-will towards the Church? As the years passed, it could not be the Roman contempt for the Jews for which the Christians had to pay the penalty. The Romans had learnt the difference between the two religions. Moreover, the Jews took care to keep open water between themselves and the Christians: if they did not the relationship could become dangerous. Judaism had possessed valuable privileges from old times. It was to a certain extent a recognized religion: the Jews could perform their worship freely and escaped civil and military duties which might bring them

A NEW DAY DAWNS

into the proximity of false gods. Also, their religion bore a national stamp.

The Christians had no privileges and were generally unpopular. Tacitus said that they were detested for their vices. Their 'hatred of mankind' was shown by their shunning of intercourse with others, i.e. heathen, and avoidance of public posts. Everyone could see that they were atheists: why, they worshipped an invisible God and refused to sacrifice to the Emperor's image. When the imperial police began to take an interest in their assemblies, they held secret meetings, and the worst construction was put upon that. Surely, people said, they would not meet in secret unless they had something to conceal. Rumours that ritual murder and cannibalism were part of their services began to go round, and the hatred of them increased greatly. Every authority who took any action against the Christians could be sure of public applause.

Curiously enough, Nero had been popular with the masses of the people—but of course they had had him at a comfortable distance. After his suicide there were persistent rumours that he was not dead at all, but had fled eastwards and was now living beyond the Euphrates. One fine day he would appear at the head of a great Parthian army and become Caesar again. Several adventurers took their chance and declared themselves to be Nero, but none succeeded. As the years passed, and Nero did not come, it was realized that he must really be dead: but then the idea was conceived that he would come from the kingdom of the dead and win back his crown. This belief in *Nero redivivus*, Nero risen from the dead, can be traced right down to the close of the second century.

To the Christians Nero was identical with anti-Christ, and the fantasies about *Nero redivivus* certainly coloured the descriptions in the Book of Revelation. In any case its pictures of the apocalypse give a vivid impression of the change which had taken place in the Christian outlook since Paul's time. He looked to the Roman administration with confidence as his protector. It was the authority a Christian should obey: it was indeed a check upon the forces of lawlessness. In the apocalyptic time there was open war between the Empire and the Church—a war which cost lives, but in which every man who held fast was assured of victory. And this latent enmity often burst into flames.

In Trajan's time there was a governor of Bithynia, a province of Asia Minor. His name was Pliny the Younger, the appellation having been given him to distinguish from his uncle, Pliny the Elder, a celebrated naturalist who lost his life in the great eruption of Vesuvius. The younger Pliny was typical of the worst kind of bureaucrat, a pedantic official who wrote endless letters and reports. Close contact with him must have been unbearable, but we can rejoice at his longwindedness, for a good deal of his correspondence has been preserved, and it throws a light on many events of the time which otherwise would have been forgotten.

There is one letter in particular which has made him famous, and it is about the Christians. He tells the Emperor of the lamentable falling off in interest in the old religion which he has noticed. The temples are not visited by so many people as before, and fewer animals are sold for sacrifices. This is connected with the rapid growth of Christianity. There are more and more Christians both in large and small towns and out in the country.

Pliny went into the matter. He interrogated a number of Christians, and if they clung to their false doctrine he had them executed or sent to Rome for further interrogation. But then he received an anonymous letter denouncing a number of people as Christians. Pliny interrogated them all. Some declared that they were no longer Christians, of which they had to give proof by offering wine and incense to the Emperor's image and cursing the name of Christ. But to obtain full insight into what Christianity really was, he had two deaconesses tortured. As a result of the whole inquiry Pliny could not see that, beyond adhering to their miserable superstition, the Christians had actually done any harm. They used to assemble on a particular day and sing hymns to Christ 'as to a god'. They bound themselves not to steal, cheat or commit adultery. In the evenings

A NEW DAY DAWNS

they met for a frugal meal. Pliny asked what further steps, if any, he should take.

Trajan replied that Pliny had acted rightly. The Christians should not be sought out, but only interrogated when they were denounced. If they were definitely proved to be Christians and refused to sacrifice to the gods, they must be punished. But no notice should be taken of anonymous complaints: 'this is not seemly in our century'.

By this imperial decision the course of action in the future was clearly defined. Trajan's letter is evidence of the religious tolerance which had now become instinctive with the Roman Emperors. But undeniably it left the Christians in a peculiar and anything but pleasant state of uncertainty. As long as they were not denounced they were left in peace, but they might be denounced at any moment. It was like having a sharp sword hanging by a hair over their heads. If there was a legal inquiry, the interrogation was cut as short as possible. The question was asked: 'Are you a Christian?' If the accused person admitted that he was, and obstinately refused to make an offering to the Emperor's image, he had clearly committed an offence against the State, and punishment followed automatically.

If pestilences came, the Christians had to be on their guard. The heathen were sure that the gods were offended, and sought for the reason. Their thoughts turned at once to those mad Christians, who would not go to the temples and had their own secret meetings, at which they slaughtered children, ate human flesh and drank blood. Of course it must be these godless, superstitious people who had brought evil days upon the Empire. Tertullian's words, written nearly a hundred years later, were already fully applicable: 'Let the Tiber overflow its banks, let the Nile cease to water the fields of Egypt, let drought, earthquake, famine or plague appear, at once the cry is raised: throw the Christians to the lions!'

Trajan himself had a personal experience of the kind. In the year 115, during the Parthian campaign, he was in Antioch, the town in which the name 'Christian' had originated. On December 13th a severe earthquake shook the city, so violently that the strongest houses collapsed, and many people were killed. The Emperor saved his life only by jumping out of a window of the palace.

The city was violently agitated: a sacrifice of atonement must be found to placate the gods. Who else should it be but the Christians? The bishop of the city was called Ignatius, an eminent man, 'whose name was on everyone's lips'. Legend has it that he was very old, and that it was he whom Jesus as a child had set up as an example. Legend says also that he made his way into the Emperor's presence and bore witness in glowing language. However that may be, he was condemned and sent to Rome to be thrown to the lions. On the long journey he wrote seven letters, which have been preserved and give a vivid impression of this fiery soul.

'Pray only', he writes, 'that I may obtain strength both outwardly and inwardly, so that I not only speak, but also will, so that I am not only called a Christian, but really am a Christian. For Christianity consists not only in being silent, but also in being strong.'

We can understand that these were times in which the Church went underground. It did so literally; it went into the catacombs. Nowhere do we obtain so colourful an impression of the conditions of the early Church as in going through the great catacombs outside the old walls of Rome.

It was the custom of the heathen to burn their dead. But both the Jews and the early Church detested this practice. When a Christian died, he should have his own grave, so that his dust could rest in peace till the resurrection. The grave should be as like the Saviour's as possible, so underground burial chambers were preferred. On the low hills near Rome the soil consists of fine-grained tufa, which is easily cut and firm enough not to collapse.

Here long galleries were cut with chambers or resting-places for the dead. There was plenty of room: the graves could be placed on top of one another, and side galleries could be dug. First one gallery was cut, then more, and if still more room was wanted, the next galleries were laid down as a new storey under

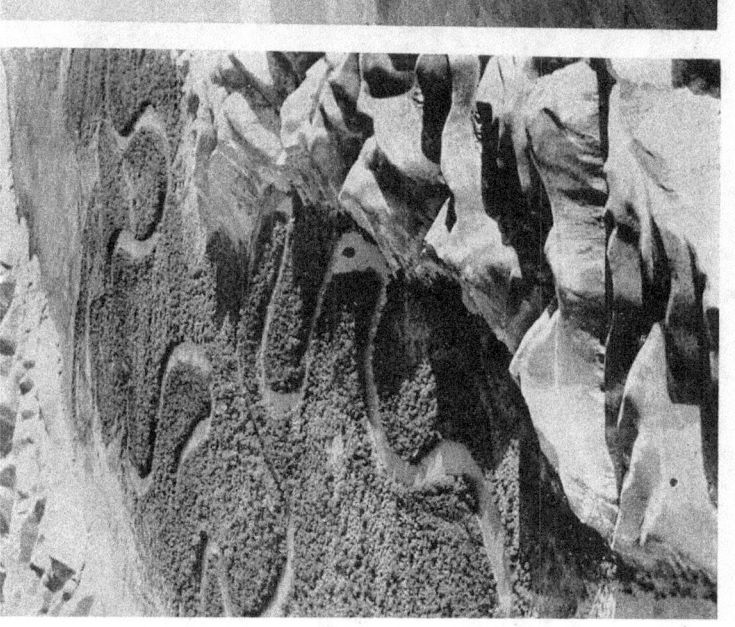

8. Wilderness of Judaea and the River Jordan  Near the Dead Sea

9. Ancient tombs of the Sanhedrin

Detail of the Sanhedrin's tombs

A NEW DAY DAWNS

the first. The catacombs became regular labyrinths, in which one can easily get lost if one does not know the place, or has no guide.

An impressive undertaking to be confronted with! It is calculated that nearly six million dead persons were buried in the catacombs of Rome. If placed end to end they would stretch for 500 miles.

The practical value of the catacombs was that they made no stir: there was nothing unusual in the custom. The Christians had in part taken it over from the Jews, but other Eastern peoples used this method, and even the Romans favoured it. The State, therefore, took no action against the catacombs. On the contrary, every burial-place was under the protection of the law.

The Christian spirit in these remote times was real and living, to judge from the pictures that ornamented the graves. We meet with Christian symbols everywhere. Most often it is the anchor, the sign of hope, sometimes with a cross-bar which reminds one of the Cross. The good shepherd carries the lamb home on his shoulders, the dove flies with the olive leaf; again we find the soul with the sign of hope. And the secret Christian sign, the fish, is constantly painted. The fish became a form of monogram for Christ: outsiders did not understand it, but Christians revealed themselves to one another by the use of it. A fish in Greek is *ichthys*, i.e. the two initials of the name Jesus Christ, Son of God, Saviour.

The catacombs were burial-places, where the Christians hid their dead. But they were also used for meeting-places, and the secret divine services of the early Church in the time of the persecution were held in these underground chambers. The Church had indeed gone underground.

The first Christian Church lived under the menace of catastrophe: it might be destroyed at any moment. But it had never expected anything else. The Saviour had ended his days on a cross, and the Church of the first two centuries continued the tale of suffering. And it survived. Every single Christian knew that beyond death was everlasting life. He who conquered would sit at table with the Saviour in glory. This strange time was an inspiration to all generations: it taught that the spirit always conquers, late perhaps and through suffering, but one day it will turn defeat into triumph.

The Church would not let itself be crushed: on the contrary, it went steadily forward despite persecutions and reverses. The martyrs' blood was the Church's seed. Even the Gentiles saw its strength. Galen was a Gentile doctor in the second century. An utterance of his is extant in which he recognizes the proud contempt of the Christians for torture and death and in particular their ability to keep their sexual propensities under control. 'There are actually Christians who, in their control of their inclinations and pursuit of virtue, are the equal of any philosopher.'

The Christian front against heathendom was as hard as steel. But between Christianity and Judaism the air cooled rapidly. After the Church had shaken off its Judaist swaddling-clothes, the relations between the two religions became more and more strained: they were always on guard against one another.

The Church did not deny its origin: on the contrary! It looked upon itself as the true Israel, the heir to both the law and the prophets, who had found their real fulfilment for the first time (in Jesus Christ). Therefore the Church defended the sacred Jewish books in the Old Testament. For the Lord they had been the Bible he was thinking of when he said: 'Man shall not live by bread alone, but by every word that proceedeth out of the mouth of God.' Therefore the Old Testament belonged to the Christian Church.

The gradual collection by the Church of Jesus' words and the narratives of his life and death is another matter—and a quite natural development. Such precious things could not be left to an uncertain oral tradition, but must be watched over as a valuable treasure. As time passed, and there came to be every reason for standing on guard against misinterpretation of the Gospel, the Church needed a standard by which to judge minds and intellects.

Externally the bonds between Judaism and Christianity were

A NEW DAY DAWNS

broken. Mother and daughter regarded one another with ever growing coolness and hostility. But round about, in the Empire, they were continually meeting.

And the far-flung Jewish dispersion had unwittingly prepared the ground for the rapid growth of Christianity.

V

IN THE DISPERSION

ISRAEL could have won the Jewish war and world history taken quite a different course from that which we know. This is a surprising statement, but it can stand the test of criticism. It has already been seen that the disintegrating influences, which set the Roman Empire smouldering several centuries later, were already at work in its early years. But at the critical moment a strong personality of the old Roman type like Vespasian seized the reins, and the vast resources of the Empire were once more co-ordinated.

But, what was still more important, the Jews did not succeed in arousing their numerous kinsmen who lived scattered about the Empire. If this had been done, if cunning diplomatists had been able to weld together Israel's latent strength for a combined effort, the picture would already have been greatly changed. If at the same time they could have roused other oppressed peoples to action, and, further, induced the Parthian kingdom to throw its weight into the scale, it is very probable that Rome would have had to say farewell for ever to all the eastern provinces, by far the richest part of the Empire.

But it is a tragic fact that the Jews in the dispersion did not support the insurrection in Judaea. That little country, for all its desperate courage, could not resist the Roman pressure alone. And when at last, many years later, the sparks of rebellion broke into flames among the Jews abroad, Judaea remained quiet, still paralysed.

Israel's fight for freedom in the vital epoch from 66 to 135 followed a curiously zigzag course. In the great Jewish war

IN THE DISPERSION

Judaea fought, but the dispersion kept quiet. Under Trajan's government the Jews in the dispersion rebelled and were suppressed, while the motherland was passive. Last came the Son of a Star's war in 132–135 as the last great attempt to free Israel. And now again Judaea fought alone, and the rebellion was choked in blood after a terrible struggle.

Here is seen a manifestation on a large scale of the old Roman principle *divide et impera*. But it was not only Roman diplomacy and shrewd statesmanship which brought about this split.

Why did it happen? An idle question, maybe: but it calls for an answer none the less. And some of the causes can be ascertained, but only up to a certain point. There must have been deeper causes behind which half-blinded historians cannot descry. So at the last it comes to depend on one's personal attitude towards the last cause history will admit—whether or not we believe that a heavenly head was at work. In the history of the Jewish people there are always riddles which can only be solved by him who looks upward.

The number of Jews in the Roman Empire was very great: of course it cannot be stated exactly, but it is estimated at six or seven millions of the Empire's total population of about 80,000,000. Thus the Jews were a conspicuous national group, the more so that most of them lived crowded together in the large towns. Until the destruction of the Temple they all looked to Jerusalem as both a national and a religious centre. Of course, living abroad as they did, they could not observe their familiar religious customs in the same way as their co-religionists in Judaea, but they clung to their Jewish faith and were far from assimilating themselves to their surroundings in religious matters. Their zeal in gaining proselytes is enough to prove this. They enjoyed good living conditions in many respects and in some countries had a wide measure of freedom to live as Jews and make themselves respected as citizens. But their hearts were faithful to the Temple and the invisible God.

In the circumstances the apparent indifference with which they contemplated the tragedy in the motherland is all the more strange. Josephus tells of emissaries from Jerusalem who sought

THE SON OF A STAR

to rouse them to action. The only positive result attained was the dispatch of an auxiliary force from a proselyte prince in the Parthian kingdom. How can this passivity be explained?

First of all the enormous distances which separated the Jews in the dispersion from each other and from Judaea must be remembered. But this was not all. The rising in Judaea took place very suddenly: there had been no time for any co-operation. Events developed suddenly at furious speed and were pressed forward by one side alone: nor was there any great leader whose name was known in far-off countries and could set men's minds ablaze. Every rising is marked by confusion and unexpected factors. The Jewish war was a victim of these circumstances on a tragic scale. So Judaea fought alone—and fell.

If we want to make a survey of the Jews in the dispersion, we find a convenient catalogue of them in the Acts of the Apostles. In the story of Pentecost it is related that Peter spoke to Jews from many different countries who were on a pilgrimage to Jerusalem: Parthians Medes, Elamites, people from Cappadocia, Pontus, Phrygia and Pamphylia, as well as Jews from Egypt, Cyrene and Crete, indeed, from remote Arabia. The mere enumeration of these many widely separated lands makes it clear from what an immense area the pilgrims came. From another quarter we know that the Jews were so numerous that 'every land and sea seemed to be full of them'. It is customary to divide them roughly into Jews from Asia, Africa and Europe. Let us make a tour of some of the Jewish centres abroad to get an idea of their life and history.

A large number of Jews had lived for many centuries in Babylonia, i.e. the fertile country between the Euphrates and Tigris, the present Iraq, then a part of the Parthian kingdom.

In the year 586 B.C. Nebuchadnezzar, King of Babylon, captured Jerusalem and carried the people away into the famous Babylonian captivity. When a change in political conditions allowed the Jews to return home, only a minority availed themselves of it: the great majority preferred a quiet and comfortable life in a large country to hard and toilsome reconstruction work

IN THE DISPERSION

in the land of their fathers. Later, conditions in Palestine became disturbed again, and still more Jews settled in Babylonia as political refugees. This meant a large increase in the number of Jews, and this great Jewish colony, growing more and more conscious of its strength, gradually came to set its stamp on Babylon.

Great seats of learning sprang up, and as their reputation grew, the Babylonian Jews actually dared to demand supremacy over Judaea! They were fond of saying that the best part of the people had remained in Babylonia, and indeed there arose a certain rivalry and emulation between these two great centres of Jewish culture. But the Jews at home insisted strongly on their right of primogeniture and compared themselves and the Jews in the dispersion as 'pure flour and mixed dough'.

None the less it was a genuine Jewish tradition that spent the winter in Babylonia. The Jews kept themselves strictly apart from the heathen and became a large and well-to-do class. They were hard-working farmers and capable business men, but they did not neglect learned studies. In these, indeed, they made such progress that they even acquired a surplus by which they were able to help the mother country. Not a few leading theologians in Judaea were of Babylonian origin: it is enough to recall that the family of the founder of Jewish theology from about the beginning of our era, the great Hillel, came from Babylon.

But so long as the secret schools continued to exist, Judaea was the supreme authority in all questions of religious belief and practice. All questions of the interpretation of the law were finally decided by the patriarch of Palestine, the Nasi, and his Sanhedrin: for example, the fixing of the exact time of the new moon, on which all the feasts depended. When Jabneh had observed the new moon, news of it was sent to Babylon by means of a kind of primitive telegraphy: fires were lighted on the hills for the whole of that great distance.

At the time of the fall of Jerusalem the greater part of Babylonia was under the influence of the Parthians. When we think of the Roman domains in the time of the Emperors, we must always remember that east of the Euphrates lay the kingdom of Parthia, which was large and powerful and the only real competitor with Rome for world supremacy. Many wars were waged between the two colossi, and neither of them ever dealt a really decisive blow at the other. One would have thought that Rome was strong enough to crush the Parthians, especially as their country was very ill organized and one revolution succeeded another, but the Parthians always held their ground. Even if the king of Parthia often had to defend himself against his rebellious subjects, they were always united in one thing, hatred of the Romans. And here they were on common ground with the Jews, to the advantage of the latter, who enjoyed unusual liberty and peace in the Parthian kingdom and possessed an advanced form of national autonomy. Certain cities in Babylon were likewise administered by Jews, for example both Nahardea and Nisibis.

According to legend King Jehoiachin of Judah, who was made prisoner by the King of Babylon and deported about 600 B.C., lived in Nahardea. He founded there a synagogue which later came to enjoy a reputation for special holiness. There was another synagogue in the neighbourhood where no less a person than Ezra had started a theological academy. One Jewish town had 90,000 inhabitants: others were strongly fortified: one was so pronouncedly Jewish that surprise was expressed at its not having over the town gate the mezuzza, the little plaque with the most important biblical words, which is always found on the right-hand doorpost of Jewish houses.

Many Jews lived in Ctesiphon, the capital. This splendid city lay in a charming district with fertile gardens and was very well irrigated. The Jewish colonies stretched all the way across to Persia proper. A quarter of Ispahan is called Jehudia to this day. But the real Jewish country in Parthia lay between the Euphrates and the Tigris: there the Jews had maintained to a special degree their national and religious purity and isolation.

The Jews in Babylonia had enjoyed peace and good conditions of life since time immemorial. But some thirty or forty years

IN THE DISPERSION

before the war in Judaea great misfortune, sudden and unexpected, came upon them.

In Nahardea there lived a poor Jewish widow. She had two sons, Asineus and Anileus, both of them tent-makers. It happened that their employer treated them badly. They were both proud and independent, and this event shook them out of their quiet bourgeois life. And then things began to happen. They collected all the weapons they could get hold of, left the town with a few young Jewish sympathizers, and settled in some inaccessible mountains. There they lived by attacking and plundering peaceful caravans. Like the feudal barons of the Middle Ages they came by degrees to levy taxation on a whole region, in return for which they let the inhabitants live in peace. The whole business was becoming a serious danger to public security, and the governor, or satrap, of the province, decided to suppress them. He collected troops in all secrecy and made a surprise attack on them. He had counted on catching them in their beds and was cunning enough to choose a Sabbath for his attack, expecting to find them disarmed on that day. But he found them wide awake and on their guard, and the lawless Jewish freebooters won a brilliant victory over his regular troops.

Now the King of Parthia was compelled to open negotiations with the rebels. As a result peace was concluded, and the King was sensible enough to appoint Asineus governor of Mesopotamia. The two brothers had triumphed over adversity: they found it much more difficult to cope with success.

They were both brave men, but were very different in appearance. Asineus was small and frail, Anileus tall and imposing. He fell in love with a Parthian nobleman's wife, his love was returned, and the difficulties were overcome by Anileus simply killing the husband and taking the woman home with him. But disaster came with her. She brought her idols, and that was the end of peace and unity in the Jewish camp. When Asineus rebuked his brother for his conduct, the foreign woman got some poison and put him out of the way.

This was going too far, and the King intervened again,

this time against the arrogant Jewish governor. But yet again fortune favoured Anileus: he defeated his enemies and took the King's son-in-law prisoner. He stripped him naked and made him ride through his camp, sitting on an ass face to tail and with bound hands.

Now the cup was full: the King could not endure such a disgrace. Large forces were sent against Anileus and the battle showed that the Jewish soldiers had been softened by good living and success. They were defeated and cut down. And, as always happens, all the Jews had to pay for the misconduct of individuals. Pogroms broke out all over the province: Jewish citizens were slaughtered in hundreds of thousands and their houses and farms burnt.

There was a wild flight from the stricken regions. And the stream of fugitives had a definite direction. The Jews knew that in Adiabene, a province of Assyria east of the Tigris, the King, Izates, had gone over to the Jewish faith. He received his unfortunate co-religionists kindly and cared for them. But this pious King stands for so much in Jewish tradition that his strange story had better be told here.

His father had married his own sister Helene, and they had been told in a dream that their first son would be specially favoured by the gods. This was Izates. When he was still a young prince, a Jewish merchant named Ananias came on a visit. He expounded his faith to the young prince and to his mother, and both were finally convinced of the truth of Judaism.

Izates was full of enthusiasm and wanted to be circumcised at once. But both Ananias and Helene were afraid of the consequences. What would the people say to a circumcised prince? Ananias had a long talk with him and explained that it would suffice for him to be a Jew in secret.

Years passed, and Izates ascended the throne. Then he had another visitor from Judaea, this time a zealous Pharisee named Eleazar. He severely rebuked the King and Ananias for their temporizing, and the result was that the King had himself circumcised and publicly announced his conversion to Judaism.

There were many pleasant stories of this noble prince.

IN THE DISPERSION

During one of the many revolutions the King of Parthia had to fly for his life. He came to Adiabene, and Izates met him on horseback. The King threw himself in the dust before him, but Izates got off his horse, made the King mount and himself walked by him on foot as a proof of his loyalty as a subject.

Helene made a pilgrimage to Jerusalem and, finding the city ravaged by famine, helped it royally. When she died, Izates had her coffin carried to the Holy City, and her tombstone is pointed out to this day.

Izates was the first foreign prince to encourage the Jews during the war and sent a force to help them. The King of Parthia, however, remained neutral and prevented his subordinate rulers from sending effective assistance. After the disastrous war many Jewish refugees took refuge in Adiabene and spread thence over the whole of Babylonia.

And it was here that in Trajan's time the Romans met with hostility and acts of vengeance from the Jews.

Israel had had close connection with Egypt from time immemoral: the Old Testament is full of examples of it. Josephus says that there were a million Jews living in Egypt, which means that every eighth person was a Jew. By far the greater number lived in Alexandria, the city which Alexander had founded and named after himself. In the time of the Emperors it was the second largest city in the Empire and by far the most important in the East. Two of the five quarters of the city were inhabited by Jews, who formed 40 per cent of the whole population. In Alexandria—as in New York in modern times—many more Jews lived than in Jerusalem.

The Egyptian Jews had their own temple in Heliopolis. It was built by a refugee high priest named Onias and was a marvellous building, rivalling the Temple at Jerusalem in both influence and beauty. It was built in the form of a tower about 100 feet high. Instead of the golden candelabra it had a gold lamp hanging before the veil. The temple was devastated after the great war.

The Jewish synagogues were scattered about the country.

THE SON OF A STAR

Where as few as ten grown men lived, they could hold divine service and accordingly built their house of God. But the great synagogue in Alexandria was world-famed for its size and splendour. Those who describe it can hardly find words strong enough. One of them writes: 'He who has not worshipped in the synagogue of Alexandria has not seen the glory of Israel.'

It was shaped as a huge basilica and was so large that it was said to have room for twice as many people as Moses led out of Egypt. Seventy golden chairs were placed for the members of the Sanhedrin. In the middle of the synagogue was the platform on which stood the priest who led the prayers and reading. But as the words uttered there could not be heard all round the building, a flag had to be waved to show what point the service had reached.

A huge congregation collected and filled the synagogue on all holy days. People did not sit just where they liked, but were placed according to class and craft, so that a stranger who had just come to the city could always find his own associates.

This splendid building also was destroyed. It was left standing till Trajan's time, but he had it pulled down as a punishment for the great Jewish rebellions during his reign.

The Egyptian Jews had a long tradition behind them and were proud of it. The Bible had there been translated from Hebrew into Greek, so that the sacred writings of Judaism became accessible to the heathen world. The story went that the great king Ptolemy II had summoned 72 learned men from Jerusalem, six from each tribe, who knew Greek as well as Hebrew. They were kept in strict seclusion on the island of Pharos, where each man worked separately under supervision. The translation went on for 72 days, and when it was completed, every single text agreed with all the others!

However much truth there may be in this story, the fact remains that this translation, the Septuagint, was of enormous importance. It accompanied the Jews all over the world and became the Bible of the first Christian Church.

Egyptian Judaism had its own individuality. A vigorous

IN THE DISPERSION

heathen spiritual life surrounded it, and the Jewish thinkers saw themselves from day to day confronted with alien ideas. This set its mark on them, which is seen most clearly in the work of the famous philosopher Philo of Alexandria.

He came of one of the most distinguished families in the country and had made a thorough study of Greek literature and philosophy. A streak of mysticism goes through his philosophy. In Palestine also at this time mysticism was growing in fertile soil. But there it was more than anything an intellectual reaction against literal belief: a great effort to penetrate the secrets of God by hard-worked minds which had grown weary of dry formalism. With the Egyptian Jews and Philo mysticism was the result of the effect and counter-effect on one another of Jewish and Hellenic culture. The result was a dreamy mysticism which set spiritual contemplation before active life. Here already may be found some of the germs which later produced curious flowers in the cabalistic systems of the Middle Ages.

Philo himself liked to retire from restless city life into the solitude of the desert, where he lived in isolation and in strict asceticism, striving to bore a way for himself into the secret nature of God. He said of these exertions that 'it is not change of place that brings good or evil'.

It is hard not to feel that in his effort to establish a bridge between the two worlds, Judaism and heathendom, he went so far that he compromised Judaism. But in his innermost heart he remained a true Jew. He went as a pilgrim to the Holy City and always acknowledged himself to be a Jew in the face of all mockery, and sought indeed to weld together Greek Platonism and Jewish mysticism, but he always urged that the laws should be observed. And when national disaster overwhelmed his people he expressed in beautiful language the profound sorrow that filled his soul.

Hard times were in store for the Egyptian Jews and for himself. They had long enjoyed freedom and peace, but under the Emperor Caligula, about A.D. 38, the storm broke. Anti-Jewish feeling had been accumulating for a long time, and for many reasons. The Jews were hard-working and often rich: perhaps they were the class which had attained the highest culture. They were many, and they held together: Jewish cohesion was proverbial. They knew how to make use of the privileges they had won in the course of time, so their businesses flourished. All this created envy and was a permanent source of annoyance to the heathen. They waited eagerly for the first opportunity to give vent to their hatred. And it came.

The Jewish King Agrippa came to Alexandria, and the mob jeered him when he entered the city. The Roman governor Flaccus intervened and punished those who had caused the disturbance: at the same time the impression was created that he had an understanding with them, which naturally gave the mob fresh encouragement.

As stated above, this was in the days of the Emperor Caligula. The most charitable thing that can be said about this Emperor is that he was a pathological riddle. It is impossible to establish, so long afterwards, whether he was impelled by madness or pure and simple wickedness. But it was at this time that he had the idea of having his statue erected all over the Empire, so that the people could worship him as a god. The consequences of the imperial order in Judaea have already been seen. In Alexandria they were bloody.

The Alexandrians obtained the long desired opportunity to humiliate the Jews. They forced their way into the synagogue on the pretext of wishing to carry out the Emperor's order and erect the statue in the sacred building. The Jews resisted this violation and hit back. Then Flaccus openly sided against the Jews: he withdrew all their privileges and gave the mob free rein.

The mob did not need to be told twice. Many Jews were shut into houses and burnt, others were killed and their bodies dragged about the streets. Mutilated bodies were seen everywhere. Neither age nor sex was spared. Jewish women were forced to eat pig's flesh, venerable members of the Sanhedrin were stripped naked and beaten, others were crucified. Meanwhile the city was given up to dancing and feasting. People

IN THE DISPERSION

discovered that plundering was the easiest way of getting money, and every evil instinct was unleashed.

At long last the Jews managed to get a complaint through to the Emperor: King Agrippa, who was a close friend of the Emperor, helped them. In one of his unaccountable moods Caligula listened to his friend's advice, and a messenger was sent to the presumptuous governor with quite new orders. Flaccus was at a grand banquet when the messenger entered. And now there was a swift change of scene. The governor was dismissed, put in chains immediately and taken to the island of Andros, where he was subsequently executed.

The Jews' relief was but short-lived. Fresh disturbances broke out, and the result was that both Jews and heathen resolved to send delegations to the Emperor to get a final decision. A man named Appion, a well-known author of anti-Jewish pamphlets, headed the heathen delegation. His writings have been preserved to our times, and we owe much of our knowledge to them. The Jews placed their most famous man, Philo, at the head of the Jewish delegation.

Both delegations arrived safely in Rome and did their best to establish connections. The Jews allied themselves to Agrippa, the heathen to Helicon, one of the Emperor's favourites. Thus fortified, they had only to await the Emperor's arrival.

Suddenly he was in the capital. But he had really had no time to talk to the disputants from Alexandria. His Majesty was going on to Puteoli at once, and the delegations had to follow in his wake. Here, on the sunny beach, the Jews received tidings of the Emperor's irrevocable decision: his statue was to be erected in the synagogue.

Nevertheless, they did not give up. At long last they managed to secure a meeting. The two delegations confronted one another in the presence of the master of the world, and a scene was enacted which deserves to be remembered.

The two contending parties were drawn up in a hall of the imperial palace, the Jews on one side, the heathen on the other. Both delegations made speeches and explained their viewpoints. But the Emperor had not time to listen! While the speeches were being made he was going in and out, busy discussing some changes in the palace with his architects. Only now and again did he stand still and catch a few words.

Suddenly he turned furiously on the Jews and asked why they, who after all were one of his peoples, would not acknowledge his divinity. The heathen shouted applause and accused the Jews of not even being willing to offer sacrifices for the Emperor's welfare.

The Jews defended themselves in vain, saying that in any case the last accusation was not true. The Emperor snarled that it did not matter whether or not they would sacrifice *for* him, when they would not sacrifice *to* him.

While these discussions were going on the Emperor continued to walk about the palace with his architects, the delegations following patiently and submissively in his wake. Again Caligula stood still for a moment and asked the Jews why they would not eat pig's flesh. There were loud bursts of laughter from the others, and the Emperor began to pour out crazy blasphemies against the Jews' God.

At last he calmed down, brought the audience to an end, and sent the Jews away with the final remark that perhaps they were not as bad as might be thought. Indeed, one should rather be sorry for them, because they could not see that he was a god.

Fortunately all problems, both in Alexandria and in Judaea, were solved by the Emperor's death. But the air was not cleared in Alexandria, and later times were to see greater terrors in Egypt than those witnessed so far.

In Italy and Rome life was more idyllic for the Jews. Julius Caesar had felt himself indebted to them and conceded them great privileges. It was the same with Augustus, who as a rule was not inclined to favour foreigners.

In Rome the Jews lived in special quarters, where they had their own civic authorities, who administered according to Jewish law and tradition. The Jewish citizens earned their living by trade and crafts. In Augustus' time the number of the Roman Jews was estimated at 40,000. They kept up an active

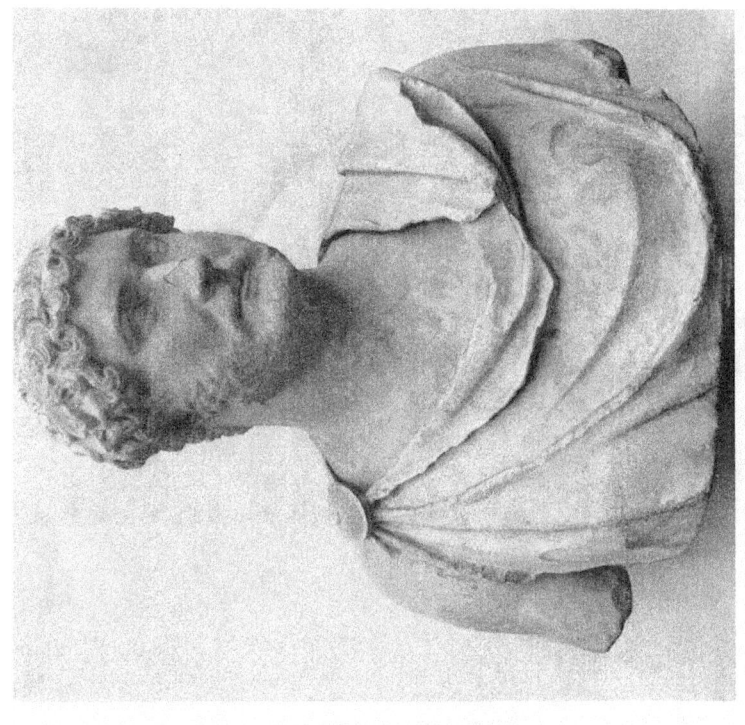
Hadrian

10. Titus

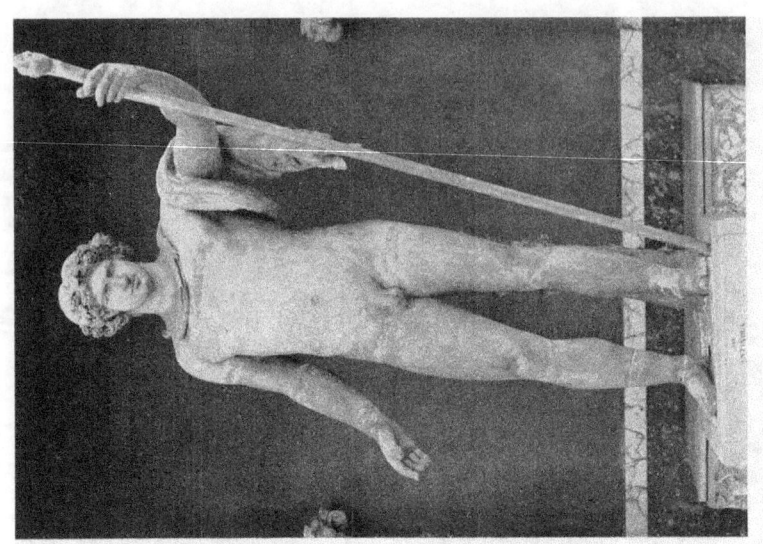

Antinous

11. Vespasian

IN THE DISPERSION

connection with Jerusalem: in one year 8,000 pilgrims from Rome visited that city. The Emperor Claudius' edict expelling the Jews from Rome has already been mentioned. It does not seem to have been thoroughly carried out, and in any case it was soon repealed. The Emperor Nero's consort Poppaea was fond of showing her predilection for the Jews.

Indeed the Roman Jews lived a peaceful life. Even the great war made no difference to them.

Millions of Jews were scattered all over the earth: in all towns of importance they had flourishing congregations. They were different from anyone else, and people could not help noticing them. And, as always happens, this strongly individual element either attracted sympathy or had to struggle against opposition.

In a world full of bewilderment and fear, like that of the crumbling Graeco-Roman heathendom, Jewish conviction was impressive. The strong moral principles of the Jews, especially in sexual problems, and no less their cohesion, had a great appeal. Many Gentiles came and sought admittance into Jewry: these were the so-called proselytes. Some maintained quite a loose connection with Israel and contented themselves with keeping the most important commandments, but the genuine proselytes were circumcised and thereby bound to the strict rules of life of the Tora.

In these centuries there was also a Jewish mission which strenuously endeavoured to win over foreigners. Of course this could only be a transitory phase. In Judaism religion and nation are so closely bound together that missionary activity will always seem an alien element. In modern times Judaism holds itself proudly aloof from religious propaganda. But there were once times when the Jews carried on a mission among the heathen.

We notice it, for example, in the New Testament, where the Gospel of St Matthew tells of Pharisees travelling over sea and land to win but one proselyte. And Juvenal talks satirically of the Jewish missionaries' skill in adapting themselves to conditions and working their way forward step by step. Even if the first generation is only won in part, victory will come in the second. Where the father respects the Sabbath, the son has himself circumcised.

There is a great deal of Jewish missionary literature, dating from the beginning of our era. Jewish writers did their best to give their thoughts Greek clothes. They made Greek authors appear in the role of Jewish spokesmen: both Aeschylus and Sophocles became speaking-tubes for Jewish philosophy. The old Bible history was decked out with legendary features which would make it attractive to heathen eyes and give an impression of the antiquity and greatness of the Jewish people. In one passage Orpheus bears witness of Abraham, or we are told how the great Greek philosophers obtained their philosophy of life from Moses.

But while the Jews won proselytes, the opposite happened just as often or, indeed, more frequently. Anti-Semitism is not a modern term: roots go as far back as the time when the dispersion began.

In the book of Esther in the Old Testament we find the classical example of antique anti-Semitism. Haman decided to exterminate the Jewish people and persuade the King of Persia to take action against the Jews. He described them in the following words:

'There is a certain people scattered abroad and dispersed among the people in all the provinces of thy kingdom: and their laws are diverse from all people; neither keep they the King's laws: therefore it is not for the King's profit to suffer them.'

And with a candour that reveals a less ideal ground for the powers he was seeking, he reminded the King that the Jews were well-to-do people:

'I will pay ten thousand talents of silver to the hands of those that have the charge of the business, to bring it into the King's treasuries.'

The whole spirit of anti-Semitism is concealed in these words: one would never think that they were uttered more than two thousand years ago. As is well-known, the King's Jewish Queen

IN THE DISPERSION

Esther succeeded by her skilful intervention in turning Haman's proposal against himself. The feast of Purim is celebrated every year in memory of this event.

Some of the factors which aroused public feeling against the Jews have already been touched upon. Their political rights and good living conditions caused envy, while their exclusiveness stirred up every popular prejudice against them. Cicero called Judaism 'a barbaric superstition', and Tacitus expressed his contempt for them in the well-known words: 'Everything which is sacred to us is unclean to them, and what we think profane they regard as sacred.'

Jews and Romans could live side by side all their lives through, but they always remained alien to one another. For the Jews Sabbaths and feasts recurred in an endless chain, watched by the Gentiles with surprise. To the Gentiles circumcision seemed revolting. And the Jews' cohesion and open contempt for heathendom embittered public opinion. All kinds of rumours were in circulation. It was declared that the Jews' secret laws commanded them to fatten and slaughter a Gentile every year. They devoured his entrails and bound themselves by oath to hate all heathen. The stories of ritual murder are old and evidently tenacious of life.

Strange ideas of Judaism were circulated and were gladly believed. The Jews originated in Crete, and took their name from Mount Ida. Later they went to Egypt, but when they became lepers the Egyptians drove them out of the country. Moses was a renegade priest who induced the Jews to be false to the gods. Under his leadership they wandered through the desert and had remarkable experiences. Once, when they were about to die of thirst, a herd of wild asses led them to a spring. Ever since, therefore, they had a golden ass's head in their sanctuary and worshipped it. The Sabbath was an expression of laziness: they wasted a seventh part of life. They hated the heathen, and would not direct a stranger properly, or tell a thirsty man where he could find a spring. And they were always charged with atheism because they worshipped the invisible God.

Not long ago a papyrus was found in Egypt. A friend had

THE SON OF A STAR

asked the writer for advice in economic difficulties. And we know the answer. It was: 'Above all, like everyone else, you must be on your guard against the Jews.'

Israel had tried to win her freedom sword in hand and had suffered a bloody defeat. To the mind of antiquity the political and military defeat of a nation was a proof of its god's weakness and its own inferiority. When a people suffered such a catastrophic defeat as the Jews had done, they became *dedicii*, i.e. those who have surrendered unconditionally. And for them there was only one fate: *vae victis*, woe to the conquered!

And yet the Jews held themselves apart and preferred their defeated God to the victorious gods of Rome, who had conquered their country and laid them prostrate.

This was a thing which other peoples simply could not understand.

VI

THE HORIZON IN FLAMES

THE old Emperor Nerva died in January 98, and the Empire looked with keen expectation to his adopted son Trajan, who was now left alone at the summit. A strong and just Emperor was awaited in him: the whole Empire needed one.

And in many ways he fulfilled expectations. He was something quite new. He came from the provinces and was the first Emperor who did not belong to one of the old Italian families. Trajan was born in the Spanish town of Italica, near Seville. His father had begun as a private soldier, had distinguished himself in the Jewish war and risen from rank to rank: he ended his career as Consul. The rise of this simple provincial family was one of the many evidences of the decay of the old Roman aristocracy and its need of reinforcement. A levelling process between Italy and the conquered countries was taking place.

Like his father, Trajan was first of all things a soldier. He had been fortunate on the battlefield and the legions admired him. He shared his soldiers' living conditions in good and evil days, and was a strict general who maintained absolute discipline. The Praetorian Guard had begun to interfere in affairs of State, but Trajan was too strong for it. He could make himself respected both by the praetorians and by the licentious mobs of Rome. When he appointed the first commander of his bodyguard, he handed him his sword with the words: 'Use this for me so long as I do my duty. Use it against me if I fail in it!' These were words which soldiers understood.

THE SON OF A STAR

He governed the great Empire firmly, always guided by his clear head. His reply to Pliny's letter about the Christians is typical of his curt decisive style, hitting the nail right on the head. Not for nothing was he the only Emperor the Senate honoured with the surname Optimus, the best.

But he did not bring the Empire peace: the whole of his reign was disturbed by wars. It would be unjust to this warlike Emperor to suppose that his great campaigns were due solely to the desire for new conquests. But he had been a soldier all his life, so it came natural to him to settle frontier disputes by the sword rather than by subtle diplomatic manœuvres. He himself preferred camp life to the refined atmosphere of the aristocracy of the capital. And he reformed the army and brought it up to the highest level of efficiency.

But Trajan's Empire was no longer the Rome which had conquered Hannibal. At that time it was a young rising State, determined to bring down older world powers and win for itself a place in the sun. Now it was old and already showing signs of degeneration, and barbaric tribes stood on all the frontiers. Of course the legions with their superior technical equipment and tactics could easily defeat these neighbouring peoples, but if the victory was to be permanent it was not enough to beat them in the field: Roman civilization and culture must be stamped on them or assimilate them. But the Empire had not the internal strength for this: it no longer possessed the surplus energy that had given it domination over the many countries and peoples which for centuries afterwards bore the marks of the Roman mind. Therefore Trajan's achievements were only successes for the moment. In reality they were fruitless, and only contributed to the decline in the Empire's strength by putting an unnecessary strain on already failing resources.

He began by turning against the Dacians in what is now Rumania. Domitian had concluded his shameful treaty with the King of Dacia, but the old Roman spirit and energy were still so strong that to have been victorious over Rome proved to be mortally dangerous to the victor. Trajan beat the Dacians

THE HORIZON IN FLAMES

in two swift and pitiless campaigns. Their defeated King committed suicide while in flight, and the country came under Roman domination.

To commemorate this victory, Trajan erected the column in Rome which still bears his name. He immortalized his victory with sculptures on the sides of the column celebrating the Roman arms. They give a vivid impression of life in the field in those remote times. A statue of the Emperor originally bulked large on the top. For a long time past it has been replaced by St Peter, a curious testimony not only to the victory of the Christian Church over heathen Rome, but to the replacement of the Empire by the Catholic Church.

When the Dacian campaign was well over, Trajan shifted the point of gravity to the Near East. The dream of a new campaign like Alexander's through the fair kingdoms of the East to legendary India had long occupied the thoughts of Roman statesmen: and cool-headed financiers and strategists had worked out detailed plans for the vast undertaking. As far back as Nero's time these preparations had been far advanced, but the insurrection in Judaea put a spoke in the wheel. Trajan made the great attempt. It failed, and he roused the Jews in the dispersion to a bloody rebellion against Roman rule, so that he saw all the fruits of his victories slip out of his hands.

The road to India ran through the kingdom of Parthia, Rome's hereditary enemy to eastward. There had been trouble between the two powers for centuries, and the question which was stronger was still undecided when both fell to pieces. The fight between them swayed to and fro: now one was on top, now the other. But the Parthians did once succeed in taking a Roman Emperor prisoner.

It happened that in Trajan's time the Parthians had one of their strongest rulers, King Chosroes, and he dared to challenge Rome. As always, the apple of discord was Armenia, the border land between Rome and the Parthians. Armenia was a vassal state of Rome, but the King of Parthia wished to extend his sway over it and appointed a successor to the Armenian throne.

THE SON OF A STAR

Trajan got moving at once and concentrated troops on the frontiers of Armenia. The King of Parthia and his designated successor saw the danger of the situation and made conciliatory advances, but Trajan decided to put a stop to Parthian expansion once and for all and to decide the matter by the sword. The legions marched in, and Armenia was conquered and turned into a Roman province. But now Trajan saw a chance of inflicting on the Parthians a chastisement that would not be forgotten—and far away in the east glimmered India and the memories of Alexander's campaign with its unforgettable romance. The Emperor organized his eastern army with headquarters at Antioch.

It is nearly two thousand years since these events. And yet when we hear an ancient historian's account of the wretched state in which Trajan found the Syrian soldiers when he had need of them, the passage has quite a contemporary ring about it. The long period of peace had made them forget their hard military ways. They were so lazy that they did not come on parade; they left their posts unguarded and were drunk from noon onwards. They would not trouble to carry their heavy equipment, and left their weapons lying about in their wake. They were so feeble that the mere sight of a Parthian soldier made them turn tail, and when the trumpets sounded it was for them the signal to retreat!

When the Emperor had restored the morale of the army, he continued the war against the Parthians. It was a victorious advance such as has rarely been seen. King Chosroes' strength was paralysed by internal quarrels, and the Romans marched swiftly onward. They conquered Mesopotamia with its large Jewish population. Trajan pushed deep into Parthia, crossed the Tigris, and set up a new province, which he called Assyria. When the Senate conferred on him the title of Parthicus it was well deserved, at any rate at the moment. Nor did he stop here; he continued his march; the Parthian capital Ctesiphon fell into his hands, and at last, following the course of the Tigris, he reached the Persian Gulf.

This was the culminating point of Trajan's life. Before him

THE HORIZON IN FLAMES

lay the sea, beyond it was India. The last leap forward, and Trajan would be the new Alexander!

It remained a dream. In those great days Trajan became aware of his limitations. He felt with sorrow that he lacked one thing, youth. He was now in the middle sixties, and the iron constitution which till now had carried him from continent to continent was beginning to fail. But what was more important, messengers were arriving daily with dispatches containing bad news. Like all conquerers, Trajan learned when just at the summit of his power how unstable is a dominion based on force. The conquered provinces could be held only so long as the legions were there. As the troops were drawn away to new battlefields, Roman rule at once began to totter.

While he tarried at the mouth of the Tigris, revolutions broke out behind him. In several towns the inhabitants rose and wiped out the Roman garrisons. Trajan himself was tired to death. And now he saw his victory crumbling away between his fingers. The whole campaign had been fruitless. He turned his back on the sea and forgot the dream of Alexander. Not dreams now, but bitter realities, made demands upon the old Emperor's mind and energies.

What had happened? Who had dared to defy the master of the world?

In Judaea Judaism still lay politically paralysed after the catastrophe in Titus' days. In old days in Jerusalem, the waves had risen high when political questions stirred them. Now Jerusalem was turned into a Roman camp: the soldiers of the Tenth Legion were there. No Jewish voice sounded from the old capital. And in Jabneh for the moment only theological problems were being considered. All political energy had been drained away from the mother country. But it had found a refuge in the dispersion. In Africa and Babylonia there lived descendants of the heroes who had survived the Jewish war. And hatred of the Romans and thirst for revenge were combined with the eternal dreams of the Messiah who was to come and redeem the people.

THE SON OF A STAR

Now the Jews saw their chance. Behind Trajan's advancing armies they and the Parthians organized irregular forces which attacked the Romans in the rear and started partisan warfare on a large scale. The relations between Parthians and Jews had generally been good, and now they stood shoulder to shoulder in fierce fighting against the Romans.

The rebellion in Mesopotamia was a spark which flew and set fire to many places where fuel was piled up. It was not long before the whole of the Jewish Orient was in flames, and some of Rome's fairest provinces were in danger of being torn away from the Empire. The time had come for the great rebellion now that mighty Rome was deeply engaged in Parthia.

In Jewish tradition black clouds envelop Trajan: he is surnamed 'the evil one'. And the relations between him and Rome on one side and the Jews on the other are significantly illustrated by the legend about Trajan's son. The Empress bore Trajan a son, and all put on festal attire and illuminated their houses. All except the Jews. It happened to be the 9th Ab, the lamentably doubled anniversary of the fall of Jerusalem, when Jews went into mourning. Then a few months passed, and the Prince fell sick and died. The whole Empire mourned—but it was just in the middle of the chanukka, the joyous festival commemorating the consecration of the Temple, when the Jews feasted and set lighted lamps in their windows. Each time, of course, the conduct of the Jews was interpreted in the worst sense: it could only be due to want of loyalty.

This was the atmosphere. There was always something wrong between Gentiles and Jews, consciously or unconsciously, always tension. Prejudices were easily awakened, nerves were sensitive. Rome had indeed warm advocates among the men of the law, but when the atmosphere was heated and panic prevailed, they spoke to deaf ears. And in the storm which now blew up all prudent voices were drowned.

Only obscure and scattered evidence of these violent events is available. Only in rough outlines can we form an idea of the

THE HORIZON IN FLAMES

tremendous blaze that sprang up, so that the Jews in the mother country must have had a feeling that every horizon was in flames.

The banner of rebellion was first hoisted in Cyrene, in North Africa. Here the Jews always had special privileges, and had grown strong. Different sources name two Jewish leaders, Andreas and Lucuas: perhaps they are the same person using different names. When the Roman garrison troops were removed to Parthia, there was nothing to resist a determined insurrection.

The Jews struck, burning with rage, and as the authorities were utterly unprepared, the rebellion grew and assumed formidable dimensions. And, as always happens, the number of adherents grew with success. The rising became a full scale civil war.

Events soon took a dangerous turn. The insurrection spread and crossed the Egyptian frontier. And Egypt was a key position in the Roman Empire. Its loss would mean a great deal. The small force of garrison troops tried to take a hand, but was too weak and found itself compelled to seek protection behind the walls of Alexandria, where it took its revenge on the large Jewish population by a regular massacre.

Outside Alexandria the Jewish rebels were masters: they controlled the country right down to Thebes. A Roman historian, Dio Cassius, gives a lurid account of the atrocities in which the Jews revelled when every evil passion had gained the upper hand. All restraint had disappeared, and ancient, accumulated hate and bitterness were absolute masters. The Jews spared no one: they literally tore their victims in pieces, sawed them in two, draped themselves in their entrails and wore their skins: the mildest punishment was that of those Gentiles who were compelled to kill each other in the arena!

Jewish sources say nothing about all this—for good reasons. When the end came no one was alive who could tell the story from a Jewish standpoint.

The great Jewish revolution was well prepared and thought out. The leaders had established contact with one another and laid their plans in time. The right moment was chosen, and the attack was made at strategically important points.

This became particularly clear when the decisive blow was struck: the revolt in Cyprus. No place could be better suited for a headquarters, safely hidden behind the sea, centrally situated for undertakings in both Africa and Asia. Here were the famous copper mines—the word copper is derived from Cyprus —and the island had from time immemorial been an important central point for numerous trade routes.

In the course of time many Jews had settled in Cyprus. The island is almost within sight of Palestine and was as a rule the first stage on the way from Caesarea out into the great world. When disasters fell upon Palestine and drove out its inhabitants Cyprus had been one of the principal places of refuge. The Acts of the Apostles relates that there were synagogues spread all over the island.

Cyprus was the first place of all that must be conquered, and there the insurrection was planned with special care. At a given signal the movement started. The rebels marched against Salamis, the capital of the island, and became masters of this important city by a daring coup. As usual, our non-Jewish sources tell of horrible massacres: 240,000 Greeks and Romans are said to have lost their lives.

Mesopotamia in flames behind the Roman armies, Egypt and Cyrene in the rebels' hands and Cyprus lost. Palestine itself was beginning to smoulder under the surface. The situation was as serious for the Romans as it well could be.

When all these calamities burst upon Trajan, he showed all his mastery of affairs. Like all great men, he grew in stature with the magnitude of his tasks. Orders were issued swiftly from the imperial headquarters, new commanders were appointed and rapid troop movements begun. It was not long before the Emperor had his eastern provinces under control. A fearful time came for the Jews in the dispersion: they experienced what their kinsmen in Palestine had been through a short half-century earlier.

One of the ablest Roman generals, Martius Turbo, was sent

to Egypt. A difficult task awaited him, but he had a strong army, in which infantry and cavalry were suitably combined. And Roman discipline and tactics decided the issue. Moreover, the Jewish insurgents had no cavalry. For all their desperate resistance the Jews suffered a decisive defeat. The Romans took a bloody revenge.

A Jewish legend from those times casts a faint, fitful light into the mist. It says that when the Emperor was about to take the field against the distant barbarians the Empress wrote him a letter imploring him first to crush the Jews. Trajan sailed off to Palestine. He had allowed ten days for the passage, but the wind was so favourable that he arrived in five days.

He found the Jewish learned men discussing a passage in the Bible which says: 'God will arouse a people against thee from afar, from the end of the world, and send it to thee on eagle's wings.' The Emperor told them that it was he who had been brought on eagle's wings to punish them.

Then he ordered the legions to surround the Jews and cut down all the men. The women had to choose between abandoning themselves to the Roman soldiers and sharing the men's fate. They demanded with one voice that the soldiers 'should treat those who were above the earth as they had treated those who now were under the earth'.

Like most legends from those times, it is all wrong when it comes to concrete details of a geographical or political nature. But it tells us something of the spirit in which the Jews remembered those tragic events. It is certain that large parts of Egypt for a long time bore the marks of the horrors of war: burned houses, withered plantations and uncultivated fields told their own tale. The famous synagogue in Alexandria was burned to the ground at the same time.

The revolt in Cyprus also was suppressed. There is no need to go into details: the campaign there was similar to that in Africa. But the imperial troops did their work so thoroughly that every single Jew in the island was killed. The inhabitants' bitterness against the hated people was so deep that henceforward Jews were forbidden to set foot on the inhospitable island. Even shipwrecked Jews were killed if they got ashore.

But Cyprus was to have the same experience as many other countries in the centuries that followed: when the Jews were expelled, economic decline followed quickly. The trade of Cyprus receded visibly, and the island, which previously had been a flourishing market for Asia, became poor, while—to use the florid language of the Jewish chroniclers—'the blood of those killed in Africa flowed out into the sea like a wide river and mingled with the stream of blood from the victims in Cyprus'.

One name from those days the Jews have since held in bitter remembrance: that of Lusius Quietus, the general whom Trajan employed to crush the rebels behind the front in Mesopotamia. The Emperor regarded the partisan war there as peculiarly dangerous, and chose his toughest general, a negro from Morocco, to suppress it. Quietus' orders were simply to exterminate the Jews to the last man. Even if he was unable to obey these orders literally, he discharged his task with unexampled severity. The so-called Quietus war did make the country quiet. And the general was rewarded with the office of Governor of Judaea, in part, no doubt, to obtain a safeguard against new Jewish insurrections in the mother country itself.

Certainly Judaea was in ferment. The Jews at home felt for their smitten kinsmen. At this time the Sanhedrin ordered that Jewish brides should no longer wear crowns on their wedding day, but show their grief at the bloody defeats the race had suffered. At the same time, Jews were forbidden to learn Greek: the gulf between the Gentiles and the chosen people was to be as wide as possible.

Here is yet another of the misty legends which have preserved strangely confused memories of those sanguinary times. Two Jewish brothers, Julianus and Pappus, had taken part in the rising. Trajan captured them, and they were condemned to death. The sentence was to be carried out at Laodicea in Syria, the present Latakia: they were taken to that place and brought before the Emperor.

THE HORIZON IN FLAMES

In his arrogant self-confidence Trajan mocked at their God and referred derisively to the freeing of Ananias, Misael and Azarias by the Jewish God in the days of old.

The two brothers answered that neither they nor the Emperor were worthy that God should perform a miracle for their sakes. But they knew for certain that God would demand their blood at his hands if he dared to kill them.

At that moment a messenger came in with a decree from the Senate in Rome for the execution of Trajan! And so the brothers were set free.

Of course all this is quite unhistorical. But in one way or another there must be some basis for the legend. It is certain that since that time the Jews have celebrated a festival on the so-called 'Trajan's day', the 12th Adar, as a rule at the beginning of March.

The explanation may be found in a confusion between Trajan and Quietus. In any case the last-named tormentor of the Jews came to a bad end. Hadrian, who became Emperor after Trajan, had good reasons for keeping a sharp eye on him. It was not long before he sent him back to Mauretania in Africa, his country of origin. There he dared to take part in a conspiracy against the new Emperor. It was discovered, and Quietus was executed along with three other highly placed men.

Trajan himself soon saw that he was not strong enough to carry the Parthian campaign through to a victorious end. He had to give up Ctesiphon and began to withdraw his forces towards Syria. The great Alexander campaign, which had begun with such favourable auguries, was petering out sadly.

Trajan, broken both mentally and physically, decided to return to Rome. He probably wished to discuss with the Senate the great question of whom he was to adopt as heir to the throne, a matter which he had long left in complete uncertainty.

He was a sick man when he reached Antioch, where he appointed his relative Hadrian governor and commander-in-chief of the army of the East. He recovered sufficiently to be able to continue his journey to Rome. Off the coast of Cilicia he fell sick again and had to go ashore at the town of Selinus. And there he died in the year 117.

Trajan had left a deep mark on the history of the Jewish people. But Hadrian had a still more disastrous influence.

VII

A SCEPTIC ON THE THRONE

A Roman legend says that when one of the old kings founded the Capitol and hailed Jupiter Capitolinus as the first of the gods, and the lesser gods respectfully made way for him, there was one god who refused to draw back. This was Terminus, the god who watched over frontiers and therefore was symbolized by a large heavy stone, which lay firmly on the ground and remained where it was laid.

In after years this was taken as a happy augury that the frontiers of Rome would never be withdrawn. This was so for many centuries, and the prophecy itself, as often happens, naturally contributed to its own fulfilment. But Terminus, who had withstood the majesty of Jupiter, had to bow to Hadrian's authority. This is how it happened.

Trajan's campaigns were the last flare-up of offensive military strength in the old Roman civilization. They have been described as flashes of lightning which for a few seconds threw a blinding illumination over the cloudy evening sky of the Roman Empire. But flashes of lightning have no morrow. Trajan could win victories over the Parthian armies, brilliant experiences for those who took part in them or heard of them. But the Empire was old and tired: it had neither the strength nor the surplus population to Romanize the vast Eastern Empire and incorporate it in the culture of the West.

If Rome had been equal to this task, world history would have followed quite another course than that which we know. It was these Eastern peoples who later achieved through Islam

THE SON OF A STAR

a mighty renewal of strength and came within an ace of overthrowing the civilized countries of the West.

When Hadrian came to the throne on Trajan's death, history was at one of its great turning points, and it was the new Emperor who took the vital decision the consequences of which gave the world the aspect it still wears today.

Hadrian was not a warrior like Trajan: peace, friendship and trade were far dearer to him than military triumphs. He decided, therefore, on a resolute change of course. He abandoned the Parthian conquests and made the Euphrates the frontier river between the two realms. The daughters of the King of Parthia, who had been made prisoners, were sent home again, but Hadrian kept the King's golden throne which the Romans had taken as war booty at Ctesiphon.

His action was a bold one, especially in the face of the legions, who worshipped Trajan's memory. Now they saw their eagles in retreat, and extensive provinces, whose soil had been moistened with their comrades' blood, given up. But Hadrian saw clearly that the Empire was large enough. Rome was sated. New land, which could not be swallowed and digested by the Empire, was unnecessary and harmful. For the first time Terminus had to give way and see his stone moved back.

Such was Hadrian's entry into history. A man who knew what he wanted and did what he thought right, even if others did not understand. But the matter was not so simple. Only seldom could Hadrian see as clearly and act as rightly as now. At other times he hesitated, and often had difficulty in collecting himself to take a big decision. And sometimes he struck out blindly, so that the consequences were unhappy. The Jewish people more than any other had occasion to feel this.

To understand fully the time, and Israel's disaster, one cannot do better than study the mind and actions of this peculiar Emperor.

The beginning of the second century was a time of ferment in the Graeco-Roman civilizations, in which widely different forces were at grips with one another. The old original Roman

A SCEPTIC ON THE THRONE

character had not yet disappeared. It was still to be found here and there, with its honesty and administrative and military efficiency, combined with old-fashioned severity and roughness. But far more conspicuous was the Greek element, which gave life its light and colour. The clear Hellenist way of thought, and the Greek sense of beauty and urge towards harmony and belief in human ideals, were advancing in triumph all the world over. And interwoven with these elements were the gloomy piety and heavy mysticism, along with furious devotion and perversity, of the Orient. Later these widely different elements were to be welded together and combined to form a queer mixed civilization which contained all the forces making for dissolution. But in Hadrian's time they could still be distinguished from one another.

Hadrian was a perfect representative of this composite and contradictory time. All that was characteristic of it was in him collected and concentrated as in a focal point. He was a full-blooded Hellenist and intellectual and at the same time an administrator and even a warrior, if one was required. But the mysticism of the East had caught and held him fast, its uncanny, sultry depths had an irresistible attraction for him. All these contradictions fought within him to win the first place, but none gained it. Despite many talents and great qualities he never became a complete character. His lack of unity and centre made him a protean nature, a psychological riddle which no one could solve. But just all that was dissonant and composite in him make him a true representative of a cleft and groping time.

Modern historical research has placed Hadrian as the first in an epoch in the history of the Roman Empire, the time of the Antonines, the happiest period of the Roman Empire, perhaps of the world. Behind it lay wars and internal convulsion, ahead of it downfall and dissolution, a time of deep shadows and thick darkness, in which the Empire collapsed. But in the half-century of the Antonines the zenith was reached, life stood still and breathed peace and happiness. On Hadrian's coins were inscriptions such as 'the golden age' and 'enricher of the world'—

THE SON OF A STAR

flattery for the Emperor from the servile Senate, no doubt, but the words are not unjustified.

The fact that another great rebellion in Judaea had shaken the Empire during his reign was quickly forgotten. And when the sceptic Hadrian deployed all the might of the Empire against the out of the way little province and the iron heels of the legions trod on Jewish necks once again and for the last time, the stillness of death at last descended on Palestine and the 'golden age' continued its quiet, harmonious life undisturbed.

The new Emperor's full name was Publius Aelius Hadrianus, and he was born in Rome in the year 76, during Vespasian's reign. But his family was of Spanish origin and consisted of veterans from the second Punic war. He thus belonged to one of the distinguished provincial families that brought new blood into Roman society, which after numerous purges badly needed renewal.

Fortune laid the cards of his destiny at an early date. His father died when he was only nine. His father's cousin, the famous general Trajan, then adopted the boy. Thus both relationship and guardianship brought him into close relationship with the future Emperor. But at that time no one dreamed of such brilliant possibilities.

The boy received the best education that could be had in those times, and in his earliest years he showed his liking for Greek literature. His friends used to call him Graeculus, the little Greek. Otherwise outdoor life, sport and hunting were his great hobbies: he trained his body so that he became a strong youth and even in boyhood laid the foundations of that physical endurance which later made people call him 'the Travelling Emperor'.

Trajan kept a sharp eye on his protégé and certainly had good reason for doing so. Hadrian was dissolute in his early years and needed firm management. The best way of subjecting him to discipline was the military career, so he became an officer. But science and art were nearest his heart: he burned continually to extend his knowledge, and learned men and artists were his

A SCEPTIC ON THE THRONE

favourite companions. He came unscathed through Domitian's reign of terror. He was still too young and unimportant to incur suspicion, and was serving far away from Rome as an officer in the Fifth Legion, stationed in Moesia, the present Bulgaria.

When Domitian fell to his murderers' daggers, and old Nerva adopted Trajan as his fellow ruler and successor, eyes were suddenly turned upon Hadrian. So far his life had followed conventional lines: it had been no different from that of any young man of the *bourgeoisie*. Now his guardian had been raised to the summit of power and he himself was the heir of the childless Emperor.

When Nerva died, Trajan was with the army of the Rhine. Hadrian determined to make every effort to be the first to tell the new Emperor that he was now alone on the throne. His brother-in-law Servian, much older than he was, grudged Hadrian this opportunity and set about intriguing to delay his journey. He put every obstacle in Hadrian's way, went to the length of having his carriage smashed up and sent an express messenger of his own instead. But Hadrian was not a trained walker for nothing. He set off on foot as quickly as possible and came in first! No one knew then that long afterwards Servian would try to murder Hadrian and that his ambition would cost him his life.

Contrary to all expectations Trajan hesitated to adopt Hadrian as his successor. He was himself a dry, prosaic man, entirely occupied with national problems, a cold thinker whose 'iron face' was proverbial. He brooded silently and critically over his young relative, over the undeniably strong complexity of his character and his fondness for art and pleasure.

But Hadrian realized what the Emperor was thinking and did his best to clear away the mists. He changed his ways and began seriously to train himself for high posts in the administration of the Empire. As the years passed, Trajan could not but recognize the manifest efficiency and zeal with which Hadrian discharged the tasks laid upon his young shoulders.

Hadrian knew enough of life, too, to know that in the long run it is women who govern the world. He became a close

THE SON OF A STAR

friend of Plotina, the Empress, and of course there was a great deal of contemporary gossip to the effect that their friendship was not quite platonic. The first result of their connection was a promising one. In the year 100 Trajan married his young ward to the only princess of the imperial house, his great-niece Sabina. He thus showed beyond all doubt that he regarded Hadrian as his heir. But he hesitated for a long time to adopt him formally.

Hadrian's house soon became one of the centres on which all eyes were turned and to which everyone sought admission. In Rome he collected round himself the intellects of the day. Pliny the younger and the historian Tacitus belonged to his regular circle. The imperial biographer Suetonius and the poets Juvenal and Martial also visited his house. This story gives a solitary glimpse of the atmosphere in his circle. Appolodorus was the greatest architect of the day: he was Trajan's right hand when the construction of new buildings was intended. One day he was sitting talking to the Emperor. Hadrian joined in the conversation, but Appolodorus cut him short with the words: 'You go and paint your cucumbers. You don't understand these things!'

This ancedote tells us that Hadrian, among his other artistic interests, was a painter, and a painter of still life. But it shows us also what freedom of speech a great artist could allow himself in conversation with the most powerful men in the world.

As the years passed, Hadrian matured. He went through the usual stages on his rise towards the heights. As Quaestor he was Trajan's reporter in the Senate. The senators did not conceal their amusement at Hadrian's provincial Spanish dialect. But he resolutely changed his manner of speech and learnt to speak Latin correctly, though Greek was always his favourite language. While the war against the Dacians was raging, Hadrian was in the field and did his best to please Trajan. He went so far as to take part in the Emperor's drinking bouts. Trajan was a heavy drinker; but such excess was repellent to Hadrian, whose weaknesses were of a different kind.

Trajan now gave Hadrian the command of a legion: it was his first independent command, and he showed such remarkable

A SCEPTIC ON THE THRONE

talent as a leader of troops that Trajan's last doubts must have disappeared. Everyone commented on his having given Hadrian the diamond ring he himself had received from Nerva on his adoption. And yet Trajan would still make no formal announcement of this important decision.

He put Hadrian to the vital test, the last examination a future Emperor should take. Hadrian was given a province to govern, Pannonia, on the course of the Danube through what is now Austria and Hungary. He did well there. He waged war successfully against neighbouring barbarians, controlled both the army and the civil authorities with a firm hand and protected the inhabitants against too rapacious taxation. He had now given proof of his capacity both as a general and as a governor, and rose to still higher posts. Hadrian became Consul in Rome.

In the eyes of all, this was a great time for the Empire! Domitian's despotism and evil moods were forgotten and buried with him. Instead Rome displayed her strength in victorious wars, her eagles flew through conquered lands. But the laurels won by Trajan in battle did not kindle fresh ambition in Hadrian. His taste was not for war, at any rate not for war's sake. If he had had to choose between Homer and Achilles, he would have preferred Homer.

Trajan may well have had some idea of the cleavage in his young relative's mind and feared that as he quite openly preferred peace to war and Athens to Rome, he would let his victories crumble away to nothing. However that may be, when Trajan left Rome in 114 and travelled to the East to begin the great Parthian war, the decision had not been made. The war followed its lamentable course, and on August 7, 117, Trajan died at Selinus in Cilicia.

Hadrian was then in Antioch, the capital of Syria, as governor and commander-in-chief of the army of the East. Here he received the Empress Plotina's letter with the news of the Emperor's death and a document signed by Trajan on his death-bed in which at last he made his decision, formally adopted his younger relative and made him his successor.

THE SON OF A STAR

Hadrian immediately had himself hailed as Emperor by the army in Syria and distributed to the soldiers a sum of money twice as large as was customary on such an occasion. He did not wait to be elected by the Senate, as he really ought to have done. Instead he sent it a polite letter, saying that the dangerous situation in the Orient had compelled him to act in this irregular manner, and begged the Senate to confirm his election. The Senate, seeing itself confronted with a *fait accompli*, hastened to send its respectful congratulations to the new Emperor.

It was not long before rumours began to circulate. It was alleged that Trajan's declaration of adoption was false, that Plotina had written it herself to secure her lover the throne. She had kept Trajan's death secret for several days so that there should be time for the forgery. She had indeed been so cunning that she had had a man put into Trajan's bed, where, hidden under the bedclothes, he played the part of Emperor and announced his decision to adopt Hadrian in a feeble voice. The rumours were very persistent, but it is impossible today to get to the bottom of the mystery.

But Hadrian had gained his object: he was ruler of the World Empire. And, as has already been seen, his first decisions were firm and far-reaching.

The heavy doors of the Temple of Janus were closed. The war was over, and now the great era of peace was to begin.

Hadrian made the Empire a unit. Formerly the Empire had been synonymous with Rome. The provinces existed only for the capital's sake: they were springs which were sucked dry by the voracious great city. Hadrian's achievement was to knit the different parts of the Empire, Rome and the provinces together into a whole, in which the hitherto overlooked provinces obtained an independent position and significance.

Hadrian spent two-thirds of his reign out in the Empire, travelling about on endless journeys. There was scarcely a town he did not visit, or a detachment of troops or a fortress he did not inspect. He wanted to see everything with his own eyes. He intervened personally in affairs, removed defects, punished

A SCEPTIC ON THE THRONE

dishonest officials, rebuilt fallen cities and erected new ones, he made roads, harbours, bridges and all the time talked to men of learning and studied art and the phenomena of nature. Where new impressions and knowledge were to be had, he was insatiable. The result of all this was that he was known all over the Empire as no other Emperor had been. He travelled everywhere and scattered his benefits freely. So he came to live in the people's consciousness as 'the Travelling Emperor'.

Here too he is a full-blown representative of an uneasy, unrestful time. The old Romans had been stationary: they stayed where they were. When not called away by war or other duties, they remained in Rome. Cicero regarded it as a misfortune when he was compelled to go away: all his thoughts and interests were bound up with life at home, i.e. in Rome.

But in this respect as in others ideas were gradually changing. People were becoming individualists and demanding to be allowed to live their lives for themselves and for their own development: they moved on from one impression to another. But if they wanted to escape from boredom, the obvious thing was simply to travel to other countries and see new things and ask new questions. Only long after it was written was the truth of Lucretius' profound observation realized, that 'boredom flows from the same source as pleasures'. It took some time for a restless, nervous, blasé generation to realize it.

Hadrian was a child of this restless time: he moved uneasily from place to place: his whole personality was uneasy. He was as unstable in his friendships as in everything else: one friend replaced another: *semper in omnibus varius* is how he was described, always changeable and uncertain.

Thirsting for knowledge and full of curiosity, he wanted to see everything made by men's hands or the work of nature. He visited Athens, Olympia, Pergamus. He climbed Etna and travelled far into Egypt, towards the sources of the Nile. A contemporary described him thus: 'Hadrian had extraordinary stamina, he went on foot through all his provinces, hurrying on ahead of the rest of the party . . . he did not mind cold and rough weather, and always went bare-headed.' He took short

THE SON OF A STAR

cuts away from the high roads, with a very few companions, and took local accommodation as he found it, however miserable it might be.

He initiated a happy time for the great Empire, a time of prosperity and contentment, above all in the provinces. Long after his reign the Christian Tertullian described the conditions then prevailing. He was writing about A.D. 200, but the prosperity he described had its beginning under Hadrian.

'The earth is provided with everything, it is becoming daily more and more civilized and is richer now than in old times. Everything is accessible, everything is known, and everywhere there is activity. Deserts which once lay desolate are now covered with pretty farms, cultivated land has replaced forest, and flocks of tame animals have ousted the wild beasts. Corn grows in the desert sand, hills are planted, swamps dried. There are as many towns today as formerly there were houses. No barren islands or mountains any longer have a frightening effect. Everywhere there are signs of human habitation, everywhere civilized government, everywhere life.'

The travelling Emperor dates from the beginning of this brilliant era, and the Christian author of one of the sibylline books paints his portrait thus: 'The grey-haired man named after the sea'—a play upon the words Hadrian and Adriatic—'who will walk unrestingly over the earth, bringing gifts everywhere'. To this day we can follow him by the coins which were struck in his honour wherever he went. They call him the world traveller and the world's saviour. One of them speaks of the 'Golden Age' and shows a half-naked genius surrounded by a circle which he is touching with his right hand, while in his left he holds the globe, on which a phoenix is sitting.

Religious movements always tell us something definite about the time whose children they are. Here too the uneasiness and scepticism of the times are concentrated as in a focal point in this strange man. The urge which ran through this time, and fumbled its way in behind the old ideas of the gods, to find the one God, had gripped Hadrian. He built temples which were

A SCEPTIC ON THE THRONE

called pantheons, consecrated to all the gods at once, in fact to divinity. Hadrian built a pantheon in Athens, but we know too that he built temples without images of the gods, which were not dedicated to any particular god, but where everyone could worship the god in whom he believed.

Past times had been extrovert and active. This time became reflective and introspective: men pondered over the dark riddles of life, death and evil. The mystery religions of the East, therefore, with their puzzling ideas and rites of penance, purification and dedication, inevitably pushed their way forward and increased their hold on men's minds. And here we meet the Emperor again. He interested himself in the Eleusinian mysteries and went from one oracle to another. Quite early in his life the Castalian spring had foretold that he would gain the imperial throne. When the prophecy was fulfilled, he walled up the spring for safety's sake: he would not risk its doing anyone else the same service!

Dreams and omens were an essential part of his life. When his death was approaching he dreamed that his father gave him a sleeping draught, and soon afterwards that a lion killed him. Every New Year he studied the positions of the stars and wrote down, according to the rules of astrology, what was going to happen to him in the New Year. An astrologer had once predicted his coming greatness. When the year of his death was beginning, he wrote down everything that was going to happen down to the day of his death. After that the paper was blank. But to obtain the fullest insight into his character the strange and unpleasant Antinous episode during his great journey to Egypt must be described.

The Pharaohs' land was the scene of the oldest culture in the world. From Augustus' time Egypt had been the Emperors' private domain and Rome's corn-growing province. The rich country was ruled by an Imperial Prefect, who administered or, to be more accurate, exploited it for the benefit of the Emperor's treasury. He kept the country down with an iron hand, but here was always feverish unrest among the swarming, overcrowded, superstitious population, especially in Alexandria, the second largest city in the Empire. It was the meeting-place of the caravan routes and shipping routes, which joined the near Orient to distant lands far away to eastward and to central parts of the Empire. Egypt was already, as it is now, a museum for the embalmed culture of the Pharaohs. Of course Hadrian wanted to see all this with his own eyes, and in the year 130 he set out on his great Nile journey. And it was there that it happened.

Antinous was a handsome lad, scarcely twenty years old. Hadrian had found him in Bithynia and had been completely fascinated by the pretty boy with the slim Adonis-like figure. He became the Emperor's dear friend and inseparable companion. As long as he lived the Emperor could not do without him. Their relationship is a profound mystery, but all the indications are that Hadrian, to whom no vice was unknown, was passionately in love with the boy. In those days people saw nothing peculiar or objectionable in a sexual relationship between a distinguished man advanced in years and a young lad. Trajan had had similar inclinations without giving offence to anyone.

On his Nile journey Antinous was drowned. Hadrian almost collapsed with grief. He declared Antinous a god, the honour which as a rule was given only to deceased Emperors. At the place where the youth lost his life he built a city which he named after him, and there later an oracle was established, at which Antinous gave answers to inquirers. Temples in his honour were erected at other places in the world, and a number of sculptures are extant showing a handsome youth with a sad face, a lad who had resigned himself to his unhappy lot.

What lay behind this strange event? Perhaps Antinous was accidentally drowned. But it seems more likely that the tragedy was in the nature of a sacrifice. Perhaps the visionary youth offered himself as a sacrifice to the gods of death, to save his imperial friend. Perhaps Egyptian priests had read in the stars that mortal danger threatened Hadrian and could only be averted by the person he loved best on earth voluntarily sacrificing himself and giving his life. This would be quite in line with the Emperor's profound belief in astrology and the

A SCEPTIC ON THE THRONE

general ideas of the time, more especially in Egypt and on the mysterious Nile.

At the funeral ceremony a new star appeared, a clear proof that Antinous had been received into the company of the gods. Dying heathendom obtained in him a new god and antique art its last ideal figure.

In later years the Christian Church looked back on Hadrian's reign with appreciation. There was scarcely any persecution, and any that there was was of a quite local nature. Fuller consideration shows us that this tolerance was only natural in a man of Hadrian's type. Uncertain, inquiring minds are tolerant. Intolerance is born of strong conviction; scepticism breeds tolerance.

But when later Christian writers suggest that Hadrian was a secret admirer of Christ, we enter the world of legend. He had no sympathy with Christianity, and certainly his knowledge of it was extremely superficial. It is sufficient to quote one of his secretaries, who called the Christians 'a kind of people with an evil and dangerous superstition'. But a letter which Hadrian sent to his brother-in-law Servian from Alexandria is also of interest. He writes:

'I have learnt to know the Egyptians as a light-minded, unstable people, who run after everything new. Those who worship Serapis are Christians, and those who call themselves the bishops of Christ worship Serapis. There is no head of a Jewish synagogue, no Samaritan, no presbyter among the Christians, who does not read the stars and work miracles. Yes, even the Christian patriarch (from Jerusalem?), when he comes to Egypt, is compelled by some to worship Serapis, by others to adore Christ. Money is their god; the Christians, Jews and all other races worship him.'

Such a letter shows how remote Hadrian was from any real knowledge either of Judaism or of the Christian Church.

Hadrian's last years were painful. He had always had a difficult temperament to contend with and felt himself in the depths of his heart a lonely man. He was more than often petty and grudging in his behaviour towards eminent men. And his

THE SON OF A STAR

friendships were quickly broken. He returned from his last journey sick, tired and depressed. He did not want to live in Rome: he had never liked the city. But he built his great villa, whose ruins still attract attention and are one of the richest mines of antique works of art, in the pleasant country at Tivoli. Here he assembled all the art treasures which had interested him, either originals or copies. And he offered immense sums to obtain copies of landscapes which had particularly impressed him on his long journeys.

He spent his last years at Tivoli. They were gloomy and sad for a man who was not made for illness, but only for activity—and now his strength was failing him.

Long before the Emperor's death those closest to him began to intrigue about the succession. Hadrian made his choice in defiance of court opinion, and chose the man he thought best qualified. But soon afterwards the chosen Emperor died suddenly. It was on this occasion that Hadrian uttered the well-known words: 'I have leant on a falling wall.'

His brother-in-law Servian, who in Hadrian's early youth had tried to bar his way to Trajan's favour, could not help conspiring. He had now become an old man, over ninety, and was working not for himself, but for a young grandson, his daughter's child, who was not yet seventeen. The imperial police got wind of his plans, and Hadrian forced them both to commit suicide. Before Servian died he swore that he was innocent and prayed to the gods that Hadrian might not be able to die when he most longed for death.

It almost looked as if the prayer had been heard. Hadrian's health grew worse and worse, and it was clear that the end was approaching. Dysentery and dropsy consumed his strength. He could not now delay the choice of a successor. Yet again his choice was unexpected. Aurelius Antoninus—he received the additional name Pius later for the way in which he preserved Hadrian's memory—was the lucky man. The condition was made that he should adopt two nephews to ensure the succession to the throne. One of these was Marcus Aurelius. Thus Hadrian on his death-bed gave the Empire the two noblest emperors in

A SCEPTIC ON THE THRONE

its history. The Senate confirmed his choice, and Antoninus took over the government.

It was high time. Hadrian was very ill and tormented by fearful pains. But he could not die. The end of his life was terrible: the strong body, trained by long travel on foot, refused to give up. It was said of him that he died every day without dying. The doctors did all they could to ease his pains, and recourse was had to magic, but without result. Hadrian himself received his doctors with his sarcastic smile, saying: 'Many doctors are the king's death.' He asked them for poison, but they dared not give it. He showed his favourite slave where he should thrust the dagger into his breast: he himself had not the strength to do it. But the slave fled; no man dared to lay a hand upon his majesty, who would become divine in the moment of his death. At long last the hour of liberation came. One July day in 138 he died in Antoninus' arms.

On one of the last days of his life he wrote a Latin poem.[1] It is a remarkable message from the dying sceptic, full of melancholy love of life and instinct with the unrest from which he never freed himself:

> Genial, little, vagrant sprite,
> Long my body's friend and guest,
> To what place is now thy flight?
> Pallid, stark, and naked quite,
> Stripped henceforth of joke and jest.

Even in death this enigmatic man could not refrain from satire and mockery. His ashes were buried in the great mausoleum he had built in Rome, for a long time the stronghold of the Popes of Rome.

[1] Many translations into English of Hadrian's stanza have been made. That used above is from *Roman Memories*, by Thomas Spencer Jerome. The original Latin is:
> Animula, vagula, blandula,
> Hospes comesque corporis,
> Quae nunc abibis in loca,
> Pallidula, rigida, nudula,
> Nec ut soles dabis jocos.

VIII

A ROCK IN ISRAEL

According to legend, when Moses ascended to heaven—for he did not die, and no one has seen his grave—he found God making little crowns for all the Hebrew letters of the Tora. He asked the Lord what they were meant to be, and received the answer:

'In times far hence a great teacher will appear called Rabbi Akiba. He will puzzle over these crowns and find my hidden intention in them, so that he can teach men to understand my law better.'

And the legend adds that long, long afterwards Moses begged the Lord to let him see the great teacher. The Lord allowed him to go to Akiba's school, but Akiba was so great a teacher that Moses was given a place eight rows behind him, and he could not understand Akiba's interpretation of the Tora!

So great was the popular veneration for Rabbi Akiba. His figure rises like a mountain over deep valleys, and in the time of Trajan and Hadrian he was the Jewish people's guide. In him Israel's faith and defiance were concentrated for the last great struggle.

His full name was Akiba Ben Joseph, but only once does tradition give his father's name, and his origin is obscure. It is said that his father was a proselyte. The family could trace its descent back to the heathen commander Sisera, who in the time of the Judges was defeated by the army of Deborah and Barak. Sisera met his death when, in his flight, he sought shelter in the tent of an Israelite woman, Jael. She killed him

A ROCK IN ISRAEL

while he was asleep by hammering a tent-peg through his temple.

But it is certain that Akiba began as an "'am ha-arez', a man of the common people, whom the rabbis despised for their ignorance. He came from the masses, and he continued all his life to love all the unknown small people. And they did the same, they were fond of Akiba and honoured his memory in the way people now do homage to those whom they look up to and love: in story and legend his life was given colour and warmth.

Of course it is said that he lived to be 120. Only the greatest men did this—Moses, Hillel, Johanan Ben Zakkai and Akiba. And as with the other great teachers his life fell into three sections: for forty years he was a shepherd, for another forty years he studied, and for the last forty years of his life he was a popular leader. As it is known approximately when he died, about 138, he must, if tradition is firmly based, have been born in the year 18 and so been a witness of the events narrated in the Gospels.

But the general course of his life is known: it began as a romantic adventure and ended in bitter tragedy. Behind legend and tales we can trace the main features of his personality and story: but the details must be taken for what they are worth, which is not much.

The learned looked down on the ignorant mob, to which Akiba in his youth belonged. Common people had no time to amass knowledge: for them life was only toil. But Akiba, who had to earn his living as a poor ignorant shepherd, repaid with detestation the contempt of the arrogant theologians.

'If I'd only got one of those learned men here, I'd bite him like a donkey,' the young man once cried.

'Why like a donkey, rather than a dog?' someone who heard him asked.

'Why,' Akiba replied, 'when a dog bites a man, it just bites him. But a donkey holds on and bites till the bones crack.'

And yet he found himself attracted by theology. Once

by a spring he saw a stone, which drops of water had fallen upon for a very long time and hollowed out. Then he burst out:

'If these drops of soft water can hollow the hard stone just by going on falling, how much more can God's strong words penetrate man's heart if it goes on listening?'

Suddenly romance entered his life. He became shepherd for one of the three richest men in Jerusalem, Kalba Shabua. He fell in love with Kalba's pretty daughter Rachel—and his love was returned.

The father violently opposed the unequal match, but the girl clung stoutly to her shepherd. Kalba in his anger threatened to disown her if she would not give up Akiba, and swore solemnly that he would not receive her into his house again if she would not obey him. But Rachel had given Akiba her hand, and the two were married.

The girl made one condition, and that Akiba had to accept. He must go away and study and not come back till he had become a teacher. Soon after the marriage Akiba went off, leaving his young wife alone.

Rachel went on living in her poor hut, with only straw to sleep on. Her father could not help her: his oath forbade him. And the proud girl asked for help from no one. When her first and only son was born, she had to cut off her lovely plaits of hair and sell them to get food for the child. But one day a beggar came to her door and begged for straw for his sick wife. Rachel gave him half her poor supply of straw and thought: 'So after all there is someone who is still poorer than I am.' Legend afterwards declared that the stranger was the prophet Elijah, who wanted to test her.

Akiba and Rachel had agreed that he should remain in the school for twelve years before they met one another again. At last the long years came to an end, and Akiba hastened eagerly home to see his loved one. When he came near the hut he heard voices inside. Kalba had come and was engaged in a vehement discussion with Rachel. He reproached her in strong language with her strange marriage and solitary life. But Rachel replied that she wished Akiba to remain away for another twelve years, that he might acquire as much learning as possible.

Akiba heard this. He did not let them see him, but went away again.

Twelve more years passed. At the end of them Akiba had become one of the most famous teachers in the country, and large crowds of disciples assembled round his chair. And now at last he could go home.

At the head of a huge crowd of enthusiastic disciples—the number of 24,000 is given!—he approached the place where Rachel was living in her misery. People gathered from near and far to get a glimpse of the great man and hail him.

As the procession advanced, a poor woman came up clad in miserable rags. Her thin cheeks were aglow and her eyes shining with joy. She made a way for herself through the crowd and reached Akiba.

Unable to control her feelings, she flung herself at his feet. The disciples were already trying to drive her away, but the rabbi checked them, saying:

'Let her alone! All that I am, and all that you are, we owe to her.'

And all ended happily. Kalba felt himself to be freed from his oath. He had sworn not to give his daughter to an ignorant shepherd. A man of learning was quite another thing. No man could wish his daughter a better match. He gave Akiba his fortune, so that the young couple, formerly so poor, became very rich.

Akiba could never tire of showing Rachel how much he loved her, and what he owed her for all that she had sacrificed. He once gave her a golden head ornament representing Jerusalem in all its beauty.

The ornament excited the other women's envy. The wife of the great Nasi, Rabbi Gamaliel, urged her husband to interfere to stop such unnecessary luxury. But he replied that if Rachel had been able to sacrifice her hair, she deserved to receive an ornament for her head.

Akiba was by far the most important of Joshua Ben Hananiah's disciples. In many fields he outshone his famous teacher: there were some, indeed, who maintained that he was greater than the great Hillel. He combined originality and genius with moral earnestness and personal independence. His intelligence was fine and keen, but the essence of his matchless personality was the feeling and enthusiasm with which he defended his convictions. He thought over a matter carefully and critically before he acted, but once the choice was made he fought with his heart rather than with his head.

Rabbi Akiba was a man with clearly defined points of view and emphatic opinions. Even today, when so much in his character and actions is shrouded in legend, his personality stands out and impresses us. But he himself was quiet and modest, as really great men are. He showed it in the way he always confessed to his humble origin. In contrast to other learned men, he respected the masses and did not conceal his disapproval of his colleagues' attitude:

'A man who gives himself airs about learning is like a piece of carrion in the road. The traveller turns his head away in disgust and hurries on.'

Among the utterances of his which have survived is a curious parallel to a famous saying of Jesus: 'Take at a feast a place lower than your rank allows. For it is better that they should say "go up higher!" than "go down lower!"' He himself lived up to this rule.

This marked the whole of his career. He was profoundly convinced that Judaism must have its central authority. He therefore subjected himself respectfully to the Nasis, who were chosen to govern, and showed both Gamaliel and Joshua complete loyalty. As long as they lived he contented himself with modest posts, although his learning and influence might have entitled him to the highest.

It is an old experience that theologians can be difficult to get on with. It is no doubt because they discuss the highest subjects in life and understand what can be at stake if they do not cling firmly to their opinions and dispute those of others. But their feelings can undeniably be expressed in such sharp words that one feels that they are fighting for heavenly things with very earthly weapons. So it was in the lecture halls at Jabneh, where the waves often ran high.

Rabbi Akiba is universally praised for the pleasant, peaceful manner in which he comported himself amid struggles of this kind. It was not at all that he modified his own points of view and agreed to dishonest compromises. On the contrary, there are several instances of his sharply attacking the patriarch's decisions when he found them not to be in accordance with the written or oral law. But he had a capacity of his own for building bridges over deep chasms between teachers at variance. He knew better than most men how prejudices are calmed, suspicions dispelled and jealousy and envy overcome. He could whisper consolation to the depressed and stimulate the hesitant. He was a spiritual guide of a high order.

Rabbi Akiba is often called the father of rabbinical Judaism. And it is true that he marked out the way for the spiritual development of Judaism in the next two thousand years. This he did, first and foremost, through his work on Holy Writ and the oral tradition.

Before his time the oral tradition had been handed on from generation to generation, being simply learnt by heart; that was why it was called the oral tradition. But every generation had had something to add to the teaching of their fathers, so that it had gradually swollen into complete shapelessness. Nor was the matter arranged methodically and connectedly, so that a quite superhuman memory was needed to remember it.

Rabbi Akiba set himself to go through the whole oral tradition critically, arranging the matter and connecting it up. Everything referring to the Sabbath, or with marriage problems, or whatever it might be, was brought together and arranged numerically, so that a general view of the questions could be obtained, and they could be remembered. Finally they were all written down in what is called Akiba's Mishna. Thus he laid the foundation of the Talmud.

Something was said earlier about the way in which the academy at Jabneh worked on Holy Writ and its interpretation.

THE SON OF A STAR

Hillel had drawn up seven rules for understanding the Bible, and later teachers had gone on building on this. But Akiba put the finishing touch to this. In him we find the Jewish allegory in full flower.

To Akiba there was a marked distinction between the text of the Bible and all other writings. Therefore, in interpreting them, quite different rules must be applied. In the Bible nothing is superfluous; every word, every syllable, indeed every letter has its hidden meaning. And if there is a single stop in the text which is not strictly necessary, it must have a secret, higher object.

In the commandment 'thou shalt worship the Lord thy God' there is, in the Hebrew text which had been handed down, a single letter which could be dispensed with. And of course there was endless discussion as to what the meaning of it might be. Perhaps it meant that there was someone or something alongside God which should be venerated together with him! And Akiba established that this must be the Tora.

All this strange, unreal form of Bible study seemed to contemporaries the highest wisdom. Accordingly they venerated Akiba and did homage to his genius. As has already been seen there were rabbis who believed that Akiba had discovered secrets of which Moses had had no knowledge.

There was more permanent importance in his work on the definition of the Old Testament, so that it should be known exactly which writings properly belonged to the Bible and which did not. It was due to Akiba's influence that the Song of Solomon and the book of Esther are in the Bible today.

Another side of his mentality must be mentioned for the picture to be complete—his interest in mysticism. Mystical theology was only for the few initiated. It centred on the mystery that God, the eternal, had connected himself with the Creation. How could the unthinkable thing happen, that eternity should touch dust? There were, therefore, certain Bible texts which the mystical theologians pondered over early and late—the story of the Creation, the revelation to the prophet Isaiah and Ezekiel's vision of the wagon.

A ROCK IN ISRAEL

This study gradually developed into theosophical speculations and strange fantasies. But the urge to deep love in the relationship to God, and the feeling that the understanding will always be knocking at the locked doors of mystery when it ventures into the field of eternity, are fundamental religious experiences. A deeply religious people like the Jews is simply bound to have pronounced experiences in the realm of mysticism. In the cabbala of the Middle Ages Jewish mystics ventured far into this closed land.

But as long ago as Akiba's time people talked of 'the closed land'. Incomprehensible things happened to the mystics there. When they were studying the law, flames burst out of their heads, and they became able to perform miracles. There was a story of four wise men who went into 'the closed garden', i.e. engaged in theosophical studies. The first looked round him in the garden and fell down and died immediately. The second lost his reason. The third tried to lay waste the garden, and only the fourth came out uninjured: he was the Rabbi Akiba!

Where Israel's national and religious hopes were concerned Akiba stood in the front rank. The whole of his personality quivered with longing for the Messiah: he was always on the look out for him. And he hated and despised the foreigners. No one could give such ready answers as he in argument with Gentiles. This is one of the stories told of him.

On one of his journeys he came to Rome and was immediately involved in a discussion with a philosopher about Judaism and heathendom. The keen-witted philosopher, who was accustomed to discussion, expected to find an easy prey. He wanted to prove that circumcision was a bad, superstitious custom, and thought he had found a clever way of driving the Jewish learned men into a corner. He asked:

'Which is the more beautiful, God's work or man's?'

He was sure the Jews would reply that God's work was the more beautiful, but if so circumcision must be a bad custom, and he had the rabbi in a fix. To his astonishment Akiba replied immediately:

THE SON OF A STAR

'The work of man is the more beautiful. For nature only supplies us with the raw material as God commands. Then we have to prepare it according to the rules of art and good taste.'

The philosopher had another try:

'Yes, but why did not God create man as he wished him to be?'

And again Akiba disarmed him:

'Because it is man's duty to perfect himself.'

But what he is most remembered for is his childlike trust in God. Endless stories have been told of this. And here are two of them.

He was travelling, and night came on suddenly. Fortunately he was close to a village, so he knocked on the door and asked for shelter. The villagers were disagreeable, inhospitable people, and turned him away. So he had to spend the night in the open air. As his custom was he had with him a torch, an ass to carry his luggage, and a cock to wake him early, so that he could use the first hours of the day for reading the Scriptures and prayer.

But one misfortune after another overtook him. The wind put the torch out, a lion ate the ass, and a fox killed the cock. But Akiba bowed his head submissively and said:

'God's will be done! Whatever happens must have some good purpose, even if I think it unfortunate at the moment.' And the learned man spent a cold, windy night in the desolate mountains.

When daylight came he discovered that in the darkness of the night robbers had come and attacked the village, stolen everything in it, and carried off the inhabitants as prisoners. But he had escaped: the torch had not burnt and the animals had not betrayed him.

Another time he was travelling with some friends past devastated Jerusalem. The others wept at the sight of the desolate ruins and a hyena prowling over the height on which the Temple once stood. Akiba alone preserved his equanimity. He reminded them that they could see how literally the prophecies of the destruction of the Temple had been fulfilled. So they were also entitled to trust that when God's hour struck, his blessings would be just as concrete a reality.

A ROCK IN ISRAEL

Tradition had handed down many of his sayings. For example:

'God loves mankind, for he created it in his image. But the love which told us that that is so is greater than that with which he created us.'

'Everything is given to us on credit. A net is spread out over all living things. The shop is opened, and the shopkeeper gives credit. But a book lies open, and God's hand writes down all that we do.'

And his favourite saying was:

'What God does he does for the best.'

It was this legendary great man who intervened in the people's hour of destiny. He did not act on a sudden intuition. He worked his way forward to it all his life. That the great Jewish revolutions in the surrounding Empire during Trajan's Parthian war were so extensive and seemed so remarkably coordinated was largely due to Rabbi Akiba's tireless activity and clever diplomacy. He often travelled about the world. It is known that he was in Rome in the years 95–96, and his tracks can be followed at many places in the Empire. Wherever he went he stayed with fellow-countrymen, as the usual custom was, and enjoyed their hospitality. But his real object was of a political nature. He met the leaders of the people out in lonely places and made plans for what was going to happen when the great hour came.

During the time of waiting he established the many connections required. And for the present he armed himself with patience. He counted absolutely on God in his hour being willing to send the help his people needed.

He waited and looked forward to the great day. And the Messiah came! Then he saw that the day had arrived, and struck.

IX

IN THE BALANCE

❦

IN these years two great men in Israel were sharply opposed to one another, the Rabbi Akiba and the Nasi Joshua Ben Hananiah. The tension between them did not take the form of disputes and tug-of-war contests: outwardly it was not noticeable, but it was there. Akiba's policy was deliberately aimed at war: Joshua was equally determined to preserve peace. The essence of the matter was that in these friends two human types met with directly contrary principles of life—boldness and caution.

Akiba waited in burning faith for the sign from God, the Messiah, who would intervene from heaven and smash the enemy and restore the glory of Israel. Joshua sought to understand the foreigners and established contact with the Emperor to get the people as good and secure living conditions as possible. Joshua's love of Israel and faith in the living God was no less strong than Akiba's. He only sought to advance by another route: he desired above all quiet development and peace. These two contending elements are found in all times of national crisis. The situation was like a balance with scales rising and falling, now one way now the other. It was many years before the decision was taken, and the weight of war sent the scale of peace flying up.

For a long time Joshua was the stronger, and Akiba bowed his head loyally and modestly before his eminent superior and friend. He did not change his opinion or deflect his course. He continued to prepare quietly for the bloody decision he was sure would come one day. But he was outwardly submissive, and

IN THE BALANCE

all the more so in that political developments in the first years of Hadrian's reign promised peace and conciliation. Before ever Hadrian came to the throne, a Jewish poet in Alexandria had predicted that an Emperor who was called after a sea would initiate a new era which would bring happiness to Israel and Jerusalem. And indeed Hadrian was called after the Adriatic, so the prophecy went from mouth to mouth.

No one knew that Hadrian, in a secret conference with his intimates, had aired a proposal simply to exterminate the Jews. Would it not be expedient to amputate a diseased limb, rather than let it infect the whole body? One of his advisers, who was a proselyte, violently opposed the Emperor's idea. He was executed. But the plan was laid aside for the time being, and no one spoke of it.

Hadrian wanted peace. He therefore abandoned Trajan's conquests and tried to bridle the restless Orient without bloodshed. And he met as many of the wishes of the peoples of the East under the yoke of Rome as he felt was practicable. Of course they applauded him, and his shares stood high. His rising popularity can be traced on many coins struck in his honour. Some have been found even in Judaea: there is one which shows the Emperor lifting a kneeling woman, Judaea, who had three children standing at her side.

Hadrian left his traces all over the Empire. He rebuilt and adorned towns which had been burnt down. It seemed to him quite natural that fallen Jerusalem should be rebuilt. And to Israel's delight he issued an imperial rescript permitting the Jews to rebuild their capital and the Temple in it. In a Jewish sibylline book there is an enthusiastic account of the situation in the first years of Hadrian's reign: 'Judaea shall be radiant in eternal peace and splendour never yet seen, and while our psalms and prayers ring out, the sacrificial altar is being made ready again.'

The permission was given just when the hated and cruel governor Quietus was transferred, to meet soon afterwards an ignoble death as a traitor. With a stroke of the pen the new Emperor had delivered the people from the tyrant and fulfilled its dearest wishes. Naturally all Israel looked to Hadrian with confidence and gratitude.

The Jews set about the work with astonishing energy. The two brothers Julianus and Pappus, who had miraculously escaped death, were given the task of obtaining money for the great work of rebuilding. They had the imperial rescript made known in all countries where Jews lived, and money began to flow in in abundance. In Galilee and Syria, all the way from Accho to Antioch, the two brothers set up money-changers' shops, where foreign money could be changed into Palestinian currency.

But things were not to go as well as they had promised. The Samaritans grudged the Jews such a triumph and began to intrigue against them. It was not difficult for them to point out to the Emperor that his takings from Jews would fall sharply if they got their own city and sanctuary again; nor could there be any certainty that Judaea's new independence would not mean new danger from this refractory people. The Emperor was persuaded and lent a willing ear to the intriguers.

He could not openly break his word. Instead he announced that the Temple which was to be built must either be on a slightly different site from the former one, or its measurements must be either about ten yards larger or smaller. But the site and measurements of the Temple were ordained by God, and no man could change a tittle of a commandment of God. The new imperial decision, therefore, really meant that the rebuilding was forbidden.

The Jews quickly saw through the Emperor's trick, and their feelings changed suddenly from joy to sorrow. And it was not long before their disappointment turned to such violent anger that the worst might be expected. Secret messengers went round the country bidding all men able to bear arms to assemble in the valley of Rimmon, in the northern part of Palestine. A huge crowd from all parts of the country collected there, and the general feeling was for a direct break and the immediate opening of a new rebellion against Rome.

But Joshua was there too, and at the stage of the meeting

IN THE BALANCE

at which all were shouting for vengeance and bloodshed he rose and began to speak. The shrewd old man knew well how easily feeling is swayed at large meetings if the intervening speaker only knows how to do it. He therefore chose to narrate an old and well-known fable. He opened his speech calmly and quietly, as follows:

'There was once a lion eating his prey. Suddenly a bone stuck in his throat: it remained there and could not be got out again. The situation became extremely serious for the king of the forest. If he could not get the bone removed he would die of hunger: it was a matter of life and death. So the lion issued a proclamation to all the other animals, saying that the one who could get the bone out would receive a great reward. The offer sounded tempting, but most of the creatures thought twice before they dared put their heads into the lion's mouth. Who could know if they would ever get it out again? After a long time the crane came up and said it would make the attempt. The lion opened his jaws as wide as he could, and the crane stuck his long bill and long neck far down the lion's throat. And it really succeeded in getting the famous bone out! But then the question of a reward came up. Alas! kings are seldom grateful. The lion told the crane to hurry off home and thank its lucky star that it had got its head safely out of the lion's jaws. It would certainly be both the first and last time it had had such an experience!'

When Joshua had told his fable, he was silent for a moment. Then he added quite briefly:

'We must thank God that we have fared as the crane did. We too have tried to have our head in the lion's jaws. And so far we have kept alive. Why stick our head in yet again?'

Joshua had calculated aright. People realized they had been on the verge of a mortally dangerous adventure. The feeling of the assembly swung round, and this time the balance inclined towards peace. The meeting broke up and all went quietly home.

Rabbi Joshua exercised all his influence for the maintenance of peace and he succeeded. So long as he lived he postponed

THE SON OF A STAR

the catastophe which loomed on the horizon. Of course the Emperor knew quite well that he had an advocate in the Nasi of Israel. There are several accounts of meetings between the two men.

Hadrian, eternally questioning and uncertain, always oscillated between scepticism and superstition. He naturally found it stimulating to discuss vital questions with the old Jewish sage. He wanted to be initiated into all mysteries, so why should he not have a peep into the secrets of Judaism? Joshua was not very successful as the Emperor's instructor in Judaism—the letter to Servian quoted earlier makes that clear—but one characteristic story handed down by tradition is worth hearing.

Hadrian once asked Rabbi Joshua Ben Hananiah:

'I am better than your teacher Moses, am I not?'

'But why?' Joshua asked in surprise.

'Because I am alive, and he is dead. And the saying goes that a live dog is better than a dead lion.'

'But can you,' Joshua asked, 'give an order that no one in the city shall light a fire tomorrow?'

'Of course I can,' said the Emperor.

The next evening they both went up on to the roof of the palace and looked out over the city. And in the far distance smoke was ascending from a chimney.

'What is that?' the rabbi asked.

'One of my leading men is desperately ill. The doctors have said that he can only recover if he has something hot to drink. So I have given permission to light a fire.'

'There, you see,' said the rabbi with conviction, 'you are alive, but you cannot be sure that your commands are obeyed. But Moses said, "you must not light a fire on the Sabbath", and so no Jew lights a fire on the holy day. You see, we obey Moses' ordinances, though he is dead. So which is the better? You or Moses?'

As long as Joshua lived he kept the peace between Judaea and Rome. When he died about 130, people said that in him a shrewd adviser and wise mediator was lost.

IN THE BALANCE

In the year 128 an earthquake destroyed Caesarea. The whole country felt that this catastrophe must have some special significance.

Caesarea was the foreigners' city: it had lain there flaunting its wealth and its heathendom in the Jews' country, while their own capital lay in ruins. They felt it as an open, festering, ulcerous wound in their side. And now it had fallen because the earth shook it. All over the country the rabbis told excited assemblies that it could only portend the speedy liberation of Jerusalem. The barometer of public feeling indeed pointed to earthquake.

Such times as these do not favour intellectual studies. Not much is heard of the academy or the Sanhedrin in these years of unrest. But a few of the Sanhedrin's legal decisions have come down to us, and these decrees contain characteristic features worthy of notice.

Parents are bound to support boys till their twelfth year and girls till they are married. If a father in his lifetime gives his son all his property, it is the son's duty to support his father. A man may give only a fifth of his fortune in alms.

We are here looking into the soul of a community which was faced with a terrible crisis—and was conscious of it. When the very ground begins to sway under men's feet, when social or political landslides are imminent, the waters divide. Some become petrified in selfishness, so gross that things which should be a matter of course have to be enforced by law, while others blaze up in fanaticism which forgets the day or in any case the morrow, so that they have to be restrained. It is these two tendencies that the Sanhedrin's decrees endeavour to check. Children must think of their parents and parents of their children. And family property must not be thrown away in a moment of enthusiasm.

Our hand is on the pulse of a people whose temperature is evidently rising from hour to hour. The crisis is at hand.

Just at this crucial moment old Joshua died—and with him disappeared the last barrier to the advance of Rabbi Akiba. Henceforward it was he who set the course, he stood alone on

THE SON OF A STAR

the ramparts. And his great qualities fully revealed themselves as the vital decision drew near. All who came near him perceived it. For this fiery soul conviction became passion, hope conviction, and every possibility, however small, a hope. He worked untiringly at his preparations.

Again he set out on long journeys, the aim of which was to weld the Jews of the whole world together in a united, concentrated effort to cast off the yoke. It is on record that he went far into Persia, where he spoke to a congregation of the sufferings of Job, which the Lord used to achieve a great purpose. In the same way God would use the sufferings his own beloved people was going through to make it worthy of a great destiny.

But he did not content himself with speaking. Active preparations for revolt were quietly made everywhere. After A.D. 70 Jewish smiths were bound to make weapons for the Romans every year. Now they began to make them so badly that the Romans condemned them. Then the smiths took them again and put them in order so that the Jews themselves could use them when the time came. All over the mountains they excavated holes for storing arms and underground passages which could be used in war, the classic Jewish form of warmaking in Palestine. Such large-scale preparations could not be made without a good many people having knowledge of them, and it was inevitable that some information should leak out.

The Romans took counter-measures. Hadrian appointed one of his toughest men to be Governor-General of Judaea, Tineius Rufus. The Jews changed his name and called him Tyrannus Rufus. He well deserved the name, for he was a stern master to the Jews for many years. Hadrian knew well that it would require energy to keep Israel down. But neither he nor any other Roman realized what a fierce and strong enemy they would have to face when war at last began. For the present there was only one thing for Akiba to do—to wait for the sign from heaven. He waited and kept his eyes open.

Rufus delivered his first blow. One day large detachments of the Tenth Legion marched up to the old Temple square in Jerusalem and fell in for a formal parade. The golden eagles

12. *Trajan*

13. River Jordan north of the Lake of Genesareth

River Jordan south of the Lake of Genesareth

IN THE BALANCE

gleamed in the sunshine, the sun glittered on bright helmets and arms, while the trumpets sounded long solemn fanfares. Sacrificial smoke ascended about a statue of Jupiter from a temporary altar, and the priests chanted.

Then suddenly a procession moved into the square. Two oxen were dragging a plough right round it. The furrow lengthened slowly behind the sharp ploughshare. Finally the square was separated from the burnt streets of Jerusalem by the long thin furrow.

It was a symbolic action. It meant that henceforward the Temple was, as it were, cut off from the rest of the country. Never more should Israel build on the site where it had once worshipped its invisible God in the white Temple.

The next blow fell soon afterwards. Rufus made it known that a new imperial edict had prohibited circumcision. Historians have subsequently proved that the edict in itself was not directed against the Jews in particular. It was a link in an imperial policy which sought to put an end to the horrible castrations which clung to the Oriental religions like a black shadow. But previous Emperors, when taking similar measures, had as a rule made an exception for the Jews.

Circumcision was to the Jews the sign of the sacred pact between God and his people. The Jews therefore felt that the order was directed against the very essence of Israel's life. If it was to be carried out literally, it would simply mean the extermination of the Jewish people. And Rufus intended to force the edict through in all its rigour.

The country was wild with excitement, and everyone expected that Akiba would at last give the signal for the long-awaited rebellion. But he hesitated: the Messiah was nowhere to be seen, so the hour of the Lord could not have come.

Suddenly the Jews were given something else to think about. The travelling Emperor came to Syria, and from there he visited Judaea. The whole resistance movement went underground. It was no use thinking of war so long as the Emperor himself was in the country.

Great festivities were prepared for the Emperor and his

THE SON OF A STAR

retinue by the Roman authorities and the Gentiles in Palestine. Here too the Emperor's route can be followed with the help of the coins he left behind. And it can be stated that the journey must have taken place after 128. Hadrian is described on the coins as P.P., i.e. *Pater Patriae*, the Father of his Country, and it was just in the year 128 that the Senate conferred this title upon him.

On this journey he decided to rebuild Jerusalem himself. But the new city was not to bear the name of the old one: it was to be called Aelia Capitolina, Aelia after Hadrian's family name Aelius, Capitolina because the new city was to do honour to the Capitoline Jupiter in Rome and contain a temple dedicated to him. There may have been no real evil intention in these plans. Hadrian certainly did not understand what an insult he was offering to Israel, and what consequences would follow. But he found out.

So now the Jews were to see the Holy City rebuilt, but to become a Gentile city. Where Jehovah had received offerings from his priests, heathen priests would worship the Capitoline Jupiter, the personification of the Roman religion itself. Israel could not have been more grossly insulted.

What more was there to wait for? Jerusalem profaned and circumcision forbidden: the cup was full. Even the hesitant and the uncertain joined the ranks of the national liberation party.

But Akiba still delayed. First, as a matter of course, he had to wait till the Emperor had left the Orient and was on his way westward again. Hadrian moved on slowly to Egypt and undertook that trip up the Nile which brought him the tragic experience of Antinous' death. At last news was received in Palestine that the Emperor had left Egypt and was sailing back to Rome. This was in the year 132.

And then events began to move of themselves: even Akiba no longer had them under control. As always happens, there were small incidents to begin with. At many places in the country the resistance groups took the offensive and attacked soldiers of the Tenth Legion. Swift, hard blows—and then they

IN THE BALANCE

withdrew to their concealed bases and underground hiding-places.

The Romans underestimated the seriousness of the rebellion. Further, their most important base, Caesarea, was partly destroyed and out of use. Rufus certainly expected to be able to quench the sparks with the troops he had on the spot. But he was mistaken. Time after time small Roman detachments were wiped out by the furious Jews. And the rebels' first successes naturally encouraged their countrymen, so that the fire spread, and the whole country would soon be ablaze.

And then Akiba suddenly came into action. He received the sign for which he had been waiting so long. The Messiah had come! The Son of a Star was proclaimed Messiah by Akiba. The decisive weight fell heavily into the balance, and the scale shot down. The great war began.

X

THE SON OF A STAR

THE man for whom Rabbi Akiba had been longing and waiting so fervently was called Simeon. This name is found on many of the coins struck in the three and a half years in which he was master of Judaea. It is now known from a letter written by himself which was found as recently as 1952, and of which more will be said later, that his full name was Simeon ben Koseba, son of Koseba. His enemies turned the name into Ben Koziba, the son of lies, but his friends called him Bar Kochba, a Hebrew word which means Son of a Star.

Interesting as it is to have light thrown on this formerly insoluble problem of his name, we would much rather have heard about his childhood and development through youth up to the great day when he came to the front. But all this is wrapped in obscurity: the only thing known is that he was of royal family and was descended from David himself. This satisfied the preliminary condition for his emergence: the Messiah was to be a shoot of David's tree.

While the tension in the country was growing and becoming wellnigh unbearable, Simeon was one of the first to take direct action against the Tenth Legion. He quickly attracted attention by his successful execution of daring coups for which both cunning and good fortune were needed. He challenged fate again and again, and always came out on top.

It was said that Simeon could run a Roman mile, a legend which probably has some basis in fact. It was a way of expressing admiration of his speed. The secret of his victories was his

THE SON OF A STAR

mobility, which always enabled him to appear where he was least expected. Other great commanders have worked on the same lines. Bonaparte said in his Italian campaign that he would rather beat the enemy by tiring his soldiers' legs than by shedding their blood.

It was not long before Simeon became a popular figure, and all kinds of fantastic stories began to circulate. He was so strong that no one could stand up against him. Once the heavy stone from a Roman catapult struck him on both knees: but the stone flew back and struck down those who had discharged it! And he could spit fire from his mouth when fighting against the Gentiles!

He was the hero whose name was on everyone's lips, and eyes sparkled when Simeon's name was mentioned. He became the personification of the liberation movement in Israel, and crowds gathered round him when he suddenly appeared in the villages with his band of brave men.

But there was one place in Israel where the stories of Simeon's exploits were followed with the keenest attention. Old Akiba collected all the reports which flowed in; he interrogated eye-witnesses and shut himself up to ponder and pray in solitude. What could it all mean? Could it be . . . ? He felt that the great hour was approaching. And one day the scales fell from his eyes. He rose and sent a message to Simeon summoning him to what would be a decisive meeting.

Simeon set off one day in early spring. As far as can be ascertained it was in February, just when winter is ebbing. A bright spring sun was shining, the peasants were out ploughing the fields softened by the late rains, and the very first signs of spring, little red anemones, were sprouting along the roadsides. And both Akiba and Simeon felt that in more than one way spring and summer were at hand for Israel.

All the roads swarmed with armed men: the army of the Son of a Star was on the move. They did not need to take any special security precautions. All the countryside in Judaea belonged to them: the Tenth Legion had withdrawn behind the ramparts of its strongholds.

THE SON OF A STAR

And there he came in person, Simeon, the Son of a Star, equipped with sword and shield and helmet, with his great black beard and a pair of dark eyes which were keen and sharp and yet full of laughter and delight in his triumph. With his highest officers at his side he strode into the circle of Israel's dignitaries, the seventy-five from Jabneh who sat there with Akiba in their midst. Simeon made a deep bow to the leading man in Israel. Then he drew himself up, fixed his dark, burning eyes on the rabbi and waited to hear what he had to say.

He saw an old man with long white hair and beard, with pale cheeks and deep wrinkles from much brooding: a frail, bent ancient. Akiba was 114 years old that day.

But then Akiba drew himself up to his full height, and the authority which emanated from him in the greatest moment of his life was manifest to all. People had collected in thousands from all sides: learned teachers and young women and rough Jewish soldiers from up in the mountains. There was a hum of voices, but dead silence followed when Akiba lifted his hand and began to speak. All eyes hung upon his lips in expectation of what they felt must happen.

He began slowly and formally, quoting a few old Biblical phrases in Hebrew:

'There shall come a Star out of Jacob, and a Sceptre shall rise out of Israel.'

Everyone knew Balaam's prophecy of the future that awaited the chosen people. And when Akiba continued, the whole audience said the words with him. The sacred words resounded from all sides like a torrent bursting a dam.

Akiba fell silent, and the huge crowd stood quivering with anticipation. It had dawned on them that the old rabbi had found a mysterious connection between the promise of the star of Jacob and the Son of a Star's name.

Then Akiba began to talk in the usual Aramaic language, and now came his message. He gave himself plenty of time and spoke at length of the sufferings of Israel and of the heathen who had dared to lay the Lord's temple desolate and hold his people

THE SON OF A STAR

in bondage. He himself was old enough to have seen Jerusalem in its glory. And now they were to see these foreigners build a temple in the Holy City for the false god from Rome, and deny the Lord's people the sign of their pact with him. He described his own ponderings and hesitations, but declared in fiery words that now the Lord had lighted up the road and raised up the man who would lead Israel on to victory and greatness.

Then, pointing to Simeon, he uttered the portentous words: 'Here is the king, he who shall come, Messiah!'

The ten thousand stood as still as the flame of a candle. A blue sunny sky arched itself over the brown spring landscape. A westerly breeze swept in cool and fresh from the sea and stirred Simeon's great beard. This was the only movement then, when for a few seconds even hearts had ceased to beat.

Then the rabbi went slowly over to Simeon, who knelt down before him. A servant held a jug of holy oil, and Akiba anointed Simeon, as Samuel had once anointed Saul and David, kings of Israel. Then he bade the King rise and led him to the throne.

And when the anointed King, the Messiah, had taken his seat, a storm of cheering broke out. Through generation after generation these feelings and longings had been dammed up, like a brook which cannot find an outlet. But now the moment of liberation had come. A violent storm seemed to sweep over the multitude as it hailed the Son of a Star and swore to be faithful to him. And from that day he stood at the head of his people and led them out into their last bitter struggle.

But amid the jubilation there were some who were silent. They withdrew hurriedly from the singing multitude, with pale cheeks and fear in their eyes. And when Akiba returned to Jabneh, one after another of the best men in the nation came and spoke to him bitterly. For they doubted. How could he have proclaimed the Messiah on so slender a foundation? Who had given him a right to proclaim the Son of a Star on behalf of Israel as the expected king? It was a hasty and ill-considered step, they said, and there was some outspoken discussion between them and Akiba. In the course of one of these disputes one of the best-known teachers in the country said to Akiba:

'Akiba, grass will grow on your cheeks before he becomes the Messiah!'

But for Akiba the dice were cast, the last doubt in his mind had been swept away. And those who have become acquainted with his personality will understand that he could not have acted otherwise than he had done. Throughout his long life he had moved forward step by step to this hour of destiny.

And to the masses of the people Akiba's proclamation was a rousing fanfare. Everyone believed that what this stood for came from God in heaven. The war, therefore, was not primarily political, like the great war against Titus. They had fought then because war broke out of itself. And then they had clung to the hope that God would intervene and at last give his people victory. But the Son of a Star's war was religious. The spiritual chief of Israel had consecrated it at the outset and pointed out the King the people had been dreaming of and praying for for centuries, God's own emissary, his Anointed, the Messiah!

The news of the event flew to distant countries, and it awakened a sensation in the scattered Jewish colonies. Many volunteers set out for the land of their fathers to offer their help and their swords in the great war. They walked for great distances to get home, in large and small parties. The rising against Trajan was fresh in their memories: here was an opportunity to avenge all those who had been killed in it. And the great hour had struck.

But this time as before there was no great combined *levée en masse* of the Jews in the dispersion and the other oppressed peoples. The Orient was still paralysed from the hard blows it had suffered. The Son of a Star's proclamation did not catch on among the leading men as it did in Judaea. The Jews in the homeland were left to stand alone.

This did not mean that Simeon was short of men. Legend even tells us of the hard test to which he put those who applied to enter the army. They were to give proof of their bravery and toughness by cutting off the little fingers of their left hands.

THE SON OF A STAR

But, the legend continues, the wise men of Israel sent him a message reproaching him.

'How long will you continue to mutilate Israel?'

But Simeon replied: 'Then how can I prove who is worthy to serve in my army?'

The wise men said: 'Any man who from horseback can pull up a cedar of Lebanon by the roots, is strong enough to be a soldier in Israel's army.'

Thus, the legend concludes, Simeon got 200,000 men with no little fingers on their left hands, and 200,000 who could pull cedar trees up by the roots when riding past them!

Simeon's prayer to the Lord when he went into battle is of a piece with these hard tests he imposed:

'Lord of the world, if thou wilt not help me, at any rate do not help the enemy. Then I shall conquer!'

These are the few glimpses we get of Simeon's personality. Really nothing more is known of him. But they indicate a rough, strong man, merciless to the enemy and bold and fierce in battle.

This was quite another Messiah from him whom the prophets had depicted and promised: neither faith in God nor spirituality can be detected in him. But he must have had them. Otherwise a spiritual leader like Rabbi Akiba would never have championed him. The fact is that his portrait has only come down to us damaged by weather and painted over by the ill-will and hatred of later times. And the hard war against Rome called for a man of steel, if there was to be even the smallest hope of victory in the unequal contest.

But it goes without saying that in any case there was one group in Jerusalem which most emphatically refused to take part in the war or to recognize the Son of a Star as the Messiah. These were the Christians. For them the Messiah had come already, so there could never be any other. And the Son of God they believed in and worshipped was of quite a different type from this hard, severe soldier. He was the meek king, and he had promised that 'the meek shall inherit the earth'. They turned away from Simeon in disgust. Of course, they did not help the

THE SON OF A STAR

heathen Romans, but neither did they fight alongside their countrymen.

Simeon punished them severely and cruelly. It was a conflict between fire and water. The fathers of the Church, among others the historian Eusebius of Caesarea, tell of it. And as it was they who wrote the Son of a Star's obituary it is not surprising that it contained many negative features.

But there are other sources, and imperishable ones, which tell their own silent story—the many coins from that time. They bear Simeon's name, and date from the first or second year after the liberation of Jerusalem. They have emblems on the reverse side—a palm or wreath, a bunch of grapes, a lyre or two trumpets. Many of them are old Roman coins which have been stamped afresh: Trajan's or Hadrian's faces can be seen under the Hebrew letters. They lie in one's hand, dumb witnesses to a time when Hebrew culture was able to efface the hard features of the Roman Emperors.

As late as 1952, quite unexpectedly, fresh and tangible evidence from the Son of a Star's days came to light. Not far from Khirbet Qumran, on the shore of the Dead Sea, where the sensational discovery of scrolls was made, and there is a ruined monastery which has remarkable news to tell of Israel two thousand years ago, archaeologists came upon the so-called Murraba'at caves. And here the find was made.

Among very many other interesting things a man suddenly came upon several letters written on papyrus which can certainly be dated from Israel's last bloody insurrection against Rome. They say that they were written 'after the liberation of Jerusalem by Simeon ben Koseba, the Prince of Israel'. But still more exciting is the fact that two of these letters were written by the Son of a Star himself. He had stationed a post in the inaccessible clefts at Murraba'at, and these are dispatches to its commander, Jeshua ben Gilgola by name. The text of the most illuminating of them is as follows:

'From Simeon ben Koseba to Jeshua ben Gilgola and the men of your company, peace! I call Heaven to witness against you that if you do not break off communication with the

THE SON OF A STAR

Galileans, all of whom you have saved, I will put your feet in chains as I did with Ben Aflul.' The letter is signed 'Simeon ben Koseba'.

Naturally the experts have flung themselves upon this document and endeavoured to squeeze the last drop of information from it. It will be perceived at once that it gives authoritative information as to the Son of a Star's name: it was Simeon ben Koseba. The text and signature do not appear to have been written by the same hand: the Son of a Star dictated it to a secretary and only signed it. This secretary was presumably one of his officers: the writing shows that he was not a professional amanuensis, for the lines are not quite straight and the letters uncertainly formed, but the spelling is correct, so he was an educated man.

The dispatch, as is seen, is an order to the commander at Murraba'at—no one knows what the place was called in those times—about some people called 'Galileans' whom he had previously saved from danger. His friendly intercourse with them is to cease: otherwise he can expect the same severe punishment as Ben Aflul, who has evidently been guilty of the same offence.

But who can these Galileans have been? One thinks at once of the Jewish Christians, who at any rate later were called Galileans. If this theory is right, here is further evidence of the Son of a Star's severity towards the Jewish Christians, who, as is known, stood coldly aside and whom he regarded as a kind of fifth column.

But it is not quite certain that this is the meaning of the letter: the text is not clear in certain places, and perhaps the passage about the Galileans ought to be read as follows: 'I take Heaven to witness that, if anyone has trouble with the Galileans whom you have saved, I will put their feet in chains.' If this is the correct text, it appears that there were both Galileans and Judaeans in the garrison, and that the unhappy tension between north and south in Israel, which cleft the kingdom in two, just after King Solomon's reign, was still smouldering even now in the country's hour of need. But the

THE SON OF A STAR

Son of a Star could not afford to have any cleavage in his army, and sought to crush it by brutal threats.

These are only one or two glimpses through the fog. But they may be indications that more is to come. It is possible that some day much more will emerge from the caves in the Judaean desert that will throw light on the great drama once played out there.

'The second year after the liberation of Jerusalem.'

Such an inscription indicates that fortune smiled on Simeon for some years. And the legends give us an idea of the fronts the war was fought on. As usual, the Romans had little understanding of Jewish customs and trampled brutally on their feelings. They paid dearly for it.

One of the old stories of the war says that it came to the King's Mountain because of a cock and hen! It was customary to carry a cock and a hen in front of a bridal pair when they went to the bridegroom's house. They were there to remind the young couple to be fruitful and multiply like fowls. But a party of Roman soldiers attacked a bridal pair on the King's Mountain and stole the two birds. The whole bridal party replied by attacking the Roman legionaries and striking them down.

And the axle of a cart brought the war to Beth-ter. There it had from old times been customary to plant a cedar when a boy was born, and a pine when the child was a girl. When they grew up, and there was to be a wedding, the two trees were felled and the posts of the bridal canopy made from them.

One day a Roman lady of fashion came driving by in her carriage. One of the axles broke, and she ordered her men to fell a cedar which stood by the road. It was one of the cedars which were shortly to be used for a young man's wedding.

When the Jews who were near by saw this new outrage, they collected and fell upon the Romans, killing the lady of fashion and her attendants. Roman troops were sent out to punish the presumptuous people. And soon the war was raging round Beth-ter as well.

THE SON OF A STAR

By the King's Mountain the highlands of Judaea are meant. But the situation of Beth-ter is a problem which will be dealt with later. The mountains of Judah were the heart of the country, and of course the rebels delivered their first blow there. And fortune was with them. The ruined city of Jerusalem was freed, but obviously could not be used as a capital in its devastated condition.

The movement swept over the country like a storm wind. In towns and villages everywhere the population rose and cut down their hated enemies, while Simeon's detachments of regular troops pushed forward and soon had liberated most of the country. Only a few strong points remained in Roman hands. It is stated that the Jews captured in all 50 fortresses and 985 villages. Simeon may have extended his campaign beyond the frontier and threatened the Romans in Syria.

One thing is certain: the Romans had not expected a rising on so vast a scale. They had noticed no doubt that the country was in a ferment, but had counted on the scattered detachments of the Tenth Legion being enough to suppress any trouble. After all, the despised Jews had been smitten to the ground again and again for many, many years. They must surely have learnt by degrees that they could not rise against Rome unpunished.

But the governor Tineius Rufus soon discovered that he was not master of the situation. One after another of his detachments was cut up. The Tenth Legion was practically wiped out. Some miserable fragments had slipped over the Syrian frontier, behind which they would have to be thoroughly reorganized, and a few cohorts were shut up behind the protecting walls of Caesarea. Caesarea could be held because its sea communications were still intact.

Express messengers in quick succession went off over the sea to Rome and reported the serious calamity which was again threatening in the always dangerous and restless Orient. When the Emperor had visited his Jewish provinces a little while before, the whole atmosphere was peaceful and there was no sign of danger. But now the country was ablaze.

THE SON OF A STAR

When Hadrian realized the scale of the insurrection, he took determined measures and dispatched reinforcements. One legion after another which lay in distant garrisons was notified of the emergency and sent eastward by forced marches. The names of some of Hadrian's generals who led these troops are known, and they were counted among the world's finest commanders.

But a number of striking pieces of evidence are available, which enable us to follow Hadrian's great troop movements in these years.

When Roman officers fell in battle and were buried, their comrades erected in their memory columns on which the officer's name, rank and unit were carved. But there were other occasions on which officers erected monuments. If, for example, one or two officers were promoted or enjoyed special marks of favour from the Emperor, they often joined forces and had a column carved in the Emperor's honour. This too had their names and units inscribed on it. Curiously enough—and fortunately for research into the Jewish-Roman war in Hadrian's reign—this custom was especially popular at the time when the Son of a Star rebelled against Rome. Tombstones and monuments of this kind have been found both in Palestine and in the remotest regions of the Empire.

To collect and compare these many inscriptions, and discover where the legions were brought from, and what routes they followed to reach the threatened front, is like sitting over a puzzle. One or two examples will show what I mean.

The Tenth Legion has set its stamp on Palestine: the country teemed with inscriptions referring to this famous unit, and when the Jews rose again it had to take the first blow. But inscriptions have been found in Palestine referring to three other whole legions which were flung into battle there, the Third Gallic, the Third Cyrenaic and the Fourth Scythian. And much more than this is known.

A tribune was serving in his legion where Vienna is today. His name was Sextus Attius Senecio, and a memorial stone records that he was ordered to Palestine. On the Roman Wall in

THE SON OF A STAR

the north of England the prefect Attius Marcus Statius was ordered to move with his detachment. Two centurions, Gaius Valerius Prudens and Marcus Ulpius Leontius, belonged to the Fifth Macedonian Legion, which was doing garrison duty on the banks of the Danube. It too went to the front in Palestine. Many other examples could be quoted.

All these inscriptions taken together form a picture which shows clearly how serious a threat this new war was in the Emperor's eyes. He was obliged to bring up reinforcements from North Africa, from Central Europe, indeed from far-off England. Not for nothing does a Roman historian who describes the war say that 'the whole earth seemed to tremble'. The insurrection was developing into a political event of the first rank.

The Roman army was a formidable instrument of war. It had developed from the experiences of many centuries of both war and peace and had been moulded into a form and given a strength which had enabled Rome to dominate the whole civilized world.

In Hadrian's time the army consisted of thirty legions, and each legion was a unit of immense striking power. A legion contained ten cohorts, which in turn were divided into sub-sections commanded by tribunes and centurions. The first cohort, which guarded the legion's eagle standard, was the smartest and was 1,105 men strong: in it the crack troops were collected. The other cohorts were each 555 men strong. The total strength of a legion was 6,100.

The soldiers wore cuirass, helmet and shield and were armed with spear and sword. A battle began with the flinging of spears, after which the legionaries came to close quarters with the enemy and attacked him with the two-edged sword, which was equally suited to stabbing and cutting. The legion usually attacked in an order of battle which was eight ranks deep. The legions also disposed of cavalry and numerous, more lightly armed auxiliary troops.

The army was an enlisted army, and the soldiers received high pay. They took an oath never to desert the colours, to obey their officers and to be willing to sacrifice their lives for the

THE SON OF A STAR

Emperor. Discipline was so severe that it was commonly said that a real soldier was more afraid of his officers than of the enemy. The oath of loyalty was renewed every January 1st after a religious ceremony; and the army as a whole was permeated with religion. Sacrifice was made to the gods every day in a special tent which always accompanied the legion, and in which the eagles were kept. Tacitus calls the eagles war gods. Worship of the Emperor was of course the central point of the legion's religious services.

The legions were trained so hard that they were always at the summit of physical fitness. And they needed all their strength when they marched off, each man carrying his own immensely heavy kit. The heavy war engines too had to be carried from place to place, the catapults and the terrible battering-rams which were run up against the enemy's walls to make them collapse.

This mighty army had immense significance not only in war, but also in peace. Wherever the soldiers went, and in particular wherever they were stationed in their many years of garrison duty, they brought Roman civilization with them. They made roads and bridges, they built towns round their permanent camps. It was through them that the conquered countries were Romanized, so that to this day they bear their Latin stamp in speech, culture and origin.

A number of these dreaded legions were now being marched by Hadrian in all haste through Europe and Asia Minor to assemble in strength to defeat the Son of a Star's army. Detachments came marching down all the roads, and the Mediterranean was covered with ships of the imperial fleet carrying troops by sea to Syria. There they were concentrated before being thrown in at critical points on the front in Palestine.

Nevertheless, in the first two or three years the Romans suffered defeat after defeat. The reports which reached Rome were more and more alarming. As always happens when the fortune of war favours a people, the Jews' success widened in scope. Many doubters decided to follow the victors, and Rome saw herself deserted by former collaborators and quislings, who

14. Lake of Genesareth

Mountain of Beatitudes

15. *Ancient coins:* (1) *Bronze, Vespasian's head, inscription:* Judaea Capta; (2) *Jewish silver coin from Bar Kochba's rebellion, inscription:* 'Simeon' *and* 'Liberation of Jerusalem'

THE SON OF A STAR

found it wisest to adhere to the stronger side. It is said that people of this kind, when the prohibition of circumcision was issued, underwent painful operations to remove this physical sign that they belonged to the despised Jewish people. Now they had the operation done over again, but the other way round!

The Emperor gradually realized that all the efforts made so far had been fruitless and that something extraordinary must be done. In remote Britain, on one of the most disturbed frontiers of the empire, was Rome's greatest general, Julius Severus. He was ordered to go to Palestine and take over the command of all the Roman troops in the Army of the East. The prefect, Attius Marcus Statius, whose column has been found on the Wall on the frontier of Scotland, and who went to the Orient with his detachment, may possibly have been in command of the general's escort on his way down and across Europe.

When Severus arrived after his forced march, the scene changed. A survey of the situation showed him that in open fighting the Jews had all the advantages on their side. They could withdraw to their inaccessible mountains, where they hid themselves in clefts or had underground passages which were easy to defend and enabled them to disappear quickly and turn up again at other points. And they could take the Romans in the rear and cut their communications if they advanced in large compact formations.

He therefore gave orders that all open fighting and troop movements on a large scale were to be avoided. He chose instead to fight the Jews with their own tactics. The Romans by rapid movements roped off small sectors of Jewish territory. These were besieged and the troops inside starved out. When they were completely exhausted the Romans, who themselves could all the time obtain reinforcements and supplies from Syria, attacked.

Gradually, by numerous small coups, they had cut the Jews off into separate groups, which they then overcame one by one. These tactics required time and patience, but they were profitable. Simeon's army suffered defeat after defeat, minor perhaps, but taken together so serious that the final catastrophe drew

THE SON OF A STAR

ever nearer. Final defeat and ruin now loomed ahead with inexorable certainty.

But Simeon still possessed one strong point, the town which he had made the administrative centre of liberated Judaea, and which now, when Jerusalem lay in ruins, was the Jewish capital, the strong fortress of Beth-ter. Here he gradually collected his defeated troops to fight the last desperate battle.

A Roman army on the march was a fine, regularly working machine. Everything was done automatically by cut and dried rules, every generation had had its experiences and handed them down to the next. At last everything had been thoroughly tested, and the result was perfection.

This was seen, for example, every evening, when the legions halted and camp was pitched. Roman camps always looked the same. The tents stood in lines on a definite system: the general's was always on the same spot, the different detachments had their fixed places, and certain elements erected the outworks which protected the camp against a night attack.

If the army was halting for a single night, the system was fairly simple. If it was to remain for several days, it was more complicated. And the permanent camps, which the army garrisoned perhaps for several years, were like fortified towns. In them there was everything for which there was use in the daily life of the army—armourers, apothecaries, and supply depots, workshops and ordinary shops of every kind.

A 'winter camp', as it was called, developed like this into a cultural centre, from which the superior Roman culture exercised a profound influence on the whole district. To this day place-names recall that a town grew up round one of these camps: for example Cassel in Germany, whose name comes from the Latin *castra*, and the many English place-names ending in 'castle', 'caster' or 'cester'. The name Cologne comes from the Latin word *colonia*, a stable form of Roman settlement round a camp. The Romans called a camp of this kind also *castra vetera*. A knowledge of these matters is necessary to anyone setting out to find the now disappeared Beth-ter in Palestine.

THE SON OF A STAR

In the mountains of Galilee, north of Nazareth, there was once a large and flourishing town called Sepphoris: today a dirty little Arab village is all that is left of this once brilliant centre. The town was populous and was well situated for commerce and general prosperity. It lay well protected on the top of a mountain, but close by both to southward and to westward were large fertile valleys. In several eras Sepphoris is named as being the chief town of Galilee, in hot competition with Tiberias.

Like all towns in Galilee, Sepphoris had a mixed population: not only Jews lived there, but a strong Gentile element set a special stamp on the place. And the good economic conditions enjoyed for many years, combined with the active Gentile influence, made the people of Sepphoris materialists: many of them forgot their Jewish origin and fatherland.

This was seen when in the year 67 Vespasian moved in across the frontier of Galilee to crush the great rebellion. No sooner was he in the neighbourhood of Sepphoris than the inhabitants sent a deputation to his headquarters, offering to surrender the town and begging for a Roman garrison to protect them against vengeance from the rebels.

Vespasian grasped the hand stretched out to him and established at Sepphoris a *castra vetera*, which remained there right up to the time of Simeon's insurrection. Ever since Vespasian's days, Sepphoris, with its Roman camp and Romanized inhabitants, had been a thorn in Israel's flesh.

Whereabouts in Palestine Beth-ter was situated is a question that has been deeply pondered over, and an old story of how its inhabitants cheered when they heard of the fall of Jerusalem has been found incomprehensible. When the place later became so patriotic that Simeon made it his capital and defended it to the last man, it does seem undeniably strange that the catastrophe of the year 70 should have caused the inhabitants to set lights in their windows.

But these speculations are unnecessary, for a little consideration makes it clear that the town's failure to mourn the national disaster is not in the least surprising. The whole of this much discussed problem has a very simple solution. The Hebrew 'b' is pronounced as 'v', and it was the Jews' habit, when they spoke of *castra vetera*, to leave out the first word and content themselves with *vetera*, which was then shortened to *veter*. If 'v' is now replaced by 'b', the word becomes Beter. In the course of time this process was forgotten, and the name assumed a more Hebrew form and became Beth-ter, 'beth' meaning house. Thus Beth-ter is the same as the old chief town of Galilee, Sepphoris.

This important town was bound to be one of Simeon's first objectives, especially as with its Roman garrison it would be a drawn sword pointed at the heart of liberated Judaea. He therefore ordered his army to advance on Sepphoris and captured it: presumably the Jews annihilated the Roman defenders. And so Simeon obtained, far to the north in the heart of Galilee, his stronghold and place of refuge, where he fought his last desperate battle.

The siege of Beth-ter was long and difficult. The Jews defended themselves fiercely. They knew that Beth-ter was the last fence between themselves and complete ruin. A few dim legends are still extant which afford fleeting glimpses of the course of the battle and its tragic end. We are given to understand that the fall of Beth-ter was due to treachery.

The foremost of the spiritual leaders who stimulated the Jews' will to resist was the old Rabbi Eleazar of Modin. He was bowed with age and exhausted by long fasts. But every day he was seen, clad in sackcloth and ashes, standing on the ramparts to instil fresh courage into the soldiers. Here, too, he offered his daily prayers. The soldiers felt that so long as he was among them they had a pledge that God was with them.

In the Roman camp impatience at such stubborn defence was beginning to show itself. Several times indeed the Romans were on the point of raising the siege. It seemed quite objectless to remain sitting before those walls that never could be stormed.

But one day the Roman commander received a visit from some Samaritans, who always hated the Jews and grudged them

THE SON OF A STAR

any success. They told the general that what mattered was to get rid of Eleazar. As long as that cock went on crowing Beth-ter would hold out. And one of them confided to the general a plan he had made. The general accepted the idea and sent the Samaritan away.

The Samaritan had discovered a secret underground passage which led right under the ramparts into Beth-ter. By this he entered the town. Eleazar stood on the ramparts, as usual absorbed in prayer. The Samaritan went up to him and pretended to be whispering something in his ear. The guards were alarmed when they saw an unknown man, a stranger, whispering secrets to Eleazar: they seized him and took him to Simeon's headquarters. Simeon interrogated him and asked what he had to say to Eleazar. But the Samaritan, carrying out his plan boldly, only replied:

'It is a secret. The Roman general commissioned me to give him a message. Why should I tell you what it was? If I tell you, the Romans will kill me. If I do not, you can kill me. You see, whatever I do it will cost me my life.'

The trick succeeded. Simeon was violently agitated at the idea that Eleazar could be a traitor, and sent for him. But the old man, absorbed in his devotions, had not noticed the Samaritan. He had nothing to say, but only looked astonished.

Simeon was beside himself with rage. He began to kick the old man in blind fury. The end of it was that Eleazar collapsed and died. And—the legend concludes—at the same moment a voice from heaven announced that now Simeon had paralysed Israel's arm and blinded its eyes, and that the same would happen to him as to Eleazar. And a few days later the Romans stormed Beth-ter.

How much, if any reality lies behind this legend? There are two things which, taken together, tell us why Beth-ter fell.

There may be something behind the talk of the secret underground passage which was known to the Samaritan. It is known from other sources that the Romans received intelligence of this kind of communication, through which the defenders

THE SON OF A STAR

remained in touch with the world outside and got fresh supplies. The assailants may have penetrated into Beth-ter by such a passage revealed to them by traitors.

But the story has a more important bearing. It tells of inner disunion, of a breach between Simeon and a spiritual leader. When there was a cleavage between Simeon, the strong warrior and hot-headed hero, and the real Israel, inspired by old-time faith and spiritual force, the end had come.

We see in a flash the tragic end of this development in Simeon's life. The sword prevailed over the spirit. And this meant ruin.

The Romans stormed Beth-ter and a fearful massacre ensued. All the inhabitants and soldiers were put to the sword: not a single one escaped. The Romans were so furious that they forbade the Jews who survived in the country round about to bury their fallen compatriots. The corpses lay and fertilized the fields or were piled up as walls round confiscated vineyards.

The Romans had had to use all their resources. They did not win the war till it had lasted three and a half years. It started at the beginning of the year 132, and Beth-ter fell on the 9th Ab (in August) of 135, the same day on which Jerusalem had fallen twice. The Romans had had such heavy losses that Hadrian, in his report to the Senate on the victory, omitted the words which ordinarily concluded such announcements:

'If things go well with you and your children, all is well. With me and the army things go well.' There are times when silence is more eloquent than many words.

Simeon fell in the battle. His body was found with the head cut off. When it was brought to the Emperor, he perceived that a snake had wound itself round the dead body, and burst out:

'God himself must have smitten him, no man could have done it!'

Quite unconsciously, the Emperor had made the right funeral oration over the fallen hero. Everything had begun for him with such brilliant promise, but when he forgot the greatest thing of all, he fell.

XI

IN THE VALLEY OF THE SHADOW OF DEATH

A FEW scattered elements of the Son of a Star's army had escaped and sought shelter in the mountain caverns where they had started the insurrection years before. They had saved only their lives, but how were they to get away? The Romans had set posts all round the mountains; all the ways out were barred, and they had nothing to eat.

It came to such a pitch that they began to devour their fallen comrades. An old story says that each man in turn had to go out and search for this horrible food. One day a young soldier found his father's body. He hid it under some stones and put a mark so that he could find it later and give his father decent burial. When he returned to his companions he lied, saying:

'I could not find anything to eat today.'

So they had no food all that day, but the next day another man went out. Unfortunately he came upon the temporary grave which concealed the corpse of his comrade's father. He cut some pieces out of the dead body and brought them home to the cave. When they had eaten, the son asked:

'Where did you find the dead man?'

His comrade explained where he had gone and what the ground there was like. The son, seized by a terrible presentiment, cried:

'Was the spot marked in any way?'

'Yes, it was,' the other man said, and described what he had seen.

THE SON OF A STAR

'Wretched am I,' the son groaned: 'I have eaten my father's body.'

This macabre story is only one of many, and horrible as it is, it has to be quoted to give a complete impression of the country after the defeat. Old Jewish tradition abounds in grisly stories relating to the time after the fall of Beth-ter.

It has much to say also about Roman hard-heartedness and faithlessness. A herald promised a safe conduct to all who voluntarily emerged from their hiding-places. Some were thoughtless enough to trust the promise. They assembled in the Valley of Rimmon, a place rich in tradition, where the rebellion had once been on the point of breaking out. And the Romans surrounded them. According to legend Hadrian gave this order:

'By the time I have finished eating this leg of chicken they must all be dead!'

And his order was carried out.

Like Titus, who had destroyed the Temple, Hadrian was pursued by the Jews' inexorable hatred. His name is never mentioned in Jewish tradition without the addition of the words 'May his bones be broken!'

It will suffice to tell just one story of the many which were circulated about the detested Emperor. A Jew passed Hadrian and saluted him.

'Who are you?' asked Hadrian.

'A Jew,' was the reply.

'Take him away and cut his head off,' was the Emperor's order to his guard.

Soon afterwards another Jew passed, but without a salute.

'Who are you?' the Emperor asked again.

'A Jew.'

'Take him away and behead him.'

Some of Hadrian's councillors who had been present at the scene were bold enough to ask:

'How are the Jews to behave to you? If they salute you, it costs them their lives. And if they do not, then too they are killed.'

Other stories were told of the innumerable prisoners who

THE SHADOW OF DEATH

fell into the Romans' hands. They were collected at the two great markets, one at Gaza and one under Abraham's tamarisk at Hebron. The price of slaves slumped: the supply altogether outran the demand. A slave could be bought for the same price as a horse. Many were not sold. These were taken to Egypt. They were made to suffer terribly on the journey, and thousands were so fortunate as to be freed by death from further misery.

But despite all this a good many Jews got out of the country and made in particular for Babylonia, one of the countries which were now free from the Roman yoke, and one in which they had many compatriots. They were gradually absorbed into the life of the Jewish community there, and their descendants lived on there for many centuries.

For the Romans the war was a war of extermination, in which all Jews were to be annihilated. And they did not limit their persecution to human beings: the whole country was laid waste. The towns were destroyed, the villages burnt to the ground: even fruit trees and vines were cut down. Galilee had once been famous for its olive trees and abundant production of oil. After the war there was not a single olive in the whole province.

The Jews were to be exterminated in Palestine and the country completely Romanized. The final result of this process was the imperial city Aelia Capitolina, where Jerusalem had once stood. It was the plans for this Roman and heathen town to replace the old Holy City that had started the insurrection. During the war it had of course been impossible to do anything. Nor had the Jews been able to rebuild Jerusalem in the three or four years they had occupied its ruins: the war had required all their attention. But now the Romans crowned their victory by building their own city in place of Jerusalem.

The city was purely heathen, built on the Greek model and provided with market-places and temples. Where the altar of Jehovah had stood a statue of Hadrian on horseback bulked large: on the site of the old Temple the Temple of Jupiter rose, and the Capitoline Jupiter was the guardian deity of the place. But the coins from Aelia Capitolina bear the images of other gods who were worshipped—Bacchus, Serapis, Castor and

THE SON OF A STAR

Pollux. Only a hundred years later the revolution was so thorough that a Christian, who was being interrogated by the governor in a foreign country and mentioned Jerusalem, found that the Roman official did not know any town of that name.

To complete the transformation, Hadrian forbade any Jew to come within sight of the city: the penalty for disobedience to the order was death. A barrier, the crossing of which was a matter of life and death, was to be set up between the people and the place where it had once worshipped the invisible God. Not till long afterwards did the Jews receive permission to visit the city on their national day of mourning, the 9th Ab, and weep over the ruined walls. And it was as late in time as the domination of Islam that the Jews were once more given access to their ancient Holy City. And today the name Aelia Capitolina in turn is so completely forgotten that only specialists in ancient history know it.

But Hadrian was shrewd enough to understand that if he wanted to destroy Judaism a crushing blow must be dealt at its religion. He knew well that the kernel of Judaism had always been its belief in the Lord. Therefore he issued a series of edicts which were intended automatically to obliterate the Jewish religion in Palestine. The old prohibition of circumcision was maintained and so strictly enforced that certain circles among the Jews found it indefensible to contract new marriages. Why carry the race on, when the sign of the pact with God could not be handed down to the coming generation?

But new prohibitions rained down steadily on the Jews who still lived in the country. It was forbidden to read the Tora, to keep holy the Sabbath, to wear phylacteries, to put the mezuzza on the door-post, and to celebrate marriages on Wednesdays. There are even traces of an ordinance giving the local Roman commandant, after a Jewish wedding, the *jus primae noctis*, the right to the first night with the bride! Not for nothing did Jewish tradition call this era of severity 'the time of danger'.

The Romans attached special importance to the closing of theological schools and the stopping of teaching by the rabbis.

THE SHADOW OF DEATH

The rabbis received strict orders not to study the Tora and, in particular, not to instruct others in Jewish doctrine and customs. This was a deadly blow at Judaism. And a strict control was established to see that these edicts were observed.

It is horrible to read that the Romans had renegade Jews to help them. The Roman authorities themselves knew so very little about the exclusive Jewish religion that they could not effectively keep an eye on the rabbis and the masses. They therefore attached twice their normal value to the quislings they could get to work for them. Notoriety was obtained in this way by a certain Elisa Ben Abuja, who was particularly dangerous. He had begun his career as a learned Jewish theologian, but during his training in mystical exercises his faith failed him and he went over to the Romans. Knowing Judaism from inside, he could look out for the right points. After he went over the Jews did not call him by his name, but contented themselves with the ominous term Acher, which means 'the other'.

This critical time produced great problems. The rabbis assembled at a secret meeting in Lydda. The discussions and the results attained were to be of classic importance for the next two thousand years, in which there were many similar eras of persecution.

The question was, which was the most important, the doctrine of the law or the carrying out of the law? Surely the former, for it was the preliminary condition for the latter. The rabbis, therefore, were obliged to keep on instructing steadily despite the risk they ran by doing so, but the people were to have extensive dispensations from many of the precepts to which special risk attached. There were some who went so far that they drew the line only at murder, impurity and idolatry. The prohibition of these three things was indispensable: everything else was of secondary importance.

When the Romans discovered these defence measures that the Jews had taken, they began to persecute on different lines. What seemed important to them now was not so much the keeping of desperate provisions of the law as the teaching of the rabbis.

THE SON OF A STAR

They even sought to make the existence of the rabbinate impossible by imposing the death penalty if the ancient custom of the laying on of hands at the ordination of new rabbis was observed. And not only would those taking part in the ceremony be punished, but the town or district in which the ordination took place was to be laid waste, and all the inhabitants killed. How, this being so, would the long succession of teachers acquire new and young blood?

Those times were never forgotten, and as in the Christian Church, which also was suffering hardships, legends sprang up and adorned the many graves like flowers. Most of the legends have no very sound historical background, but are worth hearing all the same. And the stories of Rabbi Akiba's death seem to be pretty well founded.

Rabbi Akiba had been the standard-bearer in Israel. It was he who led the people onward and summoned it to action at the moment he saw was the right one. And he had proclaimed the Son of a Star as the Messiah. It is obvious that this stiff-backed old man would never bow his neck to the foreign yoke. And despite all prohibitions and threats he went on quietly with his work as a teacher. His friends warned him, but Akiba told them a fable:

A fox was walking on the bank of a river and saw that the fish out in the water were swimming to and fro in a curious manner. He asked them: 'Why are you running away?'

And the fish replied: 'We are afraid of the nets men spread to catch us.'

'Then why don't you come up here on to the dry land?' asked the fox, licking his chops.

But the fish answered: 'Are you really the beast people call cunning? You don't deserve to be called so: you're stupid. Can't you understand that when we can't even feel ourselves safe in our natural element, we should be still less safe out of it? So we stay where we were made to be.'

For Akiba a life of study and the teaching of others was the element in which God had placed him. If it cost him his life to do what God meant him to do, so it must be. In no

THE SHADOW OF DEATH

circumstances could he think of transferring himself to any other element.

He was arrested and flung into prison. It was a long time before he was sentenced. Perhaps the Romans had the idea of keeping him in reserve for a triumphal procession. As far as is known, he did not die till the year 138.

It was a severe blow to the scattered members of the Sanhedrin when they could no longer seek counsel of the famous teacher. In old times, when he had been absent from a meeting of the Sanhedrin, the rabbis used to say: 'The law is away when Rabbi Akiba is not here!'

And now he had been brutally torn away from them and imprisoned. Every day brought new problems which they themselves found it hard to solve. But they hit on a way of getting in touch with Akiba and hearing his opinion. One of his disciples disguised himself as a pedlar and went past the windows of Akiba's prison with his wares. He pretended to be just crying his stock-in-trade, but he worked in among his cries little questions about theological problems.

'Needles and forks! Who wants good needles?' and then in a whisper: 'What about marriage with a dead brother's widow?'

Akiba quickly understood the situation and replied from his window:

'I'd like to buy a needle.' And he added in a low voice: 'It is lawful.'

Everyone in the prison respected the old man. It is said that even the great hater of the Jews, the governor Tineius Rufus, came to him several times and discussed religious questions.

Although he was in prison and soon to die, the learned theologian could not think of omitting any of his ritual customs. On the contrary, he gave to them quite special enthusiasm and meticulous care. He used the greater part of his scanty water ration to perform the ritual cleansings. He had hardly anything to drink.

When he was taken to the place of execution, he preserved his magnanimity and calm. Death by a process of refined cruelty awaited him. His flesh was slowly flayed from him with an iron comb. But in the middle of the horrible torture he remembered that it was time for prayer. All through his life every Jew declares his belief in the one God three times a day with the words: 'Hear, O Israel, the Lord thy God, the Lord is one!'

This belief accompanies the pious Jew all his life, and these are the last words which a dying man whispers.

Akiba got so far in his prayer. But at the word 'one' he drew out the syllable so long that his soul escaped from his body in the middle of it. He expired in the moment in which he declared his faith. His death was in keeping with his whole life. And it was never forgotten by the generations which followed him.

But Israel had many other heroes who stood up bravely for their faith under persecution. Tradition often returns to the story of 'the ten martyrs' who were put to death at the same time as Akiba.

There was Rabbi Hananiah, who was surprised as he sat reading his roll of the Tora. The soldiers asked how he dared disobey the imperial edict, but Hananiah replied that absolute obedience to God's law came before obedience to the Emperor. He was wrapped in the same roll of the law he had been reading, and tied to a stake. To prolong his sufferings damp fuel was used and wet wool was thrown between him and the flames. Hananiah was so much afraid of doing anything that could be regarded as suicide that he did not push it away, and so he suffered a slow and painful death.

Judah Ben Baba received later the appellation of 'the Pious'. He was particularly anxious about how the rabbinate was to be continued, and therefore taught a number of lads to be teachers. When they were to be ordained, he would not do it in an inhabited place for fear of the consequences for the people who lived there if the deed was discovered. So he took the young candidates out to a desolate spot, where he carried out the ceremonial laying on of hands and admitted them to the holy office of teacher.

Suddenly a party of Roman soldiers appeared: a traitor had been at work. They came too late to prevent the ordination,

THE SHADOW OF DEATH

but in time to punish Judah. He begged the newly initiated rabbis to flee, in order to guard their work for the future. He himself was too old to run away, so he contented himself with crying: 'Run, my children, run!'

'Yes, but what will become of you?' they asked in concern.

'Don't fear for me. I shall lie as insensible as a stone for them when they come,' the old man replied coolly and firmly.

And he looked without blinking an eyelid at the many spears which brought him down a few minutes later.

It was a great relief to the Christians in Palestine when the Son of a Star disappeared from the scene. They had endured persecution from his side because they had not taken part in his war. The Romans, in return for this, did not punish them, but, on the contrary, gave them permission to live in Aelia Capitolina.

It was indeed painful for the Christians to see heathendom spreading itself in their most sacred places. A temple to Venus was built where Christ's sepulchre had been, a statue of Jupiter was set up in the garden of the Resurrection: even Golgotha was profaned.

These profanations were probably not due to deliberate mockery. Hadrian's government did not persecute the Christian Church. But of course the Christians shuddered to see their most intimate feelings thus trodden under foot.

But the Church in Palestine grew up again quickly after the disturbance caused by the war. And just at this time it definitely changed its character. From now onwards it was no longer a Jewish-Christian Church, but acquired a purely Gentile Christian stamp. The first Gentile Christian bishop took over the leadership. After this turning point the Gentile Christians headed the Church in the place where the Jewish-Christian Mother Church had once been firmly established.

The old Jewish-Christian part of the Church was still alive, but from now onwards it cut itself off more and more and shrank to the dimensions of an insignificant sect. The Jewish Christians were called Ebjonim, a Hebrew word which means 'the poor'. And it became applicable to them in more than one way.

THE SON OF A STAR

The Ebjonites continued to observe the Tora, and they had a special view of the doctrine of Jesus' divinity. For them the turning point in the life of Jesus was his baptism. Thereby the son of Joseph and Mary was so to speak adopted by God and given the powers of a Messiah. They thus refused to believe in the Miraculous Birth, and also would not recognize Paul as an apostle. James the Righteous was their great ideal and Peter also they held in high repute.

A great deal of literature emanating from their circle is extant, and makes it possible to get a picture of this steadily decaying branch of the Church. The whole thing makes a rather melancholy impression, and in their writings one comes across extremely queer things. In a 'gospel' which they recognized we read of Jesus' temptation: 'the Holy Spirit took me by one of my hairs and carried me away to the great mountain of Tabor'. Peter has a collision with Simon the Magician, the arch-heretic, in whom, through a thin disguise, can be recognized the features of Paul. A flaming protest against Paul and his work runs through all the Ebjonite literature.

To the Ebjonites Christianity was Judaism purified. Jesus was described as the prophet who was to come. They maintained circumcision, celebrated the Sabbath and observed the ritual cleansings and other essential parts of the Tora, and they laid more and more weight upon asceticism.

Curiously enough the Ebjonite sect, for all its narrowness and spiritual poverty, showed itself to possess plenty of vitality. It continued to flourish and produced some notable men. They regarded themselves as the true heirs of the first Christian Church in Jerusalem and as a bridge between the ordinary Church out among the Gentiles and orthodox Judaism. But the inevitable happened. Judaism rejected them as apostates, and the Church branded them as gross heretics.

They are heard of as late as the seventh century in both Transjordan and Egypt. In the course of time some of them were absorbed either by Judaism or by the Church, and when the wave of Mohammedanism swept in over the Eastern countries the Ebjonites disappeared.

THE SHADOW OF DEATH

And yet to this very day there are quite small communities which seem to be heirs of the Ebjonites. There is a village in the mountains of Transjordan whose inhabitants keep the Sabbath and are circumcised, who are vegetarians and non-smokers and in other things direct their lives according to the precepts of the Sermon on the Mount, while they await the return of Christ and the millennium.

So at last the waters parted. Judaism went its way, Christianity took another. Much would have been gained if the ancient bridge-building work which the Ebjonites essayed had had spiritual force enough to live through the times of stress that destroyed it.

The persecutions in Palestine died down when Antoninus Pius succeeded Hadrian on the throne. The severe ordinances were modified to some extent, and it became just possible to live as a Jew in the Jews' old country.

But in effect the strength of Judaism in Palestine was broken. Even if some refugees returned, and even if it became possible to put the Sanhedrin on its legs again, Jewish life was as a weak and flickering flame. The best and strongest elements were either killed or living abroad.

Titus' capture and destruction of Jerusalem and the Temple in the year 70 cost Judaism its life as a state. It was able to go on living in its fatherland for a few score years more. It used the time of grace well and underwent a process which prepared the way for a future life without a State and without a temple. The Talmud continued where the Temple fell.

The defeat of the Son of a Star brought the period of transition to an end. Henceforward the Jews' lot was homelessness and exile—but with spiritual firmness and courage enough to continue their lives as Jews. The shadows had fallen deeper and deeper. The people was going through the valley of the shadow of death. But one of its singers had once declared that the Lord was the shepherd and cared for his flock so that even in the valley of the shadow of death it needed to fear no evil.

XII

AS THE STARS OF HEAVEN

It was a spring night in Haifa harbour a few years ago. The great Swedish motor ship had been lying at the quay for the last week: her brilliant white sides shone out among dirty grey sheds and warehouses. The blue flag with a yellow cross at her stern fluttered in the fresh breeze which every morning sent cool air from the sea in over the hot dusty harbour. When I walked out on the long mole at which one or two small Israeli warships were moored, I found an angle at which the northern flag flew side by side with the striped blue and white Israeli flag over the high Customs house: they went well together.

I was at the end of a long stay in Israel. But I had gone on board too soon: I had been told that my boat was to leave on Sunday, and her sailing had been delayed till Tuesday, so I had a couple of days in Haifa harbour as an extra concession. And there was always something new to detect and study.

On board and on the quay work continued by day and night without cessation. Three gangs of stevedores worked shifts through the twenty-four hours to get the valuable cargo ashore. The windlass thundered, and one huge mouthful after another of pre-fabricated houses was swung up from the gaping hold. They hung swaying high in the air for a few moments, swung out from the ship and sank down till they landed exactly on the lorry or goods wagon which was to carry them away. Strong sunburnt arms reached up towards them and guided them in the right direction. When the wagons were fully loaded they moved off on their journey up into the mountains of Galilee or Judaea. A few days later the houses were set up and provided homes for

AS THE STARS OF HEAVEN

fresh immigrants into the many newly established colonies where the stony ground was to be cleared and old, long forgotten fertility restored.

In these years Jews from every part of the world came crowding home in hundreds of thousands to take possession of the old country. Every week big ships arrived from distant lands with new immigrants.

A couple of days earlier a large steamer had entered the harbour with several thousand Rumanian Jews who had got out of one of the closed countries behind the Iron Curtain and were now coming home. They stood along the rails of several decks one above the other, head close to head like a string of pearls, and gazed shoreward. These were the homeless ones, eager to spy out the fatherland which had now become the sons' land again.

The ship was slowly worked in towards the quay. When at last she was moored I saw a scene I shall never forget. The steep gangway was lowered, and the first passenger disembarked. It was clear that the captain had planned a special ceremony.

A very old man appeared at the head of the gangway. I have never seen such an old man: he was said to be 112. He was shrunken and emaciated, dressed in a long black cloak reaching to his feet, and he wore a large black hat over his snow-white hair; his face was wrinkled and as colourless as a spider's web on a dirty wall. He tottered slowly and painfully down the gangway, with a nurse supporting his arm. He held to his chest his only belongings, old Tora rolls of his family, preserved as its most valuable property from time immemorial

As I stood there and met his almost unseeing eyes, I could feel what was passing through his mind. An old man was returning home. But he did not come alone: he had behind him seventy generations, the people homeless for nearly two thousand years. Long as they had been away, they had never forgotten the country which had once been theirs. Through all the generations, from fathers to sons, the slogan had been: 'Pray, hope, long. Some day the hour will strike, and we shall go home.'

And now he had come home in the late evening of his life,

THE SON OF A STAR

and in his mind his forefathers were with him. It was only the dirty quay in Haifa harbour on to which he slowly and wearily descended from the last step of the gangway. But it was his country—his country. An old man fell on his face and kissed the stones. He was home again.

He became for me the type of this 'exodus in reverse'—the people of Israel returning home after eighteen hundred years of exile.

At long last we had finished unloading and loading. The hawsers were cast off two hours after midnight. A small tug puffed and grunted irritably as she swung the great ship out towards the mouth of the harbour. The powerful engines developed their full strength, the ship increased her speed, and we glided out towards the sea.

It was a moonless night, but with brilliant stars. I stood up on deck and saw the harbour and town disappear astern of us. The lights on the quay sent their last greeting, and long rows of lamps marked out the bends of the roads up the steep sides of Carmel.

I stood looking back towards the country I had always known in my thoughts, but which I now had travelled up and down and come to know thoroughly, both as it had been in ancient times and as it was today. It was a country in which legend and reality are so strongly combined and intertwined that one hardly knows where legend ends and reality begins, in which legend has the appearance of reality, and reality resembles a legend.

And as I stood there half-dreaming, a few scattered details came to life in a corner of my mind and began to take shape of themselves and live their own life.

Iallius Bassus—was not that the name of one of the generals in Hadrian's army which crushed the Son of a Star's rebellion? Yes, I remembered the name from a column he erected in Palestine in honour of the Emperor Antoninus Pius. He was the commander of the Fifth Macedonian Legion, which Hadrian had hurriedly dispatched to the Orient from its distant garrison station in Moesia, on the course of the Danube.

But had I not heard that name somewhere else? Yes, it was

AS THE STARS OF HEAVEN

also on a tombstone he had set up in a Christian catacomb in Rome. It was in memory of his and his wife Clementine's dead daughter Iallia. They had also a son whose name was Aelius Clemens, so the daughter was called after her father, the son after his mother. And, as in all Christian inscriptions on tombs in ancient times, the last words were *in pace*, rest in peace. The Roman legion commander in Palestine was, then, a Christian.

Names from a far-off, forgotten time—but I could not escape them, they had taken a firm hold of my imagination. They had once been living people with a strange destiny. Iallius Bassus was one of the men who wore the Roman sword and struck down Israel in the Holy Land for the last time. And yet the God of Israel had conquered him and won his heart—for indeed Judaism and Christianity both spring from the same eternal source. It is one of the finest laws of life that the spirit always triumphs over force of arms.

The last lights of Haifa and Carmel disappeared far astern: the land dropped below the horizon which the darkness of night hid from me. The ship's lights on the bridge and at the masthead shone faintly, but myriads of stars glittered over the black sea as they had once glittered over Jerusalem and Masada and Beth-ter, where the Jews had gone under long, long ago.

And my dreams came to life again—was it not over these waters that Iallius Bassus too had sailed, when he left the country so rich in memories and so full of mystery, where he had been fighting?

When Antoninus, Hadrian's successor, began to withdraw his troops, the Fifth Legion received orders to return to its garrison duty in Moesia. Camp was struck and the long march began. The live war machine, with equipment and baggage and engines of war, set off through Syria and the provinces of Asia Minor, on its long journey back to Europe. Iallius himself, with some of his staff, embarked at Gaza on board a Roman galley bound for the Bosphorus, where he was to rejoin the main body of the legion.

On his last day in Gaza he went to the market place, where

THE SON OF A STAR

Jewish prisoners were being sold as slaves. They were drawn up for inspection in long rows, handsome young men and girls and children. The Romans had been able to get rid of the old and weak. There were such swarms of prisoners that only first-class material was wanted, the others were simply slaughtered.

Roman officers and Egyptian merchants went round casting a connoisseur's eye on those offered for sale. Iallius bought an educated young man who had been a rabbi, one of old Rabbi Akiba's disciples: he had been captured in one of the cave refuges of the escaped rebels in the mountains of Judaea.

Iallius needed a clerk, and he halted before the young man with the intelligent face and deep, burning eyes. He had read the placard setting forth the prisoner's qualifications, and questioned him closely. Perhaps, so meditative and full of knowledge as he seemed to be, he was suited to be a kind of house philosopher.

Nathan—this was the slave's name—had paid no attention at all to what was happening round him. Everything was dark now, the ruin of his people and his own personal fate. When Iallius began to speak to him he brightened up a little. Certainly this foreigner who was now to be his master belonged to the despised sect of the Nazarenes, but behind the brusque officer's manner he was conscious of a gentleness that warmed him and gave him a feeling of security. Nathan livened up visibly when Iallius bought him and took him away.

The galley glided slowly northwards along the coast. She was on her way to Berytus, the great harbour in Phoenicia. Thence she would cut across under the coast of Cyprus and on to Asia Minor, and follow the coast westward. This was the quickest and safest sailing route.

Iallius stood looking at the coast. The white houses of Joppa glided past, the plain of Sharon displayed the lush verdure of its great oak-woods: behind rose the sepia-hued mountain massifs of Judaea and Samaria. They passed Caesarea with Strato's lofty tower, but off Carmel evening came on; the stars shone out, and almost suddenly night fell.

The day had been hot, but now the night brought coolness.

Iallius remained standing on deck. He could not sleep that night, there was so much to think about. Like all busy men in high positions, he had so much to occupy him all day long that there was no time for personal thoughts and dreams. Now at last he could take his ease. Somewhere over there on the coast the legion was encamped for the night, and other people were going to administer it for the next few weeks.

The night was silent: the only sounds came from the ship. The oars were dipped and withdrawn in perfect time, the water dripping from them as they were raised in the air. The waves washed against the ship's side: the planks of the deck creaked now and again under the footsteps of sentries and look-out men. Otherwise all was still, so still that thoughts could come and go as they liked.

He sent for Nathan. It would be good to have a talk with him just now when they were sailing away from his country. And Iallius himself felt that he had a share in the country where the Son of God had lived and died and risen again.

A gentle rustling made him turn. The slave stood reverently before his master.

'Over there in the dark, Nathan, lies Mount Carmel. I have heard that it was there that the great prophet once fought against the false heathen prophets. Is that not so?'

'Yes, sir, and he overcame them in the strength of the Lord.'

'That was a long time ago,' Iallius continued, 'but do not your people expect that Elijah will come again?'

Nathan's voice trembled slightly as he answered:

'When Messiah comes to restore the glory of Israel, he will send Elijah first to announce his coming.'

Iallius threw a swift questioning glance down at the slave's face.

'Yes, but, Nathan, don't you know that both Elijah and Messiah have come? John the Baptist came to prepare the way for the Son of God, who was to redeem the whole world.'

Nathan gave a start. He raised his head and replied in a rather weak, but very firm voice:

'You mean Rabbi Jesus of Nazareth, the son of Joseph and

THE SON OF A STAR

Mary. He can never be the Messiah. Why, he suffered an ignoble death on the cross.'

There was mockery in Iallius' voice as he promptly replied:

'But what happened to your Son of a Star, who said that he was the Messiah? Was he not beaten and killed in battle?'

Nathan bowed his head.

'Yes, he fell, and we were mistaken. He was not the Messiah. But he was a hero, perhaps the greatest our people has possessed. His life was only a shooting star. It shone in the sky for a moment or two. And now the darkness is blacker than ever before.'

Iallius took a step towards Nathan.

'No, Nathan, the light is kindled, and the night is vanishing. But God is strange: he always delays and only kindles the light when the night is blackest. Have you quite forgotten what your great prophets foretold, that the Messiah should be like a lamb who is led to the slaughter, and you shall look to him you have pierced? That is a Messiah who is quite different from your dreams. You awaited a king, who would rule over all the kingdoms of the earth and make Israel the centre of the world. But God's way goes through defeat and death. The empires which are ruled by hard hearts shall all fall. It will be so with Rome too, for its power is based on the sword. You will never see your dream of a Messiah realized by force and violence. God's seed cannot grow in hard hearts, but only in the mind of a child. But it is there that God will establish his kingdom. And you, who have been brave soldiers, will learn where the way of God goes in spite of all your dreams.'

Iallius saw Nathan shrug his shoulders. He caught his hand and continued:

'Nathan, I believe that the Jesus of Nazareth, whom you reject, is really the Son of God. I believe that he rose from the dead and that he has an hour to come for you and your people. One day you will turn to him. It may take a long time, perhaps thousands of years. But God is always slow and late, and a thousand years are as a day to Him. But your only way goes through him, the greatest Jew who has ever lived. Both you and we must wait, just wait—then one day he will come in the clouds of heaven and make all things new. But it will never be by our strength, but only by his love.'

Iallius had spoken warmly, from the depths of his heart. Nathan understood: there was kindness in the Roman's voice. But he could not help taking a step backwards towards the rail. He stood there and began to speak again in the same quiet, firm voice:

'Shall we two ever come to understand one another? Here we are standing side by side on board the same ship. But we are far apart. You are travelling home victorious, but I am a foreigner and homeless. My people are wandering about in exile, and no one sees any hope for the beaten, dying nation. But though we have to wander, as our people once wandered through the desert, and this time we have neither the pillar of fire nor the cloud to show us the way—we shall not disappear. We are God's people: he once chose us as his special people. He led us by strange paths. Moses showed us the way to the promised land, Joshua led us when we won it, and kings and prophets built it up and filled it with life. And now we have failed: we have fought and lost the country which was ours. Our want of faith and disobedience are being dearly punished.'

Nathan's voice failed him, and he was on the point of breaking down. Iallius saw how he pulled himself together and drew himself up again. Then Nathan looked at his master and added:

'Forgive me for saying all this. And let me tell you one of our legends. It has thrown light on my road and shown me where I can find hope.'

Iallius nodded.

'When Titus' legions captured Jerusalem, they set fire to the Lord's holy Temple. Flames sprang up along the white walls, the smoke drifted all over the precincts, and gradually the holy place collapsed. The last survivors of the Temple priests had taken refuge up on the roof. As the fire spread they had to retreat farther and farther towards the last pinnacle. They stood there in the smoke in their white robes with blue bands, but they became fewer and fewer as one after another was caught by the fire and fell. At last only one was left. He was standing in the far corner of the last piece of the Temple. When the flames enveloped him, he flung the golden key of Jerusalem up into the sky, and as he fell down into the abyss he cried up to heaven: "Lord of the world, now you must guard your city yourself!" And at the moment a hand reached out from heaven, grasped the key and drew it away into the deep blue.

'We have gone under, collapsed hopelessly; all about us are ruins. But the Lord in heaven keeps the golden key. For our people can never die. Do you know that the Lord once promised our forefathers: "Ye shall be as many as the stars of heaven and the sand of the sea!" And God never forgets his promises. We live in hope, the best lies ahead of us. What God's thoughts are we do not know. He is God and we are only dust and ashes. But one thing I know: one day the Lord will turn his golden key and open the locked door.'

'You are more right than you know yourself,' said Iallius very quietly and with deep feeling. 'A day will come when God will open the locked doors for both you and us. Then we shall all understand God's ways and see who is the Messiah.'

Iallius stood by the rail looking out over the dark sea. He made a sign with his hand bidding Nathan go. And the slave disappeared again as silently as he had come.

Iallius stood for a long time in deep thought. One picture after another passed through his mind. He saw himself in his young days, when he was a heathen, the temples and the mysteries into which he had sought initiation to satisfy his thirst for eternity. In the midst of emptiness and hopelessness there had been glimpses of the eternal God, even in heathendom. He knew now that Christian teachers understood how God worked in darkness and kindled his own lights. And God had given him the longing, the longing which never relaxed.

Then the Christians came, some of his friends who had found the way to Christ. And all became new. Now he found an outlet for his longing, now his thirst was quenched. He found in Christ

AS THE STARS OF HEAVEN

the strength and peace he had never known before. He knew that Jesus was the way and the truth and the life.

But tonight he had met something great. What should he say to Nathan and his people? It was in this country that God had revealed his truth: Israel was the root from which Christendom had grown. Why, then, would the Jews not accept the truth thus made manifest? Iallius had led his soldiers against the Jews and seen their courage and spirit. And now, amid disaster and despair, he saw Nathan holding the torch of hope on high and looking up to the stars.

The stars! Was there not a Son of a Star in every single Jew who really was a Jew? Were they not going through pitch-dark night and yet seeing God's light over them all the time? And would they not always wander in the star-glitter till they found their home at last?

Why were Jews and Christians as far apart as star-glitter and sunshine? It was a riddle he could not solve. But some day God would open the locked doors. He held the golden key of Jerusalem in his hand.

There came to Iallius a sudden realization of God's greatness, a greatness that passed all understanding. God was everywhere, in every place and always manifesting the same eternal goodness. He kindled a light to lighten the Gentiles. And he gave life and strength to Judaism, to the people he had lived with and would live with through the centuries, the people whom he would never abandon or fail. And through humiliation and hopeless struggle and homelessness Israel would gain everlasting values, treasures which it would some day distribute, making others rich thereby. And even the longest night must end some day, and star-glitter become sunshine.

I started suddenly. The second officer was sauntering past to take over on the bridge. He had given me a comradely pat on the arm as he passed me. Sparks from his newly filled pipe flew overboard and were swiftly extinguished.

I looked out over the sea towards the coast. The stars were paling as night gave place to morning. Behind the dark shadows of the mountains of Lebanon the dawn was breaking. The sun was about to rise. But for a few fleeting moments the last starlight melted into the first sun-rays of the new day. Then the sun rose, and it was full day. A couple of hours later our ship glided into the harbour of Beirut. In ancient times it was called Berytus, and it had been the first stage on Nathan's journey out into two thousand years of exile.

Now the ships were going the other way.

INDEX

Aaron, 57
Abba Sikra, 48
Abgar, 104
Abraham, 59, 130
Absalom, 58
Accho, 19, 172
Acilius Glabrio, 108
Acts of the Apostles, 17, 31, 80, 94, 98, 104, 118
Adiabene, 122-3
Adonis river, 74
Aelia Capitolina, 178, 201
Agrippa I, 71, 126-7
Agrippa II, 31
Akiba, 50, 102, 160-70, 175-85, 204-6, 214
Alexander the Great, 100, 135-7
Alexandria, 23, 123-8, 139
Alityrus, 24
Ananias, 122
Andreas, 139
Andrew, 104
Andros, 127
Anileus, 121-2
Antinous, 155-7, 178
Antioch, 24
Antiochus Epiphanes, 25
Antonia, 28-9
Antonines, 147
Antoninus Pius, 158-9, 209, 212-13
Antony, 13
Apocrypha, 65
Appian Way, 107
Appion, 127
Appolodorus, 150
Armenia, 135-6
Armilius, 66
Ashmedai, 61
Asineus, 121
Assyria, Assyrians, 100, 122, 136
Astrology, 87-8
Athens, 72, 81, 153, 155
Attis, 84-6
Augustus, 82
Aurelius, Marcus, 158-9

Babylon, Babylonians, 61, 65, 100, 118-20, 123, 137, 201
Balaam, 182
Barak, 160
Baruch, 65
Beirut (Berytus), 214, 220
Ben Aflul, 187
Berenice, 31
Beth Horon, 22
Beth-ter, 188-9, 194-8, 213
Bethlehem, 94
Bible, translation of, 124
Britannicus, 76

Caecina, 31
Caesarea, 12, 20-1, 31, 38, 40, 63-4, 73-4, 80, 91-6, 175, 178, 186, 189, 214
Caligula, 19-20, 125-8
Capernaum, 44
Cappadocia, 118
Carmel, Mount, 70, 212-15
Carthage, 32, 74
Cassel, 194
Catacombs, 108, 113
Cattle, 46
Cestius Gallus, 21-2, 24
Chosroes, 135-6
Christian Church, foundation of, 94-9
Christians, Christianity, 67-8, 93-115, 124, 185-7, 204, 207-9, 218-19; *and see* Rome
Cicero, 131, 153
Cilicia, 144
Circumcision, 167, 177
Claudius, 75, 105, 129
Clementine, 213
Cleopatra, 13
Constantinople, 32
Cornelius, 95
Crete, 45, 118, 131
Ctesiphon, 120, 136, 143, 146
Cybele, 81, 84-5
Cynics, 82
Cyprus, 45, 140-2, 214
Cyrene, 118, 139-40
Cyrus, 65

221

Dacia, Dacians, 77, 134–5, 150
'Dagger-men', 16–18
Damascus, 44, 97
Daniel, 65, 102
Danube, 77
David, 13, 57–8, 66, 107, 180, 183
David's Tower, 32
Dead Sea, 11, 13, 34, 38–9, 186
Deborah, 160
Decapolis, 43, 100
Dio Cassius, 139
Dispersion, 69, 116–32
Domitia, 78
Domitian, 33, 77–9, 103, 107, 134, 149

Ebjonim, 207–9
Edessa, 104
Egypt, 21, 45, 72, 83, 100, 118, 125–8, 131–2, 139–41, 153, 155–7, 178, 201
Eighteen Prayers, 54
Elamites, 104, 118
Eleazar (at Masada), 11, 13–15, 19, 34–8
Eleazar (Pharisee), 122
Eleazar (of Modin), 196–7
Elijah, 66, 215
Elisa Ben Abuja, 203
Enoch, 65
Ephesus, 81, 103
Epicureans, 82
Epistle to the Galatians, 98; to the Romans, 89, 105
Esdras, 68
Esther, 130–1, 166
Etna, 153
Euphrates, 109, 118, 120
Eusebius, 99, 101, 186
Ezekiel, 166
Ezra, 50, 65

Festus, 31
Fifth Legion, 149, 191, 212–13
Flaccus, 126–7
Flavius Clemens, 107–8; — Josephus, see Josephus; — Silva, 35–6, 38–40; — Vespasianus, see Vespasian
Florus, Gessius, 20–1, 73
Forum Romanum, 81
Fruit-growing, 45–6

Galatians, Epistle to, 98
Galea, 114
Galilee, Galileans, 16, 25, 27, 40–4, 61, 172, 187, 195–6, 201, 210
Gallus, Cestius, 21–2

Gamaliel, 53–6, 102–3, 163–4
Gaza, 95, 201, 213
Gessius Florus, 20–1, 73
Gibeon, 22
Gospel of St Luke, 16, 94; of St Matthew, 129
Graeco-Roman culture, 24, 72–3, 90–1
Greece, 23, 75, 81
Greeks in Caesarea, 72–3

Hadrian, 143–60, 170–2, 174, 177–8, 186, 190, 198, 200, 202, 207, 212
Haggada, 52, 57
Haifa, 70, 210
Halacha, 52, 57
Haman, 130
Hananiah, 206
Hasmonaean princes, 31
Hebrew language, 61
Hebron, 15, 201
Helene, 122–3
Heliopolis, 123
Hellenism, 147
Herod the Great, 13–14, 31, 71–2
Hezekiah, 52
Hillel, 50, 53, 119, 161, 166
Horace, 81
Hosea, 51

Iallius Bassus, 212–19
Ida, Mount, 131
Ignatius, 112
India, 45, 135–6
Isaiah, 33, 67, 103, 166
Isis, 80, 83–4
Israel, State of, 32; people of Israel, passim
Italica, 33
Italy, 45, 81, 128
Izates, 122–3

Jabneh, 49–53, 55, 102, 119, 137, 165, 182–3
Jael, 160–1
Jaffa, 49, 74
James, son of Zebedee, 97, 104
James the Righteous, 97–8
Jehoiachin, 120
Jeremiah, 33
Jericho, 34
Jerusalem, 11–12, 14–24, 26; destruction of, 29–30; 33–4, 37, 47, 49, 65–6, 68, 71, 76, 95–6, 98–101, 117–19, 123, 129, 171–2, 175; rebuilding of, 178; 186, 188, 194, 201–2, 209, 213, 217–18

INDEX

Jeshimon, 12
Jeshua ben Gilgola, 186
Jesus, 50, 67, 97–8, 101–6, 164, 208, 215–16
Jews, Jewry, *passim*
Johanan Ben Zakkai, 47–53, 161
John (evangelist), 103–4
John the Baptist, 13, 67, 215
Jonathan (prince), 13
Jonathan (high priest), 17
Joppa, 40, 95
Jordan, 34, 43–4, 47, 64, 74
Josephus, 23–7, 30, 49, 95, 117, 123
Joshua Ben Hananiah, 55–6, 163–4, 170, 172–4
Jotapata, 25–6, 49
Judaea, *passim*
Judaean desert, 11–12, 34–5, 39
Judah Ben Baba, 206–7
Judas the Galilean, 15–16
Julianus, 142–3, 172
Julius Severus, 193
Jupiter, Capitoline, 42, 79, 148, 178, 201
Juvenal, 81, 84, 129–30, 150

Kalba Shabua, 162–3
Khirbet Qumran, 186
Klopas, 101

Lamentations, 33
Laodicea, 142
Law, written and oral, 50–2, 57–9
Legion, organization of, 191
Legion, Fifth, 149, 191, 212–13; Tenth, 28, 32, 40–2, 47, 63–4, 69, 74, 176–8, 180–1, 189–90; Third (Cyrenaic), 80, 190, (Gallic) 190; Twelfth, 21
Lucuas, 139
Luke, Gospel of St Luke, 16, 93–5
Lusius Quietus, 142–3, 171
Lydda, 12, 203

Maccabaeans, Maccabees, 13, 21, 24, 31, 65
Magna Mater, 84
Marcus Aurelius, 158
Mariamme, 31
Marriage, 59–60
Martial, 90, 150
Martius Turbo, 140–1
Masada, 11–16, 18–19, 21, 34–9
Matthew, Gospel of St Matthew, 44, 129
Medes, 104, 118
Melcarth, 74

Menahem, 14, 16, 18, 21
Mesopotamia, 136, 138, 142
Messiah, 16, 53, 57, 64, 66–8, 97–8, 101–2, 105, 137, 167, 169–70, 177, 179, 183–5, 204, 208, 214–16, 218
Messina, 40
Mishna, 52, 165
Modin, Eleazar of, 196
Moesia, 149, 212–13
Moses, 50, 52, 57, 64, 124, 131, 160–1, 166, 174, 217
Murraba'at, 186–7

Nahardea, 120–1
Nathan, 214–20
Nazarites, 101–3
Nebuchadnezzar, 65, 118
Nehemiah, 65
Nero, 23, 75–6, 106–7, 109, 129, 135
Nerva, 79, 103, 131, 149, 151
New Testament, 61, 67, 95, 99, 103, 105, 129
Nile journey, Hadrian's, 156, 178
Nisibis, 120

Old Testament, 62, 97, 101, 114, 123, 166
Olives, Mount of, 28, 41, 64
Osiris, 83

Palestine, 19, 33, 42; provinces of, 42–3; trade and industry, 45; Roman power in, 71, 73, 91; thereafter *passim*
Pamphylia, 118
Pannonia, 151
Pappus, 142–3, 172
Parthia, Parthians, 19, 79, 104, 109, 111, 116, 118–21, 123, 135–6, 139, 143, 145–6, 151, 169
Passover, 58
Patmos, 103
Paul, 31, 71, 80, 89, 93, 97–9, 104–5, 107, 208
Pax Romana, 79
Pella, 100
Pentecost, 58, 104, 118
Peraea, 42–3
Persia, 130, 176
Peter, *see* Simon Peter
Petronius, 19–20
Philip, 93–5, 103
Philo, 124
Philosophy, schools of, 82
Phoenicia, 72, 74
Phrygia, 118
Piraeus, 72

Pliny, the Elder, 110; the Younger, 79, 110–11, 134, 150
Plotina, 150, 152
Pompeii, 76
Poppaea, 24, 129
Praetorian Guard, 133
Prayers, Eighteen, 54
Precepts, 59
Proverbs, 61–2
Ptolemais, 19, 44
Ptolemy II, 124
Purim, 131
Puteoli, 127

Quietus, Lusius, 142–3, 171
Quirinius, 16

Rachel, 162–3
Rasha, 76
Red Sea, 64
Revelation, 109
Rimmon, valley of, 172, 200
Roman Wall, 190–1, 193
Romans, Epistle to, 89, 105
Rome, Romans, *passim*; Empire, extent and power of, 79–80; religion, 81; moral dissolution, 89–90; Christian mission in Rome, 105–14; persecution of Christians, 106–7

Sabina, 150
Salamis, 140
Samaria, Samaritans, 42–3
Samson, 58
Sanhedrin, 51, 53, 58, 101, 119, 124, 126, 142, 175, 205, 209
Saul, *see* Paul
Schools, 61
Scopus, Mount, 28, 31
Sebaste, 73
Selinus, 144, 151
Sennacherib, 21
Sepphoris, 195–6
Septuagint, 124
Serapis, 157
Sermon on the Mount, 209
Servian, 49, 157–8
Severus, Julius, 193
Sharon, 70, 214
Sicarii, 16–18
Silva, Flavius, 35–9
Simeon ben Koseba, *see* Son of a Star
Simeon, son of Klopas, 101
Simon the Magician, 208
Simon the tanner, 95

Simon Peter, 61, 95, 107, 118, 135, 208
Slaves, Slavery, 30, 61, 90, 107, 200, 214
Snake Path, 13
Solomon, 65; Song of, 166
Son of a Star, 49, 55, 65, 117, 179–90, 192–9, 204, 207, 209, 216, 219
Stephen, 95
Strato's Tower, 71, 214
Suetonius, 150
Suffering Servant, 67, 103
Sun-worship, 88–9
Syria, 16, 19, 21, 42, 61, 151–2, 172, 177, 189, 192–3, 213

Tabernacles, 58
Tacitus, 106–7, 109, 150, 192
Talmud, 45, 51, 61, 165, 209
Temple, 19–21; destruction of, 28–30, 32; 42, 50–1, 54–5, 57, 72, 74, 97, 117, 123, 168; rebuilding of, 171–2; 177, 200–1, 209, 217–18
Tenth Legion, 28, 32, 40–2, 47, 63–4, 69, 74, 176–8, 180–1, 189–90
Terminus, 145–6
Tertullian, 111, 154
Thebes, 139
Theudas, 64
Third Legion (Cyrenaic), 80, 190; (Gallic), 190
Tiber, 111
Tiberias, 44, 195
Tiberius, 106
Tineius Rufus, 176–7, 179, 189, 205
Titus, 12, 28–33, 42, 49, 63, 75–7, 184, 200, 209, 217
Tivoli, 158
Tora, 57, 61, 129, 160, 166, 201–2, 206, 208, 211
Trajan, 79, 101, 111–12, 117, 123–4, 133–8, 140–6, 149–52, 158, 169, 171, 184, 186
Transjordan, 208–9
Translation of Bible, 124
'Travelling Emperor', 153–4, 177
Twelfth Legion, 21
Tyre, 74

Vandals, 32
Vespasian, 23, 25–8, 32–3, 42, 48–9, 74–5, 107, 148, 195
Vesuvius, 76, 110
Virgil, 81

Woman, Jewish view of, 59–60

Zealots, 16–17, 25, 47–8

For Product Safety Concerns and Information please contact our EU representative GPSR@taylorandfrancis.com
Taylor & Francis Verlag GmbH, Kaufingerstraße 24, 80331 München, Germany

www.ingramcontent.com/pod-product-compliance
Lightning Source LLC
Chambersburg PA
CBHW061441300426
44114CB00014B/1788